The City and the Court
1603–1643

The City and
the Court
1603–1643

ROBERT ASHTON

PROFESSOR OF ENGLISH HISTORY
IN THE UNIVERSITY OF EAST ANGLIA

CAMBRIDGE UNIVERSITY PRESS

CAMBRIDGE

LONDON · NEW YORK · MELBOURNE

CAMBRIDGE UNIVERSITY PRESS
Cambridge, New York, Melbourne, Madrid, Cape Town, Singapore, São Paulo

Cambridge University Press
The Edinburgh Building, Cambridge CB2 8RU, UK

Published in the United States of America by Cambridge University Press, New York

www.cambridge.org
Information on this title: www.cambridge.org/9780521224192

First published 1979
This digitally printed version 2008

A catalogue record for this publication is available from the British Library

Library of Congress Cataloguing in Publication data
Ashton, Robert.
The city and the court, 1603–1643.
Bibliography: p.
Includes index.
1. Business and politics – England – London – History.
2. Big business – England – London – History. 3. London –
Commerce – History. 4. Elite (Social sciences) – Case
studies. 5. England – Politics and government.
6. London – Politics and government. I. Title.
HD2356.G72L663   301.18′32   78–67296

ISBN 978-0-521-22419-2 hardback
ISBN 978-0-521-07137-6 paperback

TO JACK FISHER
with gratitude

For I consider the most part of rich Subjects, that have made themselves so by Craft and Trade, as Men that never look upon any thing but their present Profit, and who to every thing not lying in that Way, are in a manner blind . . . If they had understood what Virtue there would have been in preserving their Wealth in obedience to their lawful Sovereign, they would never have sided with the Parliament against him.

Thomas Hobbes, Behemoth, in
F. Maseres (ed.), *Select Tracts Relating*
to the Civil Wars in England . . .
(1815), II, 592.

Contents

Tables

Preface and acknowledgements

This book was conceived more than fifteen years ago as a volume in a popular series. By the time that this series was discontinued, however, it was already uncomfortably outgrowing these requirements and was well on the way to becoming a very different sort of study. The transformation of what was originally designed as a history of early Stuart London into a study of the relations between the business world and the crown and court is chiefly attributable to the influence of two historians. From the beginning I felt myself drawn powerfully by the influence of my former master, the late Professor R. H. Tawney, in the direction of that borderland country between business and politics which his own work, and not least his last book, so brilliantly illuminated, and which I began tentatively to explore in my book on the money market published in 1960. But my final decision to make this the subject of the whole book rather than of a part of it I owe to the advice of Professor G. R. Elton, who confirmed my uneasy impression that my original draft was not one book but two and who made very specific and most valuable recommendations as a result of which the present book is lighter by at least a third, and I hope more readable and coherent, in consequence. I also owe him a very great debt for the perspicacity of his comments and criticisms on the detailed text, and for invaluable words of encouragement about it at a time when I was experiencing one of those fits of disenchantment which periodically affect scholars who have worked at a theme too intensively and for too long.

If my other direct academic acknowledgements are few they are also deep. The first is to Professor Valerie Pearl with whom

I have discussed my work from time to time and who has generously read and criticized a much earlier draft of this book. My next, and perhaps greatest, debt is to the scholar who, together with Professor Tawney, was my original research supervisor almost thirty years ago, and who once again has given me the benefit of his sharply critical comment, which is as penetrating and constructive as it is astringent. No one who has been fortunate enough to submit drafts to Professor F. J. Fisher and tough-minded enough to survive the onslaughts of devastating but enormously fertile criticism to which he subjects them will require any elaboration by me of the nature and extent of this obligation.

I have had the benefit of intermittent words of encouragement from a number of scholars, among them Dr Christopher Hill, Professor G. E. Aylmer and Dr G. D. Ramsay. Dr Ramsay has also been kind enough to read and criticize three of my chapters and to allow me to draw upon his extensive knowledge of English commercial history. I am also indebted to Professor Lawrence Stone for providing the answer to my inquiries about the concessionary interests of some of his aristocrats; to a young American scholar, Dr Frank Foster, now (I believe) of Stanford University, whose Columbia University doctoral thesis on Elizabethan London I helped (unofficially) to supervise, and from whom I learnt a good deal; to Dr R. G. Lang for permission to cite details from his doctoral thesis; to my former research student, and present colleague, Mr Victor Morgan, who was always on the lookout for evidence which was useful to me as well as to his own work; to the much-enduring Keepers of Archives and their assistants in the Public Record Office, the British Library, the London Guildhall Library, and, perhaps above all, the Records Office of the Corporation of London, whose lives I have intermittently plagued ever since the days immediately after the war when these records were housed in Lloyd's Bank Buildings in Moorgate. One acknowledgement must by convention remain anonymous since I can only guess at the identity of the historian who read the manuscript of the book for the Cambridge University Press and offered a number of most valuable suggestions, which included drawing my attention to new source materials not used in my original draft.

I would like to thank Mrs Elizabeth Wetton and Mrs Jane Van Tassel of Cambridge University Press for their efficiency and consideration in seeing the book through the press. I owe a great debt to a succession of secretaries, Mrs Mary Haigh, Miss Susan Annis and, perhaps above all, Miss Sue Brierley and Mrs Vera Durell who have had the unenviable task of reading my manuscript and converting it into a miraculously accurate typescript, and to my daughters who have helped with the proofs. During the academic year 1968–9 I benefited greatly from the sabbatical year granted me by the University of East Anglia, during which time a good deal of research for the book was done and at the end of which preliminary drafts of chapters began to emerge. Finally, what I owe to the encouragement and forbearance of my wife and other members of my family is beyond my powers to express.

Brundall, Norwich R.A.

Note on dating, spelling and abbreviations

All dates are old style but the year is taken to have begun on 1 January, not 25 March.

Spelling is where possible reproduced in the original, but all abbreviations have been extended.

The following abbreviations have been used in the footnotes.

Amer. Hist. Rev.	*American Historical Review*
Amer. Phil. Soc. Trans.	*Transactions of the American Philosophical Society*
A.P.C.	*Acts of the Privy Council*
B.L.	British Library
Bull. Inst. Hist. Res.	*Bulletin of the Institute of Historical Research*
Cal. Clarendon S.P.	O. Ogle and W. H. Bliss (eds.), *Calendar of Clarendon State Papers preserved in the Bodleian Library*, 3 vols. (Oxford, 1872)
Cal. S.P.D.	*Calendar of State Papers Domestic*
Cal. S.P. East Indies	*Calendar of State Papers East Indies . . .*
Cal. S.P. Ven.	*Calendar of State Papers Venice*
C.D. 1621	W. Notestein, F. H. Relf and H. Simpson (eds.), *Commons Debates 1621*, 7 vols. (New Haven, 1935)
C.D. 1628	R. C. Johnson et al. (eds.), *Commons Debates 1628*, 3 vols. (New Haven, 1977)
C.D. 1629	W. Notestein and F. H. Relf (eds.), *The Commons Debates for 1629* (Minneapolis, 1921)

Church Q. R.	*Church Quarterly Review*
Clarendon S.P.	R. Scrope and T. Monkhouse (eds.), *State Papers Collected by Edward, Earl of Clarendon, Commencing 1621*, 3 vols. (Oxford, 1767–86)
C.L.R.O.	Corporation of London Record Office
C.M.E.I.C.	E. B. Sainsbury (ed.), *Calendar of Court Minutes of the East India Company 1635–43*, 2 vols. (Oxford, 1907–38)
Coll. Sign Man.	Collected Sign Manual Grants and Warrants
D.N.B.	*Dictionary of National Biography*
Econ. Hist. Rev.	*Economic History Review*
Eng. Hist. Rev.	*English Historical Review*
H.M.C.	Historical Manuscripts Commission
H. of C. J.	*House of Commons Journal*
H. of L. J.	*House of Lords Journal*
J. Ec. B. H.	*Journal of Economic and Business History*
Jor.	Journal of the Court of Common Council of the City of London
J. Mod. Hist.	*Journal of Modern History*
MS. Cal. of Sackville MSS.	Manuscript Calendar of Sackville MSS. (A. P. Newton's transcripts)
P. & P.	*Past and Present*
P.C.	Privy Council
P.C.R.	Privy Council Register
P.R.O.	Public Record Office
Remembrancia Index	*Analytical Index to the Series of Records Known as the Remembrancia. Preserved among the Archives of the City of London* (1878)
Ren. & Mod. Stud.	*Renaissance and Modern Studies*

Rep.   Repertory of the Court of Aldermen of the City of London

Roy. Hist. Soc. Trans.   *Transactions of the Royal Historical Society*

S.P.   State Papers (Domestic)

V.M.   Vestry Minutes

Introduction

On 3 March 1642, nearly six months before the outbreak of the Civil War, King Charles I set out from his capital, to which he was not to return until the end of 1648. Driven from London, as he claimed, by the dangers to himself and the royal family from tumultuous assemblies fomented by his enemies, he was to return a prisoner to face trial and execution. The government of the City which Charles abandoned in 1642 was already falling into the hands of his enemies, even though the events of the preceding months had produced, in London as in England as a whole, serious heart-searchings about the movements which had been set in train by what seemed to many to be dangerously radical programmes of reform in church and state.[1] In the event Charles was deserting a city whose adherence to the cause of his opponents in the Civil War was probably to be the most important single factor in his defeat.

Why was the City of London parliamentarian rather than royalist in the Civil War? From the time of the earl of Clarendon, the first and greatest historian of the Great Rebellion, to that of Valerie Pearl[2] historians have recognized the crucial importance of this question and have offered a variety of different answers to it. But until the publication of Pearl's outstanding book in 1961 most of these explanations have tended to be of a rather simplistic sort, more especially insofar as they purport to treat of the economic interests of the principal participants and the relationship between their interests and their political sympathies. 'The City' then as now, of course,

[1] See below, pp. 210–21.
[2] V. Pearl, *London and the Outbreak of the Puritan Revolution: City Government and National Politics* (1961).

is a term of art which covers two distinct phenomena. There is
the idea of the City as the centre *par excellence* of big business;
and secondly, the term is made to do service to describe the
municipal government of that metropolitan square mile east of
Temple Bar, the geographical area where the most important
of these business activities had their being. It is especially in
their notions about the relationship between these two distinct
but connected entities and their further significance in connection with royal policy and the court that many historians of
the period have laid themselves open to the charge of grossly
oversimplifying extremely complex historical phenomena; not
least in their tendency to view these relationships as basically
static rather than being in process of continual change and
evolution.

Down to the appearance of Pearl's book in 1961, insofar as
the problem of the City's allegiance was faced at all, its parliamentary sympathies tended to be explained largely in terms of
the assumption that, since the municipal government was
composed of the élite of the world of business, it could confidently be expected that the City fathers would be alienated by
government policies which imposed vexatious restrictions on
the freedom of economic enterprise. The reasoning behind
this conclusion would be employed more appropriately to
describe the reaction of citizens to the economic controls of
Labour governments in the twentieth century than to the very
different circumstances of the seventeenth. By contrast,
Pearl's more sophisticated and complex thesis sees the municipality throughout the period as controlled by men whose
economic interests, general inclinations and official civic
position bound them closely to crown and court; in which
circumstances something of a municipal revolution was necessary in 1641–2 if the City was to be secured for the parliamentary cause. The central argument of the second part of this
book presents a view of the City's rôle which differs crucially
from both of these versions, and which, while conceding the
importance of the ties binding business concessionaires and
City fathers to crown and court, views the crisis in their
relationship as something of far longer standing than is envisaged by Pearl. It will argue that, more than a decade before

1642, the relations between many members of the concessionary business interest and the crown were in process of disintegration and that the crown's relations with the City fathers (many of whom were themselves concessionaires) were being put to an intolerable strain. In consequence, the majority of the City fathers, far from being the natural supporters of Stuart absolutism at the end of the period of Charles I's personal rule in the late 1630s, were as alienated from royal policies as were the vast majority of the political nation. As a corollary of this, the royalism of the bulk of the London aldermen at the beginning of 1642 needs to be explained by reference to the events of 1640–2 rather than in terms of their unchanging and steadfast adherence to royal policies from the beginning, unaffected by the eleven years' tyranny which alienated so many other pillars of society in the 1630s. It is in this alternative interpretation to that provided by what has been, since 1961, the current orthodoxy, that this book's chief claim to importance and originality lies.

I

Institutions and oligarchy 1:
the municipal and business élites

The central concern of this book is the relations between the
crown and the City of London. In the early seventeenth
century, as today, the latter term has two distinct connotations
which are not always clearly distinguished by historians; it is
used to describe both the municipal government of the metropolitan square mile between Temple Bar and Aldgate and the
big-business activities which are so thickly concentrated within
that area. Accordingly it will be necessary to distinguish carefully between the impact of royal policies on, and the relations
of the crown with, each of these elements. The present chapter
deals with the ruling class of the City in both these senses, and
the chapter following it with the City livery companies,
membership of which was a necessary passport not only to the
exercise of a trade or craft within the City, but also for those
who wished to attain municipal distinction via entry into this
ruling class.

I

The freedom of the City of London could be obtained in any
one of three ways – by apprenticeship, patrimony and redemption (purchase). After attaining the freedom many years might
elapse before the aspirant to high municipal office entered the
ranks of the lesser city notables, if indeed he got even as far as
this. During the intervening period he might engage in a
variety of forms of parish work, serve as a leading member of
the yeomanry or lower sector of his gild,[1] hold a number of

[1] For the significance of the distinction between yeomanry and livery, see below,
pp. 43–5, 51–8.

minor offices in his City ward, such as scavenger or constable, rise in the parish hierarchy perhaps becoming the member of a closed vestry or a churchwarden, be elevated to the livery or upper half of his gild, and finally (if lucky) be elected a member of the court of common council.

Common council, which numbered 196 at the opening of the seventeenth century, was the less powerful of the two central City courts. In both its functions and its powers it bears a certain not altogether superficial resemblance to the contem-porary House of Commons, though the functions of the superior City court, the court of aldermen, were perhaps more analogous with those of the privy council than with those of the upper house of parliament. Like M.P.s in the Commons, common councilmen were elected, though, unlike them, they were subject to re-election annually, the municipal equivalent of the parliamentary constituency being the ward. Although each ward sent only one representative to the court of aldermen, the number of common councilmen elected for each ward varied between sixteen in the huge extramural ward of Farringdon Without and in that of Bridge Within to none in the exceptional case of the relatively newly created and underprivileged ward of Bridge Without.[2] Elections were held at the annual meeting of the wardmote, where all freemen had the right to vote, though in some cases the election was virtually decided in advance by more select bodies drawn from the more wealthy and privileged members of the various precincts into which each ward was split up, and which often corresponded in actual fact with the vestries of City parishes, more especially when these were closed rather than open vestries. The fact that the boundaries of the precincts and the parishes rarely coin-cided seems to have offered no obstacle to this practice.

The first and perhaps the most important of the common council's functions was to give or withhold its consent to the assessment of the citizens for financial levies and loans. Valerie

---

[2] For the numbers of common councilmen in each ward at the beginning of the seventeenth century, see J. Stow, *A Survey of London by John Stow Reprinted from the Text of 1603*, 2 vols., ed. C. L. Kingsford (Oxford, 1908), I, 129, 138, 150, 163, 175, 186, 200, 205, 211, 216, 223, 229, 238, 250, 258, 276, 285, 290, 303, 310, 343–4, 352, II, 11, 20, 51, 69.

Pearl, whose admirably lucid and informative description of the functions and powers of the courts of common council and aldermen[3] has been drawn upon heavily in this account, has suggested that in practice these powers seem to have extended only to assessments made on the citizens via the wards, and that a number of the assessments of the gilds and livery companies of the City were made by the court of aldermen which thus bypassed the court of common council. If true, this was an important limitation on the latter's power, but it is perhaps worth noting that an exhaustive examination of the loans which were raised for the crown in the early seventeenth century reveals that, although the money was frequently raised via assessment of the livery companies rather than via assessment of individuals through their wards, this was invariably done through the agency of the common council and not the court of aldermen, and that, in the matter of loans at least, the only cases where the latter acted independently was when assessment was limited to the aldermen alone.[4]

Common council also had legislative functions, but just as the bills passed by the House of Commons might be rejected by the Lords, so did the court of aldermen have the right to reject any legislation proposed by the common council, in which they also sat and deliberated, while voting separately from the general body of commoners. But in actual fact there was small need for them to exercise this right. Even more successfully than those Elizabethan privy councillors who sat in the House of Commons and endeavoured to monopolize the initiating of legislation, the court of aldermen was able to insist that only those bills which came down from the aldermen to the common council were in fact discussed by that body. Finally, just as the king could summon, prorogue and dissolve parliament whenever he thought fit, so did the chairman of the court of aldermen, the lord mayor, exercise the same power vis-à-vis the common council. In many respects, then, the court of aldermen may be said to have exercised an effective stranglehold on the freedom of action of the inferior court. The single

---

[3] Pearl, pp. 53–62.
[4] Ibid. p. 56; R. Ashton, *The Crown and the Money Market 1603–1640* (Oxford, 1960), pp. 26–7, 114–31, 135–41, 180–2.

alderman who represented each ward was, moreover, elected for life and was therefore in practice not nearly so vulnerable as the common councilmen to changing currents of popular feeling. While it is true that aldermen occasionally chose to change the wards which they represented, thus becoming liable to fresh election, City custom sought to limit this practice to aldermen who had already served for at least two years for their existing ward, and the court of aldermen on occasions intervened to maintain this custom.[5] As in the case of the common council, elections were, technically at least, made by the freemen of the ward at the wardmote, but the rights of the electorate extended no further than the nomination of four candidates from whom the court of aldermen itself selected one, while retaining the right to reject all four if it deemed them to be unsuitable. The court of aldermen, therefore, with its powers of initiating and vetoing legislation and of preventing the election to its ranks of anyone whom it considered unacceptable, was a perfectly designed piece of oligarchical machinery. From these facts and from Pearl's description of the other functions of the court, the patronage which it dispensed and the offices to which its members had access culminating in the mayoralty itself, it must be abundantly clear that it was the aldermen who formed the governing élite of the City *par excellence*.

Many of those who hopefully reached the status of common councilmen never became aldermen, even though some of them succeeded in obtaining quite important City offices such as auditor of the Bridgehouse and second warden or even master of their livery companies. On the other hand it is perhaps worth pointing out that there were many men who rose to the aldermanry and some who succeeded to the highest City offices who never became masters of their companies. Only half of the twenty-eight men who served as aldermen in the year 1603 were also at one time or another in their careers masters of their companies. Of these, three became masters before becoming

---

[5] For an example of intervention to prevent the nomination of aldermen for a vacancy before they had served two years in their existing wards, see C.L.R.O., Rep. XLVIII, fos. 401(b)–402. For a discussion of this problem at its most acute in relation to the ward of Bridge Without, see D. J. Johnson, *Southwark and the City* (1969), pp. 146, 149–52.

aldermen, though one of them, Sir Henry Billingsley, served as master on three subsequent occasions. Of the remaining eleven, five served as masters in the year of their elevation to the aldermanic bench, while the other six became aldermen before becoming masters of their companies.[6]

On the other hand, many of those who became masters of their companies, more especially if these were minor companies, never succeeded in becoming aldermen at all, so that the mastership even of one of the twelve major companies was not necessarily a qualification for admission to the aldermanic élite, although there is perhaps a sense in which the reverse is true and a man was more likely to become master of his company if he were an alderman than if he were not. The attainment of the office of sheriff was, however, at least at the beginning of the seventeenth century, a clear indication that one had arrived. Of the twenty-eight aldermen of 1603,[7] only two served as sheriff before becoming aldermen and both of them were sheriffs in the year immediately preceding their elevation to the aldermanry. Of the remainder, fourteen served as sheriff in years subsequent to those in which they became aldermen, while twelve served in the year of their elevation, which suggests that the office of sheriff, while marking out its holder either as one who had arrived or was on the point of arrival in the municipal élite, did not denote any marked seniority within that élite. However, if the same simple calculations are made for the twenty-nine aldermen listed by Pearl as holding office between October 1640 and December 1641, a striking contrast emerges. More than half (fifteen) of these aldermen served as sheriff before becoming aldermen, while one of them, Sir George Garrett, who served in 1641–2, the year of his election as alderman, had been chosen but had declined to act as sheriff two years previously. Only one alderman served as sheriff in a year subsequent to becoming alderman, while twelve (including Garrett) became aldermen and sheriffs in the same year.[8]

---

[6] Details about the aldermen and their offices obtained from A. B. Beaven (ed.), *The Aldermen of the City of London*, 2 vols. (1908–13), *passim*; G. E. Cokayne, *Some Account of the Lord Mayors and Sheriffs of London (1601–1625)* (1897), *passim*.
[7] This figure includes both the aldermen who died or retired in 1603 and their replacements.
[8] Pearl, app. I, pp. 285–308; Beaven (ed.), *Aldermen, passim*.

While it is easy to make too much of a contrast between two arbitrarily selected years, it is more than likely that this is at least partially explicable by the fact that, as in so many of the shires during the 1630s, the shrievalty was becoming increasingly unpopular, in which circumstances there may well have been a tendency for it to be made a hurdle which had to be overcome before accession to the aldermanry. The attack of parliament on Sir William Acton, one of the two sheriffs of 1629, for taking action against merchants who refused to pay tonnage and poundage to the crown,[9] and the association of the shrievalty with the implementation, in the City as elsewhere in England, of the unpopular royal policies of the 1630s, and notably the collection of ship money, would contribute powerfully to these developments.[10]

Within the ranks of the aldermanic élite the most decisive division of status was marked by the office of lord mayor.[11] The lord mayor was chosen annually by a process which is a characteristic blend of the elective and the oligarchical principles. Two names were submitted to the court of aldermen by the liverymen of the City assembled in a body known as Common Hall, which also elected the Members of Parliament for the City and one of the sheriffs, the other being chosen personally by the lord mayor.[12] In normal circumstances there was nothing incompatible between the presence of this elective element and the gradual accumulation of aldermanic seniority as a means of attaining the mayoralty, since it was usual both for one of the nominees of Common Hall to be the senior alderman below the mayoral chair, and for the final decision of the court of aldermen to be made on the basis of seniority. Those aldermen who had served as lord mayor were in a very real sense the élite of élites, distinguished by the weight which was attached to their opinions in the highest councils of the City and by their tenure of very senior offices such as presidencies of City hospitals and offices such as comptroller-general and surveyor-general of hospitals, as well as colonelcies of regiments of the City trained

---

[9] See below, pp. 184–5.
[10] On the shrievalty and other offices below the lord mayor, see Pearl, pp. 64–8.
[11] On the office of lord mayor, see ibid. pp. 62–4.
[12] On the functions of Common Hall, see ibid. pp. 50–3.

bands. Some of these offices may well have been to a very high degree honorific and especially suitable for senior aldermen who had passed the mayoral chair. Among the aldermen of 1603, however, Sir Henry Billingsley had become president of St Thomas's Hospital in 1594, two years before becoming lord mayor, while Sir Leonard Halliday became president of Bethlem and Bridewell in 1605 in the year of his mayoralty.[13] These two cases may be regarded as exceptions which prove the rule. Of the fourteen hospital presidencies which were to be held by the aldermen of 1640–1, however, only seven were obtained after their holders had been lord mayor.[14] And in the case of colonelcies of trained bands, mayoral experience seems to have been a consideration of even less crucial importance, a fact which is almost certainly connected with the constitutional revolution of 1640–1, which is dealt with in the final chapter of this book.[15]

II

The concept of a business and a municipal élite naturally overlap. The men from whom the rulers of the City of London, the lord mayors and the aldermanic bench, were drawn were among the wealthiest and most successful business men of their day. Needless to say, eminence in the world of business did not always lead to municipal eminence. There were some business men, like the celebrated – or notorious – projector Sir Arthur Ingram, who deliberately remained members of minor livery companies and therefore consciously cut themselves off from advancement in municipal affairs. There were others, like Lionel Cranfield, Ingram's collaborator in so many business ventures, who, while prominent members of one or another of the twelve major livery companies – in Cranfield's case of the Mercers' Company – seem not to have aspired to office either in their companies or in the municipality. Cranfield, of course, had much bigger fish to fry.[16] Nevertheless, while some success-

---

[13] Beaven (ed.), *Aldermen*, II, 42, 45.
[14] Ibid. I–II, *passim*.
[15] See below, pp. 204–21.
[16] On Ingram and Cranfield, see A. F. Upton, *Sir Arthur Ingram, c. 1565–1642: A Study of the Origins of an English Landed Family* (1961); R. H. Tawney, *Business and*

ful business men viewed municipal office as an unwelcome
chore to be avoided if at all possible, there is no disputing the
fact that, in general, business success was a prerequisite of
municipal advancement. Although the business élite and the
municipal élite were not quite one and the same thing in terms
of personnel, the latter was inevitably drawn preponderantly
from the former.

London business society was a hierarchy in which there was
an almost infinite number of grades of affluence and respectability ranging from the humble master craftsman through
the retailing shopkeeper, the domestic wholesaler and the
'mere merchant' engaged in foreign trade, and culminating in
the tycoons who made substantial and often spectacular fortunes in each of these two latter spheres of commercial activity,
and from whom many of the members of the business élite of
the city were drawn. In an age in which the key to economic
enrichment was to be found in commerce rather than in manufacture the members of this élite were in a real sense the seventeenth-century equivalents of the Cobdenite manufacturers of
early Victorian Manchester. But the attitude of many of them –
and certainly of those whose main interests lay in foreign
rather than domestic trade – to the rôle of government in
business was very different from that of their Victorian successors. As members of privileged companies which enjoyed area
monopolies of trade they were in fact concessionaires of the
crown and owed their privileges to that *mariage de convenance*
between the government and big business which had been a
central feature of royal commercial policy since the days of
conservative economic and social reconstruction in the opening
years of the reign of Elizabeth I.[17]

The Elizabethan alliance between the government and
London big business had been founded on the firm belief of
both parties that the economic depression of the middle
decades of the sixteenth century had been due in no small

Politics under James I: Lionel Cranfield as Merchant and Minister (Cambridge, 1958);
M. Prestwich, *Cranfield: Politics and Profits under the Early Stuarts* (Oxford, 1966).
[17] See G. Unwin, *Studies in Economic History*, ed. R. H. Tawney (1927), pp. 133–
220; F. J. Fisher, 'Commercial Trends and Policy in Sixteenth-Century
England', *Econ. Hist. Rev.*, x (1940), 95–117; L. Stone, 'State Control in
Sixteenth-Century England', ibid. xvii (1947), 103–20.

measure to the relative ease with which persons other than professional merchants had been allowed to participate in foreign trade with a resultant overcrowding of trade and over-competition amongst those who engaged in it. In this view the pursuit of foreign trade was a profession, and, as such, beyond the capacity of the retailers and shopkeepers who had so readily engaged in it during the early Tudor period. If chaos was to be averted, entry into foreign trade must be severely limited to 'mere merchants' and to this end conditions of entry must be stiffened. The main instrument whereby this policy was put into effect was the chartered company with limited member-ship and a monopoly of trade with a particular area. Such companies were not an Elizabethan invention, but the ten-dency whereby the membership of existing companies such as the Merchant Adventurers became increasingly limited and new companies were formed on the now established restrictive pattern of the old was viewed with approval by the more substantial merchants of Elizabethan London and by the Elizabethan government, which also proved responsive to such additional arguments as that the companies would act as a counter-check on the payment of customs duties as well as fostering the building of substantial ships which could be used as a sort of supplementary naval reserve. Most of these com-panies were 'regulated companies' whose members traded under the protection of the company and within the frame-work of its ordinances, but on their own individual capital. Membership was limited to 'mere merchants' and premiums for entry were relatively high. Each member was, in theory at least, 'stinted' as to the amount of goods in which he could trade, a device which, one apologist claimed, kept 'the wealth-ier sort . . . from engrossinge the whole trade contrarie to the use and maner of a well ordered common wealth or familie, wherein all are provided for and not some starved for want, whilst others are swollen up to the eyes with fatt and plentie'. Such benefits were, of course restricted to members of the chartered companies, who were 'wealthie and well experi-mented Merchantes', and the conduct of overseas commerce was viewed in strictly professional and conservative terms. Profits tended to be big and to that extent enterprise was unnecessary. The sober, dignified, well-ordered trading of 'mere merchants' was contrasted favourably by John Wheeler and other apologists of the companies with the chaos prevalent in more open conditions. Similarly, the wardens of Trinity House predicted in 1604 that a consequence of the overthrow of the Merchant Adventurers' Company would be that

> the ritch Cloathe of the land will be had in noe estimacion, for it will be conveyed awaye in small vessells and in boates out of every Creake to the great losse of his magesties custom & to the over throwe of so manye of people as are daylye sett on worcke about the sayde Cloathes, and that because everye place beyond the seas will be filled withe pedlers and not with merchauntes.[18]

The pattern of the Elizabethan regulated company which has just been described was not universal. Some branches of commerce, such as the trade in Newfoundland fish and the trade with the western Mediterranean, were open to all merchants. This was emphatically true of Anglo-Spanish trade once the short-lived Spanish Company had gone into dissolution as a consequence of the long Elizabethan war. Early Stuart attempts to revive it were totally unsuccessful, and although attempts to control Anglo-French trade had more success, notably in the formation in 1609 of a London-dominated French Company on the regulated pattern, even this branch of trade does not appear to have been an area of tightly regulated control, despite numerous complaints to the contrary from some of the outports. And if not all trades fell within the control of companies, neither were all companies regulated companies. The trades with Russia and with the orient both involved a longer period between investment and return than was the case with the trades of most of the regulated companies. Accordingly, both the Russia or Muscovy Company, which had been founded in the reign of Mary, and the East India Company, which received its charter in 1600, were joint-stock companies, which invited subscriptions from the investing public, though control of policy remained firmly in the hands of a relatively few bigwigs. The Levant Company had at one

---

[18] P.R.O., S.P. James I, vIII/58; R. H. Tawney and E. Power (eds.), *Tudor Economic Documents*, 3 vols. (1924), III, 280–304.

time also been a joint-stock company, but by the beginning of the seventeenth century had settled down on the more normal pattern of a regulated company. The increasing importance of these trades, and more especially the intimately connected Levant and East India trades, together with the relative decline in the importance of the traditional trades to northern Europe, and most notably the trade of the Merchant Adventurers, is a central feature of early Stuart commercial history, whose significance has been stressed by Robert Brenner.[19]

Few informed contemporary observers would have disagreed that the organization of so much of overseas commerce on the basis of chartered companies with strictly limited membership was a factor which aided the expansion of London at the expense of the provincial ports. It is perfectly true that most of the companies were open to provincial merchants, but the restriction of membership to 'mere merchants' inevitably favoured London at the expense of the outports where the division of commercial labour was far less highly developed and specialized wholesale merchants were in much shorter supply. In short there can be no doubt that the privileged overseas traders of London were among the chief beneficiaries of the commercial policies of the Elizabethan government. Correspondingly, the commercial fortunes of those rich merchants whose main interests were in domestic rather than foreign trade, and who, as Lang's researches have demonstrated, represent a highly significant sector of both the business and the aldermanic élites, were less intimately connected with the crown. Such were merchants engaged in the domestic marketing of imports, the internal trade in textiles and in the provisioning of the metropolis with food, fuel and other products. The fact that much less is known about their activities than about those of merchants whose interests lay preponderantly in overseas trade has perhaps obscured their importance. Lang's work has revealed that, of the 140 aldermen serving between 1600

[19] On these companies see T. S. Willan, *The Early History of the Russia Company 1553–1603* (Manchester, 1956); K. N. Chaudhuri, *The English East India Company* (1965); A. C. Wood, *A History of the Levant Company* (2nd impr., 1964); R. Brenner, 'The Civil War Politics of London's Merchant Community', *P. & P.* no. 58 (1973), 53–65, 73–6.

and 1625, only a hundred can be shown to have actively engaged in overseas trade at any time, and more significantly, only 67 were men of whom it can be confidently asserted that overseas rather than domestic trade was a mainstay as distinct from a by-employment; of the remainder the reverse would seem to be true. Domestic trade might not offer quite the same range of opportunities for enrichment as it was to do in post-Restoration England, but it loomed a great deal larger in the economic interests of many wealthy Londoners than is often realized.[20]

III

Among those whose main interests lay in overseas trade some of the members of the business élite are distinguished from the rank-and-file members of privileged chartered companies by the scale rather than by the nature of their economic interests. They too were full-time professional merchants, but men whose interests were spread over a wide variety of enterprises and companies, in some of which they held directive interests. Such men were Sir Thomas Smythe and Sir Ralph Freeman. It may, however, legitimately be doubted whether such persons were altogether typical of the London business, and still less of the aldermanic, élites. Inheriting enormous wealth from his father, the celebrated Elizabethan concessionaire Mr Customer Smythe, the son engaged in activities which were more purely commercial in character. Unlike his father, he is not to be found in the forefront of those merchants who dabbled extensively in government financial concessions. But there can be no doubt about his pre-eminence in the world of Jacobean commerce. Governor for fifteen years in all of the East India Company, he was also in his time governor of the Russia, French, Levant, Virginia and Somers Islands com-

---

[20] R. G. Lang, 'The Greater Merchants of London in the Early Seventeenth Century' (D.Phil. thesis, University of Oxford, 1963), pp. 99, 103, 300. I am deeply indebted to Dr Lang for permission to consult his thesis. Some of his more important conclusions are summarized in Lang, 'London's Aldermen in Business: 1600–1625', *Guildhall Miscellany*, III (1971), 242–64. See also R. Grassby, 'English Merchant Capitalism in the Late Seventeenth Century: The Composition of Business Fortunes', *P. & P.*, no. 46 (1970), 96.

panies. Smythe was to become one of James I's most trusted
allies in the business world, and the government made extensive
use of his talents, not only in his capacity as governor of so
many great chartered companies but also as a member of
government commissions, including the navy commission in
1618 and the treasury commission in 1619. Like Smythe a
foundation member of the East India Company, Freeman was
one of the most prominent members both of this company and
of the Levant and Newfoundland companies, and unquestionably the greatest Muscovy merchant in his day. He was the
leading figure in organizing the take-over bid for the Russia
Company in the early 1620s, and in 1624 exported more than
half the total number of cloths which were sent to Russia. He
became lord mayor in 1633, and, indeed, it is surprising only
that he had to wait so long before receiving the ultimate civic
honour. Like Smythe he sat on a number of government
commissions, in this case on committees set up to discuss the
causes of the depression of the early 1620s.[21]

But powerful as the ties which bound such multiple commercial concessionaires to the government undoubtedly were,
there were other members of the business élite whose fortunes
were more intimately associated with the crown and the court.
These were magnates whose economic interests, while resting
on a firm foundation of commodity trade, spilt over into the
exploitation of concessions on the periphery of government
finance and economic policy. Some of these concessions arose
out of that familiar conjuncture of circumstances whereby a
government with an ambitious programme of economic and
social controls lacked the administrative machinery to make
that programme effective and filled the vacuum by using
private enterprise. Many of the patents of monopoly of the
period fall into this category; so, in a sense, does the expedient

---

[21] B.L., Harleian MSS., 2243, fo. 72(b); *Cal. S.P. East Indies, 1513–1616*, p. 100;
C. T. Carr (ed.), *Select Charters of Trading Companies* (1913), p. 54; Beaven
(ed.), *Aldermen*, II, 57; A. Friis, *Alderman Cockayne's Project and the Cloth Trade: The
Commercial Policy of England in Its Main Aspects* (1927), pp. 56–7 n, 161, 168, 177,
412, 424; Chaudhuri, *East India Company*, pp. 29, 34, 36, 58; Wood, *Levant
Company*, pp. 31, 205. For the political significance of Smythe's activities in the
East India, Virginia and Somers Islands companies in the later years of James
I's reign, see below, pp. 114–16.

of customs farming. Other concessions were the product of the crown's shortage of income which forced it back on the expedient of rewarding its servants and those whom it delighted to honour by concessions in kind rather than by payments in cash – by such devices as patents, licences and customs farms. The courtly recipients of these privileges had in turn to call upon the aid of the business world to put their concessions to profitable use.

The use of the royal dispensing power to grant licences *non obstante* penal statutes was both an undisputed part of the royal prerogative and a practice for which it is not difficult to find justification in economic terms. Parliament met relatively infrequently and occasions might often demand a relaxation of statutes in the interests of the economic welfare of the realm. An impecunious government can perhaps hardly be blamed if it also saw in the licensing system a means whereby it might kill the economic and the fiscal birds with the same stone, since it was often convenient to give such concessions direct to those who had a claim upon its bounty and thus save disbursements from the exchequer. A number of courtiers were the beneficiaries of licences similar to that which was granted to Esmé Stewart, Lord Aubigny, in 1603 to export strong beer. And the licences were always in demand in the City not only by those who ultimately used them but also by syndicates of business speculators who interposed themselves between the courtly concessionaire and the ultimate user. Such dealings can be illustrated by the licences to export unfinished cloth. As events were to prove in the second decade of the century, the English cloth economy would rapidly have gone to pieces if the statutes which forbade the export of unfinished cloth had been strictly observed.[22] The Merchant Adventurers' Company held one such licence direct from the crown, but the holder of another and more valuable licence was the earl of Cumberland, and the Merchant Adventurers found the purchase of Cumberland's privileges a great deal more expensive than those which they held direct from the crown. In 1603 a

---

[22] I am reminded by Dr G. D. Ramsay that the statutory restriction applied only to cloths worth £3 and upwards.

similar licence to export 2,500 unfinished cloths over two years was granted to the earl of Argyle, and in the following year there was a spate of further grants, among them a licence to Peter Vanlore to export 15,000 unfinished cloths over ten years, and another to Sir Philip Herbert and Sir James Hay to export 17,500 over the same period. These two last grants differed widely from one another in terms of their basic *raison d'être*. Vanlore was a foreign merchant resident in London, a jeweller, bullion dealer and moneylender, who was among the most prominent of the recurrent lenders to the crown in the reign of James I. The concession which he received was made in return for sums which were owed to him by the king. Hay and Herbert, on the other hand, were courtiers, both of them Gentlemen of the royal Bedchamber, the former the future earl of Carlisle whose name was soon to become a byword for courtly extravagance, and the latter the future earl of Pembroke. Both stood high in the royal favour. Vanlore had no difficulty in disposing of his licences at a profit to the Merchant Adventurers' Company. In addition he seems to have been instrumental in providing a means whereby the two courtiers could dispose of theirs. A crucial figure here was one John Harris, a man with courtly connections who had come into contact with Vanlore in the latter's capacity as a jeweller. Harris and Vanlore seem to have been the key figures in the formation of a syndicate in 1605 which contained a number of persons to whom such concessions were part of their normal stock-in-trade. Such men were the customs official John Wolstenholme, Richard Wright and Arthur Ingram. The function of the syndicate was to act as intermediary between the courtly owners of the licences and the members of the Merchant Adventurers' Company who ultimately exploited them. Five of the six partners in the syndicate each contributed £450 and Vanlore contributed £750 to take the licences off the courtiers' hands at a total cost of £3,000 with the idea of reselling to the Merchant Adventurers at a profit. But before the licences reached their ultimate destination, there was still room for further transfers of shares in them – again, of course, at a profit – a fact which made the licences even more expensive to the ultimate purchasers. For instance, Lionel Cranfield, though not a member of the original syndicate, had put up half the money for Ingram's share and later purchased the whole of it, only to resell half of his share later at a substantial profit to Samuel Hare and Richard Venn. Indeed, over a period of two years and four months his personal speculation in the licences showed a spectacular profit of £193. 14s. 6d. on an investment of £291. 5s. 6d.[23]

Needless to say, the most spectacular of the domestic concessions unloaded upon court and city during the period, the farms of branches of the royal customs revenue, offered rich financial pickings for both courtly and business concessionaires. The rôle of the courtier might take several forms. He might be the principal lessee of a customs farm which he exploited by subletting to city capitalist interests. The farm of the duties on silks, velvets, cambrics and other fine materials offers a good example. This had been granted by Elizabeth to Robert Cecil in 1601 and was sublet by him at a profit. On the queen's death Cecil's concession automatically lapsed and it was rumoured that his under-farmers were seeking a lease direct from the crown. While it is true that a direct arrangement between the crown and the City syndicate which actually worked the concession was likely to be far more profitable to both, the practice of rewarding government servants and courtiers by grants of this kind was by now far too well established and Cecil stood far too high in the royal favour for there to be much chance of this happening. Well aware of this, William Massam, a prominent member of the Cranfield–Ingram circle, approached Cecil, advising him that he should either 'retain the patent wholly to yourself, placing honest men to see the execution thereof, or farm it out unto any man of account'. Either of these expedients would, he suggested, satisfy those merchants who were currently complaining about the patent. Such mercantile discontent, explained Massam disingenuously, related solely to Cecil's old under-farmers, 'who for the most part are men very evil thought of, and such as . . . do now deal very rigorously

[23] B.L., Lansdowne MSS., 151, fos. 143–4; ibid. 172, fos. 387–412; P.R.O., S.P. James I, xii/48, xiv/2; *Cal. S.P.D. 1603–10*, pp. 31, 33, 67, 102, 141; H.M.C., *Salisbury MSS.*, xvii, 92; H.M.C., *Sackville MSS.*, i, 118–21, 323; Tawney, *Business and Politics under James I*, p. 89; Stone, *The Crisis of the Aristocracy, 1558–1641* (Oxford, 1965), pp. 430–1; Prestwich, *Cranfield*, pp. 60–1.

and discourteously with all merchants in general'. Massam calculated that Cecil would almost certainly decide to sublet, in which circumstances his own good advice and the previous connection of his partner Arthur Ingram with Cecil were factors which might well predispose the latter to favour the syndicate which had just been formed by Ingram, Massam and their associates. The members of this syndicate must have been bitterly disappointed at Cecil's decision in June 1603 not to sublet but to entrust the collection of the duties to a salaried customs officer acting on his behalf. And even when he changed his mind their troubles were not over, for they were faced with the competition of a rival syndicate headed by Samuel Hare and Richard Venn, men who were to be intimately associated with Ingram, Cranfield and Massam in a variety of speculative enterprises in the early years of the seventeenth century. The Massam group, however, had another card up its sleeve, and once again court influence was called into the struggle in the person of the earl of Mar, a nobleman in high favour with the king and therefore someone who might decisively influence Cecil in his choice of under-farmers. The ultimate outcome, however, was a compromise between the two groups and the farming of the duties by a joint syndicate consisting of members of both. In the meantime one of the members of Massam's syndicate, Lionel Cranfield, appears to have withdrawn, perhaps because he feared that competitive bidding would raise the rent of the farm too high, though he appears again in the next year as the purchaser of a 1/48 share for £103. 6s. 8d., which he was able to sell a year later at a profit of £201. 13s. 4d. The members of the syndicate of sublessees were to profit still further in 1606, when, as a result of the new tariff of 1604, Cecil, now earl of Salisbury, decided to farm out the increase in silk duties, this time in return for a capital sum of £3,286. 4s. 7d. instead of an annual rent. Cranfield, who had profited spectacularly from his speculation in the original farm, now tried his hand again with the purchase of a one-fifth share in the new concession.[24]

[24] B.L., Lansdowne MSS., 172, fos. 297–335; H.M.C., *Salisbury MSS.*, xv, 96, 124, xvi, 354; H.M.C., *Sackville MSS.*, I, 57–9, 69–70, 122, 124–5; Tawney, *Business and Politics under James I*, pp. 101–2; Ashton, *The Crown and the Money Market*,

Next to the great farm of the customs, the most sought-after customs-farming concessions were the three farms of the duties on sweet wines, French and Rhenish wines and currants. At the beginning of the reign of James I all three came into the hands of noblemen who made a substantial profit by subletting to business syndicates of the City. The earl of Southampton farmed the duties on sweet wines and, in 1605, the reversion of the lease of the farm of the duties on French and Rhenish wines, currently held direct from the crown by the prominent citizen Sir John Swinnerton, was obtained by the earl of Devon. Devon's under-farmers, William Godolphin and Joseph Earth, were bought out by a syndicate whose principal members were William Garway and Nicholas Salter, who already farmed the great customs, and worked their new concession as Devon's under-farmers until his death in 1606, and afterwards as principal lessees from the crown.[25]

Details are hard to find about the precise financial arrangements which prevailed between noble patentees and their under-farmers, but it could well be that those obtaining in the case of the farm of the currant duties were the norm. In 1604 the earl of Suffolk received a grant of this farm, though the farmers in actual practice were his sublessees, a syndicate led by Roger Dallison and Richard Wright, in which Lionel Cranfield held one-eighth of a share for a time. The lease was made out to Dallison and Wright on behalf of Suffolk, and it was they, not Suffolk, who were responsible for the payment of the annual rent of £5,322 into the exchequer. The remainder of the £6,000 per annum which they contracted to pay to Suffolk for the farm was paid by them direct to him. The yield of the farm to Suffolk was therefore not spectacular in the early years of the concession. The under-farmers did rather better. According to one account, the duties on currants yielded

p. 87; Upton, *Ingram*, pp. 3–4; Stone, *Crisis*, pp. 427, 773, and 'The Fruits of Office: The Case of Robert Cecil, First Earl of Salisbury, 1596–1612', in F. J. Fisher (ed.), *Essays in the Economic and Social History of Tudor and Stuart England* (Cambridge, 1961), pp. 94–6, 98.

[25] P.R.O., Close Roll 4 Jac. I, pts 38, 39; S.P. James I, XL/23, LXXI/18; S.P. 15/XXV/35; Grant Book James I (S.P. 14/CXLI), fo. 125; *Cal. S.P.D. 1603–10*, p. 34; H.M.C., *Sackville MSS.*, I, 285; Ashton, *The Crown and the Money Market*, p. 106.

£8,652. 18s. 7d. in the year ending at Michaelmas 1606 and £8,585. 6s. 0d. in the following year. Since the annual charges of managing the farm were calculated at £450, the under-farmers must have netted well over £2,000 in both years. In 1608 the imposition on currants was lowered, and in the next year a new lease was granted reducing the rent payable to the crown to £2,800 per annum. The under-farmers, however, were not allowed to gain proportionately, since, although they were now responsible for the payment of a rent of only £2,800 into the exchequer, Suffolk increased his personal cut to £3,000, making the rent due by the sublessees £5,800, only £200 less than what they had paid before 1609. According to one account Suffolk's cut had risen to £3,500 by 1612. In the next year, fearing a parliamentary onslaught on the royal right to levy impositions, Suffolk decided to relinquish his grant, which still had seventeen years to run. He received in compensation a cash payment of £10,000, and the farm was now let direct by the crown to the Garway–Salter–Wolstenholme group, who managed it, like the French and Rhenish wine farm, in close conjunction with the great farm.[26]

By the second decade of the reign of James I, then, the practice whereby the various petty customs farms were granted, usually at beneficial rents, to courtly concessionaires and sublet by them to syndicates of City business men had been superseded in most cases by the buying out of the courtly interest and the substitution of a direct relationship between the crown and the members of the working syndicates. And from the very beginning it was the latter arrangement which had prevailed in the case of the greatest of all early Stuart concessions, the great farm of the customs. In these circumstances the rôle of the courtier became limited, but his influence was by no means entirely excluded. Those with influence at court might still have scope for turning that influence into

---

[26] P.R.O., S.P. James I, vii/15, S.P. 38/vii (Docquets James I, bk vii); Grant Book James I (S.P. 14/cxli), fo. 125; *Cal. S.P.D. 1603–10*, p. 92; *Cal. S.P.D. 1611–18*, p. 216; *Cal. S.P. Ven. 1603–7*, pp. 192–3, 198, 217, 225; H.M.C., *Salisbury MSS.*, xviii, 305–6; H.M.C., *Sackville MSS.*, i, 69, 173; F. C. Dietz, *English Public Finance 1558–1641* (2nd edn, 1964), pp. 329–30, 347; Ashton, *The Crown and the Money Market*, p. 106; Upton, *Ingram*, p. 7; Stone, *Crisis*, p. 773, and information kindly supplied by Professor Stone.

cash, by throwing it into the scales on behalf of one or another of the competing City syndicates. From the point of view of the crown, the result might not be all that different from its practice of leasing at undervalues to courtiers who sublet to City capitalists. For although it could be argued that in the case of the latter practice the crown was the loser to the extent of the difference between the rents which it received and those at which its courtly grantees sublet the concessions, in cases where the rôle of the courtiers was limited to the use of influence to obtain a concession which a City syndicate leased direct from the crown, the syndicate in question undoubtedly had to pay for this influence being exerted on its behalf, and this was a factor which governed the amount of rent it was prepared to pay to the crown. Thus one of the objects of the rigorous government scrutiny of the conduct of the farmers of the duties on French and Rhenish wines in 1612–13 was to discover 'what Pencions are annuallie given to those who were there helpers in deceaving his Majestie'. As one observer put it, 'there was never any valuable Consideracion given to his Majestie, but great somes of money unto others which the Fermers haue received sufficient satisfaction for'. The earl of Nottingham, himself one of the greediest of Jacobean courtly seekers after this sort of gain, was none the less willing to criticize James's first two lord treasurers, the earls of Dorset and Salisbury, for the way in which they had profited from the first lease of the great farm of the customs, and had 'pared down the robe imperial for their own profit'.[27]

Something is known about the rôle of Salisbury, at that time Lord Cranborne, in this connection. He appears as head of a syndicate of business men whose principal figure was the customs official Francis Jones, and which was in the market for the first lease of the newly established great farm in 1604. Two rival groups were also in the field, the first led by Sir John Swinnerton, who had farmed the duties on French and Rhenish wines under Elizabeth I, the second by the wealthy Levant merchants William Garway and Nicholas Salter. It is interesting to find Cranborne's creature, the projector Arthur Ingram, playing an

[27] B.L., Harleian MSS., 1878, fo. 146; P.R.O., S.P. James I, LXXI/3, LXXIV/37.

important part in organizing the latter syndicate, not least because the upshot of the competition was that the prize went to a coalition of the Garway–Salter and Jones groups, Cranborne having meanwhile withdrawn from the field, richer to the extent of a gift of £6,000 from the successful syndicate.[28]

Domestic concessionary interests of the types outlined above were often held concurrently with a wide variety of more orthodox commercial investments. The two most prominent members of the Garway dynasty of customs farmers provide an excellent example of such diversified interest. Bishop Goodman says of Sir William Garway, who was one of the original group of the farmers of the great customs and who remained a farmer until 1621, that he was 'known to be a very poor man when he entered upon the customs, yet left great treasures behind him', but this notion of capital flowing from the ill-gotten gains of a customer, 'by deceit and fraud become rich', into legitimate commerce does not do justice to Garway's renown as a foundation member of the East India Company and one of the most prominent Levant merchants of the early years of James I's reign.[29] But an even better example is William Garway's son, Sir Henry, the royalist lord mayor of 1639–40, who succeeded to his father's interest in the great farm from 1621 to 1625, and retained an interest as an investor in a number of farms throughout the 1630s. Henry belonged to the very top flight of merchants engaged in three branches of foreign trade – that to the eastern Mediterranean, which brought him the governorship of the Levant Company from 1635 to 1643; the East India trade (he was deputy governor of the East India Company from 1636 to 1639 and governor from 1641 to 1643); and the trade to Russia and Greenland (he became governor of the

[28] Dietz, *English Public Finance 1558–1641*, pp. 330–2; Stone, *Crisis*, p. 427, and 'Fruits of Office', p. 96; Prestwich, *Cranfield*, p. 22; A. P. Newton, 'The Establishment of the Great Farm of the English Customs', *Roy. Hist. Soc. Trans.*, 4th ser., 1 (1918), 148–50.

[29] *Cal. S.P. East Indies 1513–1616*, pp. 100, 117; G. Goodman, *The Court of King James I*, 2 vols., ed. J. Brewer (1839), 1, 305; Friis, *Cockayne's Project*, pp. 177–8; Wood, *Levant Company*, p. 22; Ashton, *The Crown and the Money Market*, p. 89; Chaudhuri, *East India Company*, p. 75.

Greenland and Russia companies, an office from which he was deposed in 1643 on account of his royalist sympathies).[30] One of Henry Garway's partners in the customs-farming syndicates of the early 1620s was an even more spectacular figure, Sir Morris Abbot, the brother of the archbishop of Canterbury, who was for thirteen years governor of the East India Company as well as being one of the ruling clique of the Levant Company and an influential member of the Virginia and Somers Islands companies. To these interests he added extensive trade with France, Italy and Russia, and his dabblings in government financial business included, besides his customs-farming interests in the early 1620s, a share in the farm of the pre-emption of tin in the first decade of the reign of James I and a collectorship of the impositions on lawns, cambrics and silks after 1638, in which year he became lord mayor.[31] Similarly widespread commercial interests can be found among the customs farmers in the later 1630s. Sir Nicholas Crispe, described by Clarendon as 'a citizen of good wealth, great trade and an active-spirited man', was a member of the Merchant Adventurers' Company, a substantial shipowner, a holder of a considerable stock in the East India Company and a dealer in oriental commodities on a very large scale. He was also the leading spirit in the foundation of a new company for trade with Guinea in 1630. His speculations in government financial business, which were facilitated by his success in commerce, included loans to the crown, membership of the syndicate of customs farmers which was heavily fined by the Long Parliament, and monopoly interests in the sale of dyestuffs, copperas stones and vending beads.[32] His partner in

[30] *Cal. S.P.D. 1641–3*, p. 99; Beaven (ed.), *Aldermen*, ii, 60; R. R. Sharpe, *London and the Kingdom*, 3 vols. (1894–5), ii, 122–31; *D.N.B.*; Wood, *Levant Company*, pp. 42, 52; Ashton, *The Crown and the Money Market*, pp. 92, 105–6, 107; Pearl, pp. 299–301; Chaudhuri, *East India Company*, pp. 34, 86, 171, 181, 184, 186; M. C. Wren, 'The Disputed Elections in London in 1641', *Eng. Hist. Rev.*, LXIV (1949), 40–1.

[31] *Cal. S.P.D. Addenda 1580–1625*, p. 498; Beaven (ed.), *Aldermen*, ii, 60; *D.N.B.*; Friis, *Cockayne's Project*, pp. 222, 353, 404; Wood, *Levant Company*, p. 42; Ashton, *The Crown and the Money Market*, pp. 92–3, 96–7; Pearl, pp. 285–8; Chaudhuri, *East India Company*, pp. 34, 59, 86, 175, 185.

[32] Bodleian Library, Bankes MSS., 11/68; *Cal. S.P.D. 1631–3*, pp. 186, 237; *Cal. S.P. East Indies 1625–9*, p. 438; *Cal. S.P. East Indies 1630–4*, pp. 268, 412, 414–15,

the great farm, Sir Job Harby, was a prominent member of both the East India and Muscovy companies who had contracts with the government for the supply of cordage to the navy, as well as being a farmer of the pre-emption of tin.[33]

A characteristic of the operations of all these persons is their simultaneous large-scale involvement in a variety of branches of privileged import–export trade and in activities on the periphery of government business. Indeed the two types of activity were in a real sense mutually fructifying. Capital from orthodox commerce flowed into customs farms, collectorships, the acquisition of patents and other concessions, and the fruits of this investment in turn flowed back into commerce. Moreover, the two forms of investment were on occasions complementary. For example, Sir Job Harby's connection with the trade of the Russia Company was vital to his position as a supplier of naval stores to the government, while his farm of the pre-emption of tin facilitated the important private business which he built up as a large-scale exporter of English tin to the Mediterranean.

Frequently, of course, the growth of interest in government concessions involved a measure of disinvestment in orthodox commodity trade. Sometimes such disinvestment was on quite a large scale and on occasions it was total. Two examples will serve to illustrate this. In the first decade of the reign of James It Lionel Cranfield combined export–import trade with the Netherlands and Germany as a member of the Merchan, Adventurers' Company with investments in a wide variety of syndicates which were formed to exploit government concessions,

418, 429, 473, 497; W. Notestein (ed.), *Journal of Sir Simonds D'Ewes from the Beginnings of the Long Parliament to the Opening of the Trial of the Earl of Strafford* (New Haven, Conn., 1923), pp. 312 & n, 497, 540; Edward, Earl of Clarendon, *The History of the Rebellion and Civil Wars in England*, 6 vols., ed. W. D. Macray (Oxford, 1888), iii, 42; W. R. Scott, *The Constitution and Finance of English, Scottish and Irish Joint-Stock Companies to 1720*, 3 vols. (Cambridge, 1910–12), i, 200–1, ii, 14–15; Carr (ed.), *Charters of Trading Companies*, pp. xliv–xlv; Ashton, *The Crown and the Money Market*, pp. 102–3; Pearl, pp. 119, 194, 266; Chaudhuri, *East India Company*, pp. 34, 127, 156, 185, 186, 188.

[33] *Cal. S.P.D. 1629–31*, pp. 19, 100, 136; *Cal. S.P.D. 1634–5*, p. 586; *Cal. S.P.D. 1635–6*, p. 347; *Cal. S.P.D. 1636–7*, p. 376; *Cal. S.P.D. 1637–8*, p. 83; *Cal. S.P. East Indies 1617–21*, p. 229; Ashton, *The Crown and the Money Market*, pp. 84, 86, 102, 105. Harby disposed of his East India investments in 1635 (*C.M.E.I.C. 1635–9*, pp. 10, 73).

including syndicates for the purchase and resale of export licences, the bestowal of titles of honour, the cornering of supplies of dyewoods, the regulation of the manufacture of starch, the purchase of crown lands, the issuing of licences to sell wine and the farming of various branches of the customs revenue. Such investments on the periphery of government business came to occupy an increasingly large share of his capital and attention until in 1613 he finally abandoned his export–import trade altogether. Similarly, Sir William Russell's purchase of the office of treasurer of the navy from Sir Robert Mansell in 1618 was preceded by large-scale, though not total, disinvestment of his extensive holdings of East India stock. During the 1630s Russell added further to his concessionary interests by joining both the new exclusive group of merchants trading to Barbary and the notorious Westminster Company of Soapmakers.[34]

IV

From the foregoing account it would seem clear that there is a very real sense in which Namieriste analysis in terms of an 'in–out' hypothesis might be applicable to the business interests of the City. It will be one of the main objects of this book to distinguish not only between the interests of the 'ins' and those of the 'outs', but also between the interests of the different groups of 'ins' – between the mass of privileged merchants in general and merchant princes who had directive interests in the great chartered companies: and between those whose interests were confined to orthodox commodity trade, and those who dabbled extensively in domestic concessions, such as customs farms, licences and patents of monopoly. Both of the first two groups were likely to be drawn to a greater or lesser degree towards dependence on the crown, partly because they owed their privileges to royal charter, and partly because these privileges were viewed with hostility by the House of Commons.

[34] Tawney, *Business and Politics under James I*, pp. 33–120; Prestwich, *Cranfield*, pp. 49–93; Ashton, *The Crown and the Money Market*, pp. 18–19, 192–3, and 'The Disbursing Official under the Early Stuarts: The Cases of Sir William Russell and Philip Burlamachi', *Bull. Inst. Hist. Res.*, xxx (1957), 163.

But their connection with the court was less intimate and regular than was the case with those business men who – like the celebrated silkman and moneylender Sir Baptist Hicks – regularly provided the court and courtiers with goods (often on extended credit), and, above all, with those who regularly exploited the multitude of domestic concessions which were unloaded by courtly grantees upon the city. These were concessionaires with a difference, and, just as the interests of different privileged companies in overseas trade often conflicted with one another, so was there ample scope for dispute between different groups of domestic concessionaires and between them and the chartered companies. Export licences provide one of the many examples of this. Given the fact that the Merchant Adventurers could not obtain direct from the crown all the licences they needed, they were by no means averse from buying them at higher prices from courtiers provided that the profits of the latter were kept within reasonable limits and the Merchant Adventurers' profit margins were not squeezed too tightly, as was certainly happening, for example, in the 1630s, when Cumberland's licence had come into the hands of the duke of Richmond and Lenox, who raised his price to a level which the company was not prepared to pay. But, above all, what were the Merchant Adventurers to think of City speculators – some of them, like Cranfield himself, members of their own company – who interposed themselves between the court and the exporting interest, and, not even content with this, were prepared to unload the licences on yet another group of intermediaries before they came into the hands of the ultimate users? Both the Merchant Adventurers and the City speculators in cloth licences were unquestionably concessionaires of crown and court, but in a real sense their privileges were conflicting rather than complementary.[35]

Similarly, it was not only the consumers of monopolized commodities and the producers whose livelihood was threatened, or who, at best, had to pay the patentees or their sub-

[35] On Hicks, see Ashton, *The Crown and the Money Market*, pp. 11, 19–20, 25, 36–7, 73–4, 158–9, 160, 168–9, and 'Usury and High Finance in the Age of Shakespeare and Jonson', *Ren. & Mod. Stud.*, IV (1960), 31–2. On Richmond and Lenox and the cloth licences, see Stone, *Crisis*, p. 432; Ashton, 'Charles I and the City', p. 156.

lessees for the right to continue to do what they had formerly done as of right, who were offended by patents of monopoly. As in the case of export licences, the interests of more powerful and exalted persons, and notably of commercial concessionaires of the crown, were often adversely affected. For instance, both the monopolies of the manufacture of pins and playing cards, as well as the arrangements for the control of production of the latter by a royal patentee, involved the prohibition of the importation of these commodities and therefore aroused the hostility of merchants who imported them from the Low Countries and France no less than that of the haberdashers who sold them on the home market. The tobacco monopoly was, similarly, an important grievance of the merchants of the Virginia and Somers Islands companies in the early 1620s, while the soap monopolies of the successive Westminster and London soapboiling companies in the 1630s were, in their different ways, both detrimental to the interests of the Greenland and Eastland companies via the artificial restrictions which they imposed upon the demand for whale oil and potash, staple imports of each of these companies. Finally, it was owing to the complaints of the gunpowder monopolist John Evelyn that the East India Company's right to make gunpowder for its own use out of the saltpetre which it imported was curtailed in 1632; and, even though this right was revived in 1635, it appears to have lapsed again two years later.[36]

It is, of course, possible to push the distinction between the interests of different groups of concessionaires too hard. It needs to be emphasized that royal domestic concessions, such as monopolies and customs farms, interested a far greater number of persons than those principal directors whose names appear on the patent rolls. Customs farms, for instance, were divided into shares, a controlling interest in which would

[36] B.L., Lansdowne MSS., 160, fos. 291–304(b); P.R.O., P.C.R., P.C. 2, XLII, fos. 87, 294; *Cal. S.P.D. 1625–6*, pp. 99, 376, 407; *Cal. S.P.D. 1629–31*, p. 496; *Cal. S.P.D. 1635*, pp. 311–12, 513; *Cal. S.P.D. 1637*, pp. 53–4, 100, 480, 513; *Cal. S.P.D. 1639*, pp. 45, 363–4; *Cal. S.P. East Indies 1630–4*, pp. 266, 273, 289, 315, 317–19; *A.P.C. 1629–30*, p. 201; *C.M.E.I.C. 1635–9*, pp. 49–50, 76, 101–2, 131–2; *C.D. 1621*, II, 371–2, III, 50–1, 232–3, VII, 455–7; W. Lefroy (ed.), *Memorials of the Discovery and Early Settlement of the Bermudas or Somers Islands 1615–1685*, 2 vols. (1877), I, 339–40, 347–8; S. M. Kingsbury (ed.), *The Records*

normally be retained by the principals, and the remainder marketed in the City. The free assignability of such shares and, above all, their fractional subdivision, meant that an enormously wide range of persons might become financially interested in domestic concessions. But it would be a mistake to stress too strongly the permanence of the interest of the majority of these investors. Unlike the principal patentees, their interest was marginal, and disinvestment normally presented no problems. While the general pervasiveness of investment opportunities in domestic concessions might foster a measure of community of interest between the privileged export–import interest and the domestic concessionary interest, especially when both were under attack in the House of Commons, there is no reason to assume that it prevented friction arising between the two groups.[37]

For instance, the more efficient methods of customs collection employed under the system of customs farming produced a proliferation of complaints about 'the extreame course taken with the Subiect to paie to the vttermost exaction, with which severitie it Cannot be denyd that they were not formerly vsed'. That such complaints might come from commercial concessionaires of the crown as well as from other merchants is clear from a report made to the privy council in 1612 which, after making the usual complaints of mere merchants that 'many Retaylers, Shopkeepers, Artificers and others being unskilfull in the feate of Merchandizing and yet vseing the same . . . are a great discouragement to auncient Murchantes', went on to attack the level of customs and impositions and to affirm that 'the severe vsage of the ffarmers towardes the Murchantes in their goodes

---

of the Virginia Company of London, 4 vols. (Washington, D.C., 1906–35), I, 442–3; Scott, *Joint-Stock Companies*, II, 291; G. Unwin, *Industrial Organization in the Sixteenth and Seventeenth Centuries* (2nd impr., 1957), pp. 144–5, 164–9; R. W. K. Hinton, *The Eastland Trade and the Common Weal in the Seventeenth Century* (Cambridge, 1959), pp. 45, 81; Ashton, 'Charles I and the City', pp. 142–3. Under the inspiration of Sir Edwin Sandys the Virginia and Somers Islands companies became associated for a time with the tobacco monopoly in 1622 (see W. F. Craven, *Dissolution of the Virginia Company* (Gloucester, Mass., 1964 edn), pp. 221–50).

[37] B.L., Stowe MSS., 326, fo. 81(b); P.R.O., S.P. James I, XXII/23; *Cal. S.P.D. Addenda 1625–49*, p. 568; H.M.C., *Sackville MSS.*, I, 101: Ashton, *The Crown and the Money Market*, pp. 86–7.

is a great discouragement to them in their Trades'. Again, in the parliament of 1621, it was the view of the Merchant Adventurers' Company that one of the causes of the slackness of trade was 'the strictness of Farmers in exacting the Custom without anye allowances'. However, it is also true that some of the export–import companies benefited from numbering farmers of the customs among their members. This was certainly true of the Garways and Sir Nicholas Salter, members both of the Levant Company and the customs-farming ring. In 1617 the merchants of Plymouth complained that Sir William Garway had, in his capacity as farmer of the great customs, forbidden commodities to be imported from the Levant into that port by persons who were not free of the Levant Company. Other companies, however, were less fortunate. The Eastland Company, for example, appears to have suffered more than once from the fact that, unlike the Levant Company, none of its members held a place of power and influence at the receipt of custom, with the solitary exception of Sir William Cockayne in the last year of his life. In these circumstances, it was inevitable that the customs farmers would be tempted to ignore the interests of some of the chartered companies insofar as considerations of private profit dictated that they might maximize their returns by winking an eye at the activities of interlopers so long as the latter paid duty. And even the Levant Company's feelings about customs farming were by no means unmixed. They bitterly opposed the farm of the duties on currants being granted to the earl of Suffolk in the first decade of the century, and again to the earl of Arundel in the 1620s, while, useful as Garway's and Salter's influence might be, it bred arrogance in them and a refusal to come to heel when the Levant Company insisted that their exalted position as customs farmers did not automatically confer on them exemption from the ordinances of the company, which they showed an increasing tendency to treat with disdain. In such incidents we can see the germs of a potential divergence of interest between the rank and file of chartered companies and their more opulent brethren with economic eggs in a wide variety of baskets. As long as outport merchants and M.P.s such as Sir Dudley Digges were determined to stress the point of view that the restrictive activities

of the chartered companies and the operations of the customs
farmers were parts of a single plot to secure the aggrandizement
of London at the expense of the outports – that, as another
writer put it, as a result of customs farming, no less than of
cartelization, a situation ensued in which 'the Commons
become disquieted, the prices of all things are daily raised, the
Merchants discoraged . . . the Townes and Out Portes of the
Kingdome decayed, and only London by abridging of Trades
and Trafficke swelles beyond proportion' – there was bound to
be some closing of the ranks of the various privileged groups of
the City. But if there should later come a time when the need
for solidarity was less apparent, it was likely that a split might
be opened in the ranks of the City concessionaires.[38]

The conflict of interest between privileged export–import
merchants and other forms of domestic concessionaires such as
monopolists and speculators in licences has already been
noticed in dealing with these concessions. Nevertheless, so long
as the members of export–import cartels, no less than the domestic concessionaires and the City sublessees of court concessionaires, owed their privileged position to the crown, and, more
important, so long as both of them met with hostility from the
bulk of the members of the House of Commons, it was unlikely
that this potential and actual divergence of interest between the
two groups would be sufficient to dislodge either of them from
leaning towards the court rather than the country. They would
continue, that is, to perceive their best interests as lying in
support of the royal prerogative and hostility to the pretensions
of the House of Commons. After all, it was, for example,
through the exercise of the royal prerogative of enlarging and
restraining – as Bacon put it in 1601 – that internal monopolists
derived their privileges, and the Merchant Adventurers were
reminded from time to time in the House of Commons that one
of their most valued privileges – that of exporting unfinished

[38] B.L., Harleian MSS., 1878, fos. 79–80; Lansdowne MSS., 152, fo. 231; P.R.O.,
S.P. James I, xiii/70, xviii/127–8, xxii/23; S.P. Charles I, xciv/107; P.C.R.,
P.C. 2, xlii, fos. 324–5; *Cal. S.P.D. 1611–18*, p. 476; *Cal. S.P. Ven. 1603–7*, pp.
192–3, 198, 217, 225; *Cal. S.P. Ven. 1628–9*, pp. 552–3; H.M.C., *Salisbury MSS.*,
xvi, 380–1; Ashton, 'Charles I and the City', pp. 143–4; M. Stonehewer,
'Economic Policy and Opinion in the House of Commons, 1621' (B.A. dissertation, University of Nottingham, 1955), pp. 38–9, 77–8.

cloth – rested on a royal licence *non obstante* a parliamentary statute. On the other hand, if issues arose which produced a change in the attitude of the Commons or which accentuated the potential divergence of interest between different types of concessionaires, the London concessionary interest might become disastrously split.

V

It remains to illustrate the intermeshing of the personnel of the concessionary business and the aldermanic élites. For these purposes an analysis has been made of the concessionary interests of two samples of London aldermen. The first sample comprises the twenty-eight aldermen serving at one time or another during 1603, and the second the thirty aldermen serving between October 1640 and December 1641 and who are numbered in Appendix I of Valerie Pearl's book. The result is given in table 1, but it should be borne in mind that a more searching investigation of aldermanic business interests would probably reveal that domestic trade bulked at least as large as such concessionary interests in aldermanic fortunes. Lang's investigations of the aldermanry over the first quarter of the century suggest that more than half of the aldermen may have owed their fortunes principally to this source.[39]

The interests here represented relate to the whole careers of the aldermen in question, including those which were developed after as well as before the years 1603 and 1640–1 respectively. It also needs to be emphasized that the figures represent a minimum degree of involvement, and that a more extensive search would undoubtedly reveal wider interests. However, at least half of the aldermen of 1603 and 46.6 per cent of those in 1640–1 had or came to have directive interests in overseas

[39] Lang, 'Merchants of London', *passim*, and *Guildhall Miscellany*, III (1971), 243–4. The details in the tables which follow are drawn from Beaven (ed.), *Aldermen, passim*; Pearl, pp. 285–308; and an enormous number of mainly printed sources and secondary works which are too many to be listed in detail here. Some idea of the range of these sources can be obtained by consulting the footnotes relating to the individual cases which follow. An exhaustive account of the economic interests of the élite such as has been provided by Lang for the reign of James I and Brenner for the latter part of that of Charles I would involve the use of an even wider range of source materials.

TABLE I. *Aldermen of 1603 and 1640–1 compared*

	Aldermen of 1603	Aldermen of 1640–1
Total	28	30
Master of livery company	15	20[a]
Master of livery company more than once	9	10
Interests in overseas trade	22	18
Interests in more than one branch of overseas trade	18	10
Directive interests in overseas trade	14	14
Directive interests in more than one overseas trade company	7	8
Member of government commission	9	17
Member of more than one commission	6	8
Holder of domestic economic concession, viz.	9	9
(i) Customs farms	4	9
(ii) Revenue collector	4	3
(iii) Pre-emption of tin	0	1
(iv) Monopoly	0	3
(v) Contractor for crown lands	2[b]	0
(vi) Prize-goods contractor	2	0
(vii) Licensee	4	0
(viii) Aulnage	1	0
(ix) Purveyor	1	0
Moneylender to court circles	17	4

[a] Includes one minor company, the Brewers.
[b] Later in the reign under the administration of Lord Treasurer Salisbury.

commerce, while 25 per cent of the earlier group and 26.6 per cent of the aldermen of 1640–1 had or came to have directive interests in more than one company, often held concurrently. Pearl's biographical sketches and an earlier section of the present chapter[40] have provided an account of some of the concessionary interests of those aldermen of 1640–1, who, like Sir Morris Abbott and Sir Henry Garway, were also commercial magnates of the first order. One of their equivalents of 1603 was Sir John Hart, who had been lord mayor as long ago as 1589–90, and who, like many merchants prominent in Elizabethan privateering, was a Levant merchant, a founder member of the East India Company and one of its original

[40] See above, pp. 25–6.

board of directors as well as serving seven times as governor of the Russia Company over the whole of his distinguished commercial career.[41] Others were Sir William Romeney, governor in his time of both the Merchant Adventurers' and East India companies as well as engaging in a substantial trade to Spain and Portugal;[42] and Sir Thomas Lowe, who was to be lord mayor in 1604–5, and was later to be concurrently governor of the Merchant Adventurers', Eastland and Levant companies.[43] Finally we may cite the case of Sir John Watts, who succeeded Lowe as lord mayor and had been described as 'the greatest pirate [viz. privateer] that has ever been in this kingdom'. Watts was a substantial shipowner, a Levant merchant and a founder member and the second governor of the East India Company. He had been one of the directors of the ill-fated Spanish Company at its foundation in 1577 and, despite the failure to refound that body after the Peace of 1604, he developed extensive Jacobean interests with the Iberian peninsula, as well as with France, the Levant and America.[44]

Although there were top-ranking merchants like Richard Stapers, one of the greatest Levant merchants, who never became aldermen, the aldermanic bench of 1603, like that of

[41] *Cal. S.P.D. Addenda 1580–1625*, p. 376; *Cal. S.P.D. 1595–7*, p. 222; H.M.C., *Salisbury MSS.*, x, 214, 236–7; G. Birdwood and W. Foster (eds.), *The Register of Letters . . . of the Governor and Company of Merchants . . . Trading into the East Indies, 1600–1619* (1893), p. 164; H. Stevens (ed.), *The Dawn of English Trade to the East Indies* (1886), pp. 1, 225, 226, 249, 250, 256; Beaven (ed.), *Aldermen*, II, 41; Scott, *Joint-Stock Companies*, II, 49; Willan, *Russia Company*, pp. 24, 221, 245n, 286; K. R. Andrews, *Elizabethan Privateering: English Privateering during the Spanish War 1585–1603* (Cambridge, 1964), pp. 77, 217.

[42] H.M.C., *Salisbury MSS.*, XIX, 178–9, 443; Birdwood and Foster (eds.), *Register of Letters*, p. 46n; Stevens (ed.), *East Indies*, pp. 2, 7, 63, 111, 225, 239, 255; Beaven (ed.), *Aldermen*, II, 48; *D.N.B.*

[43] H.M.C., *Salisbury MSS.*, XVIII, 226; H.M.C., *Sackville MSS.*, II, 135; Beaven (ed.), *Aldermen*, II, 45; Friis, *Cockayne's Project*, pp. 82–4, 100, 130, 183, 242, 268n, 424; Wood, *Levant Company*, pp. 41, 205, and app. IV; G. D. Ramsay, *English Trade during the Centuries of Emergence* (1957), p. 110. As Friis points out, Lowe's numerous governorships are not necessarily a guide to the extent of his active trade and are probably more indicative of a high degree of past than of current commercial activity.

[44] *Cal. S.P.D. 1595–7*, pp. 75–6; *Cal. S.P.D. 1603–10*, p. 176; H.M.C., *Salisbury MSS.*, v, 489, XI, 304, 323, XIX, 55–6, 443; Birdwood and Foster (eds.), *Register of Letters*, pp. 10n, 164n, 281; Stevens (ed.), *East Indies*, pp. 256, 261; J. K. Laughton (ed.), *State Papers Relating to the Defeat of the Spanish Armada* (Navy Record Soc., vols. I–II, 1894), I, 350 & n, II, 337; Beaven (ed.), *Aldermen*, II, 45;

1640–1, contained some of the outstanding commercial magnates of the day. But as Brenner has pointed out, there is a significant change in the nature of their commercial interests as between these two dates. It was remarked earlier that Lang's study of the economic interests of the aldermen in the first quarter of the seventeenth century has revealed that over half of them owed their wealth to domestic rather than to foreign trade. Of the remainder, however, despite the prominence of East India and Levant pioneers like Watts, Hart and Romeney, there can be no doubt of the preponderance of the Merchant Adventurers. In contrast, by 1640, almost half of all the aldermen were Levant or East India men.[45]

The numbers of holders of domestic concessions, as distinct from members of privileged trading companies, were the same in both years, but the fact that there were more aldermen such as Sir Henry Garway and Sir William Acton with financial interests in customs farming among the 1640–1 group than among the alderman of 1603 is in no way surprising. Although there were several piecemeal customs farms in existence in 1603, the government had not yet plumped decisively and publicly in favour of the farming as opposed to the direct administration of the customs revenue; above all, the great farm of the customs was not established until the end of the following year. Nevertheless, both Sir Thomas Bennett, who was lord mayor in 1603–4, and Sir William Ryder, who had distinguished himself during his mayoralty by playing a prominent part in foiling Essex's abortive *coup* of 1601 in the City, had some customs-farming interests, while Sir John Swinnerton, who was to be lord mayor in 1612–13, has already received mention as a farmer of wine duties and unsuccessful competitor for the great farm in 1604. He was also purveyor of wines for the royal household and the sum of his domestic concessionary interests probably brought him substantially greater returns than his commodity trade with Spain, France and the orient, even though he was to be frustrated in his wider customs-farming ambitions. Both Bennett and Ryder were later to play a notable

---

D.N.B.; D. B. Quinn, *Raleigh and the British Empire* (1947), pp. 122–3, 125–6; Stone, *Crisis*, p. 364; Andrews, *Elizabethan Privateering*, pp. 104–9. 194–5.
[45] Lang, 'Merchants of London', p. 194; Brenner, *P. & P.*, no. 58 (1973), pp. 63–4.

part as contractors for the purchase and resale of royal lands.[46] An even more striking contrast between the concessionary interests of the aldermen of 1603 and those of 1640–1 is to be found in the matter of monopolies, but the fact that there were no monopolists among the former group probably reflects absence of opportunity rather than lack of inclination. In 1603 the great furore over monopolies in Elizabeth I's last parliament was only two years away, and had, of course resulted in the cancellation of many patents and the leaving of the remainder to the tender mercies of the common law. Monopolies were again to proliferate under the Stuarts, but by 1603 there had hardly been sufficient time for them to become a significant feature of the economic and political landscape, and the aldermen of 1603 provide no parallels to some of the concessionaires of 1640–1, such as the detested wine monopolist Alderman William Abell, who was also an under-sharer in the customs farms – and Sir Edward Bromfield, the leading figure in the London Society of Soapmakers which, perhaps because it consisted of manufacturers who had previously been ousted by its predecessor, the notorious soapboilers of Westminster, was one of the few monopolies to survive the Long Parliament's onslaught. But while there were no monopolists and relatively few customs farmers among the aldermen of 1603, a number of them held other sorts of domestic concessions, some of which have already been mentioned when dealing with those aldermen with customs-farming interests. In addition to these, Sir Thomas Lowe, for example, besides his directive interests in the Levant, East India and Merchant Adventurers' companies, is found during the early years of James II's reign investing in the purchase and resale of royal lands and acting as a com-

---

[46] *Cal. S.P.D. Addenda 1580–1625*, p. 423; *Cal. S.P.D. 1595–7*, pp. 18, 19, 42, 436; *Cal. S.P.D. 1598–1601*, pp. 72, 445–6; *Cal. S.P.D. 1603–10*, pp. 89, 137, 296, 312, 378, 459, 492, 524; *Cal. S.P. East Indies 1513–1616*, p. 101; H.M.C. *Salisbury MSS.*, IX, 249–50, 253, 304, X, 269, XIV, 138–9, XV, 124, XVII, 168; H.M.C., *Sackville MSS.*, I, 58, 144, 182; Stevens (ed.), *East Indies*, pp. 4, 252; Beaven (ed.), *Aldermen*, II, 44, 48, 60; Cokayne, *Lord Mayors and Sheriffs*, pp. 1–4, 15–18, 54–7; Dietz, *English Public Finance 1558–1641*, pp. 74–5, 88, 90–1, 124, 153–5, 316, 324–5, 332–3, 347, 358; Tawney, *Business and Politics under James I*, p. 105; Ashton, *The Crown and the Money Market*, pp. 87, 90, 106–7, 192; Upton, *Ingram*, pp. 24–5; Pearl, pp. 291–301; Prestwich, *Cranfield*, pp. 29, 117–20, 126, 128–9; Newton, *Roy. Hist. Soc. Trans.*, 4th ser., I (1918), pp. 145–6.

missioner for the issue of starch licences. Sir John Hart, another alderman with widespread commercial interests, was a royal contractor for the sale of prize goods, a concession which dovetailed neatly with his extensive privateering interests, but which, like them, was to fold up with the end of the war in 1604. Finally, Sir Thomas Hayes, a substantial Merchant Adventurer and investor in the early voyages of the East India Company, was also a patentee for the lease of the aulnage and subsidy of the new draperies, and had in 1597 subleased from Lord Hunsdon a licence to export unfinished cloth.[47]

Moneylending may well have absorbed a greater proportion of the funds of the aldermen of 1603 than of those of their counterparts in 1640–1. Certainly the earlier group contained far more of the outstanding moneylenders of the day than did the latter. Among them were aldermen whose activities have already been mentioned such as Bennett and Hart, and others such as Sir Thomas Cambell, Sir Henry Rowe, Sir Thomas Middleton, Sir John Moore, Sir Stephen Soame and, perhaps above all, Sir William Craven and Sir John Spencer. Craven was perhaps the wealthiest cloth wholesaler of his day and a particularly spectacular example of Lang's thesis about the importance of purely domestic trade in the creation of aldermanic fortunes. At his death in 1618 he was reported to be worth half a million, and a recent more conservative estimate of his estate in 1616 puts him as worth at least £125,000. His bequests amounted to £42,167, of which more than £8,600 took the form of charitable benefactions of one sort or another. During his lifetime he numbered among his debtors the second earl of Essex, the ninth earl of Northumberland, Sir Robert Cecil, the later earl of Salisbury, the Mercers' Company – he was himself a Merchant Tailor – and King James I himself. Both Essex and Northumberland were also on the books of Sir

[47] *Cal. S.P.D. 1603–10*, p. 63; *Cal. S.P.D. 1637–8*, pp. 39–40; *Cal. S.P.D. 1638–9*, pp. 21, 101–2, 583, 634; *Cal. S.P.D. 1639*, pp. 110, 131, 167, 168–9, 183, 186, 196, 241, 256, 300–1, 529–30; *Cal. S.P.D. 1639–40*, pp. 161, 395, 408; *Cal. S.P.D. 1640–1*, pp. 289–90, 325, 410; *Cal. S.P.D. 1641–3*, 32–3, 226; H.M.C., *Salisbury MSS.*, v, 94, vii, 523–4, 525; H.M.C., *Sackville MSS.*, i, 155; Birdwood and Foster (eds.), *Register of Letters*, p. 278; Stevens (ed.), *East Indies*, pp. 3, 177, 261; Beaven (ed.), *Aldermen*, ii, 59, 63; Friis, *Cockayne's Project*, pp. 93, 472; Pearl, pp. 289–91, 293–4; Prestwich, *Cranfield*, p. 38.

John Spencer, who had made his pile in overseas trade, notably to the eastern Mediterranean. In 1591 he had been accused, along with two other merchants, of engrossing all the English trade to Tripoli. One of the early directors of the East India Company, at the opening of James I's reign he was said to be 'one of the half dozen richest men in the city'. Spencer had been the projected victim of an abortive kidnapping plot devised by Dunkirk pirates whereby they planned to abduct him from London and exact a ransom of £50,000. Perhaps the most prominent of all lenders to the courtly world of fashion of his day, Spencer's fortune at his death in 1610 was variously estimated at figures between £300,000 and £800,000, but unlike Craven, he left not a penny to charity, and legend has it that the spectacular Spencer inheritance temporarily unhinged the mind of his son-in-law, Lord Compton.[48]

Finally it may be asked whether there is any significant difference between the concessionary and other economic interests of those aldermen who ultimately rose to the mayoral chair and became senior aldermen and those who never rose as high as this. On this subject tables 2 and 3 may offer some guidance.

The fact that a much higher proportion of those who were aldermen of 1640–1 never reached the mayoral chair is due, in part at least, to the revolution in City government in the early 1640s which forms the subject of part of the last chapter of this book.[49] Too much attention should not be paid to the fact that

---

[48] H.M.C., *Downshire MSS.*, II, 251, 259, 261, 263, 268, 272; H.M.C., *Salisbury MSS.*, IX, 425, X, 214, 377, 487, XI, 397, XII, 495, 498, XIII, 288, XIV, 169, XVII, 526–7; Birdwood and Foster (eds.), *Register of Letters*, pp. 164, 281; Stevens (ed.), *East Indies*, pp. 179, 181, 244, 256; G. R. Batho (ed.), *The Household Papers of Henry Percy, Ninth Earl of Northumberland (1564–1632)* (Camden Soc., 3rd ser., XCIII, 1962), pp. 166, 168; Beaven (ed.), *Aldermen*, II, 42, 47; *D.N.B.*; Wood, *Levant Company*, p. 22; Tawney, *Business and Politics under James I*, p. 82; W. K. Jordan, *The Charities of London 1480–1660* (1960), pp. 53, 107, 110–11, 237–8, 258, 286, 295, 337, 339, and *The Charities of Rural England 1480–1660* (1961), pp. 328–9; Ashton, *The Crown and the Money Market*, pp. 116, 117n, 121 & n; Stone, *Crisis*, pp. 534, 535–6, and 'The Peer and the Alderman's Daughter', *History Today*, XI (1961), 48–55; Lang, *Guildhall Miscellany*, III (1971), 245, and 'Social Origins and Social Aspirations of Jacobean London Merchants', *Econ. Hist. Rev.*, 2nd ser., XXVII (1974), 30. Lang's tentative figure for Spencer's fortune is around £400,000.
[49] See below, pp. 205–7, 215–20.

TABLE 2. *The aldermen of 1603*

	Aldermen who never became lord mayor	Aldermen who became lord mayor	Total
Total	9	19	28
Master of livery company	3	12	15
Master of livery company more than once	2	7	9
Interests in overseas trade	8	14	22
Interests in more than one branch of overseas trade	8	10	18
Directive interests in overseas trade	4	10	14
Directive interests in more than one overseas trade company	3	4	7
Member of government commission	1	8	9
Member of more than one commission	1	5	6
Holder of domestic economic concession, viz.	3	6	9
(i) Customs farms	0	4	4
(ii) Contractor for crown lands	0	2	2
(iii) Prize-goods contractor	0	2	2
(iv) Licensee	2	2	4
(v) Aulnage	1	0	1
(vi) Revenue collector	1	3	4
(vii) Purveyor	0	1	1
Moneylender to court circles	4	13	17

a higher proportion of those who ultimately became senior aldermen had active interests in more than one branch of overseas commerce. One quite striking difference between these two years does, however, emerge, for while in 1603 only 47.3 per cent of the aldermen who passed the mayoral chair held directive interests in great merchant companies as against 44.4 per cent of the junior aldermen with such interests, in 1640–1 53.3 per cent of those who ultimately became lord mayor, as opposed to 40 per cent of those who did not, had such directive interests. Domestic concessions were held by 32.1 per cent of the aldermen of 1603 and 30 per cent of those of 1640–1. Among the former those who held or were to hold domestic concessions of one sort or another formed a higher proportion (33.3 per cent) of those who remained junior aldermen than of those who did pass the mayoral chair (31.5 per cent). But the reverse obtains in the case of the aldermen of 1640–1, when only 20 per

TABLE 3. *The aldermen of 1640–1*

	Aldermen who never became lord mayor	Aldermen who became lord mayor	Total
Total	15	15	30
Master of livery company	9[a]	11[a]	20[a]
Master of livery company more than once	2[a]	8	10[a]
Interests in overseas trade	7	11	18
Interests in more than one branch of overseas trade	3	7	10
Directive interests in overseas trade	6	8	14
Directive interests in more than one branch of overseas trade	3	5	8
Member of government commission	11	6	17
Member of more than one commission	2	6	8
Holder of domestic economic concession, viz.	3	6	9
(i) Customs farms	5	4	9
(ii) Revenue collector	0	3	3
(iii) Pre-emption of tin	0	1	1
(iv) Monopoly	1	2	3
Moneylender to court circles	1	3	4

[a] Includes one minor company, the Brewers.

cent of those who remained junior aldermen had such concessionary interests as opposed to 40 per cent of those who ultimately became lord mayor.

If these figures are somewhat inconclusive, they do at least
demonstrate the intermeshing of the personnel of the aldermanic and business élites, and the intimate concern of a significant number of them with government concessions of one sort
or another to which the rôle of moneylender to court circles
had on more than one occasion provided the initial entrée. In
later chapters of this book an attempt has been made to separate
the impact of the policies at court and in the country on the
municipality (that is, in effect, the aldermanic élite) from their
impact on the business-concessionary élite. If this chapter has
demonstrated nothing else, it has at least served to emphasize
that such an exercise is legitimate and rewarding only if it is
remembered that, in the final analysis, the two considerations
are not separate, but inextricably connected.

2

Institutions and oligarchy 11:
gilds and companies

I

The London livery company which emerged out of the medieval gild in the course of the later Middle Ages has been described by the greatest of its historians as 'a social hierarchy . . .
organized on the principle of selection from above'.[1] Unwin's
definition clearly implies that membership of the company did
not necessarily confer equal rights upon all of its members. A
convenient starting point for illustrating the oligarchical
tendencies within the livery company is the institutional
bifurcation of that body into an upper section, usually known
as the livery, and a lower, usually known as the yeomanry. The
distinction corresponds roughly with that between those who
exercised trade in the products of a craft or crafts and those
who manufactured them. The livery consisted of the more
affluent members of the society, and since the surest way to
affluence in pre-industrial England lay via the pursuit of trade
rather than the exercise of a craft, it was inevitable that, at
least in the case of the greater companies, the vast bulk of the
members of the livery were traders rather than craftsmen. The
conflict within the ranks of the livery company with which
Unwin was especially concerned was that between tradesmen
and craftsmen or, in other words, between livery and yeomanry.
But discussion of the oligarchical tendencies which characterized
the London livery companies is by no means exhausted by
reference to this conflict and its institutional expression. The
merchant members of the livery may normally have been
united in opposition to the aspirations of the yeoman craftsmen,
but, on other crucial issues, they were by no means invariably

[1] G. Unwin, *The Gilds and Companies of London* (4th edn, 1963), p. 217.

united among themselves. Nor it is quite true that the distinction between livery and yeomanry was invariably a distinction between a preponderantly trading and a preponderantly handicrafts body. For one thing the bulk of the liverymen of many and perhaps most of the minor companies certainly consisted of handicrafts masters rather than tradesmen, though, as independent producers, most of them also traded from their shops; and, for another, there were some trades which totally lacked a manufacturing element. To cite two fairly obvious examples from the twelve major companies, Fishmongers sold but did not catch fish, and Drapers sold but did not manufacture cloth. Finally, in the larger companies, a significant, if minority, sector of the yeomanry consisted of traders rather than handicraftsmen.

An examination of the constitutional arrangements which prevailed within a large number of the livery companies makes it clear that, while it may be true that the livery was a privileged body as compared with the yeomanry, some of the members of the former body were more privileged than others. The executive authority within each company was normally vested in a master and a number of wardens – normally between two and four – who exercised their functions in conjunction with a select body which was usually known as the court of assistants. In the larger companies there was an important tendency for the latter body to be composed of anything from a highly significant sprinkling to a complete preponderance of those who had previously been masters or wardens. New masters and wardens were often either nominated by their immediate predecessors or, at best, by the court of assistants. And, often enough, the rôle of the court of assistants, let alone that of the livery as a whole, in the election of new officers was severely circumscribed. In the new charter granted to the Drapers' Company in 1607, the apparently democratic method of election of a new master and wardens by 'the men of the Gild or Fraternity' was replaced by election, not by the gild as a whole, not even by the livery as a whole, nor even by the court of assistants, but by those members of that court who had already held the offices either of master or warden. In the Mercers' Company the members of the court of assistants had the right to produce a list of names out of which the existing master and wardens chose their successors. Since the membership of the court of assistants itself had been confined by an ordinance of 1504 to 'sad and discreet persons' who had themselves previously been masters or wardens, the prevailing impression which is conveyed by these electoral arrangements is that of one oligarchy superimposed upon another. In these circumstances it is hardly surprising that the oligarchical structure of many of the companies aroused protests from liverymen as well as from yeomen. As early as 1529 the indirect modes of election which had already become prevalent within the Goldsmiths' Company had precipitated a sharp constitutional crisis in the livery of that company, and during the succeeding century, membership of its court of assistants was whittled down to an even narrower clique, which violated the interests not only of the craftsmen but also of many of the more substantial goldsmiths who were liverymen. The constitutional disputes within the Cutlers' Company in 1621 reflect similar circumstances, for these were not disputes between the livery and yeomanry, but between 'the Master, Wardens and Antienst [*sic*] of the companie of Cutlers and those of the livery of that Companie'. The occasion of this dispute was the attempt of the vast majority of the livery who were not office-holders to break down the prevailing oligarchical arrangements by directly electing a new master without observing the now normal procedure whereby nomination was made by the existing office-holders.[2]

Now while the division of companies into livery and yeomanry and the disputes which prevailed between the members of the two bodies can obviously lend themselves to an Unwinesque interpretation based upon the distinction between traders and craftsmen, the type of dispute which has been outlined above is hardly explicable in these terms. It is, of course, a common practice for large and unwieldy bodies to entrust a measure of executive and administrative power to select

---

[2] P.R.O., S.P. James I, cxviii/119, clxiii/10, 11; C.L.R.O., Rep. xxxiv, fo. 133; Rep. xliii, fo. 64; Rep. xliv, fos. 15–15(b), 84(b)–85; Unwin, *Gilds and Companies*, p. 219; A. H. Johnson, *A History of the Worshipful Company of Drapers of the City of London*, 5 vols. (Oxford, 1914–22), iii, 76–7. For a good description of the dominant rôle of the court of assistants in one company in the later sixteenth century, see F. Consitt, *The London Weavers' Company* (Oxford, 1933), pp. 114–22.

committees consisting of a small number of persons. But arguments from administrative efficiency can hardly be adduced in explanation of the sorts of electoral restrictions of which examples have been given above. In the light of such facts it seems reasonable to entertain serious doubts about the notion that there was an inevitable community of interest between all the members of a company who possessed the right to wear the livery.

II

Some of the grounds for divergence of interest between members of the same company may be illustrated from conflicting notions about the purpose of gild membership. Unquestionably to many of the liverymen of the greater companies the central object of their membership was to dominate and control the crafts. In early Stuart England, as in Tudor and late medieval times, the growth of industrial capitalism in relation to the craft gilds, with their traditional obstacles to technological progress and their insistence on equality between small master craftsmen, took two main forms. In the first place, the obstacles to expansion posed by the gilds could be circumvented by the migration of capital and enterprise to rural and suburban areas where the writ of the gilds did not run. But although this is the most momentous and important way in which industrial capitalism overcame the obstacles posed by the medieval craft gilds, it is not the only one. In London, in particular, a second strand of development was the attempt to capture the institutional machinery of the gilds and to use it for ends which were fundamentally different from those for which it had originally been designed. The process whereby craft gilds were transformed into livery companies was – in part at least – one whereby in addition to being an association of master craftsmen – with or without journeyman employees – the gild had also become an association of traders, in whose interest it was to exercise some degree of control over production. This is the classic thesis of George Unwin,[3] and although it is arguable that

---

[3] Unwin, *Gilds and Companies, passim*; also his *Industrial Organization, passim*.

he overstated its importance as the principal factor behind gild development, in considering the *raison d'être* of gild membership to many liverymen, it is unquestionably a consideration of primary importance. Some of these liverymen had originally been master craftsmen, who, by virtue of their enterprise or their occupation of strategic positions in a productive process (the final stage of production, for example), had developed marketing functions and aspired to control their less enterprising or less fortunately placed fellows. Others had always been traders and had often been members of a purely trading association which had amalgamated with craft gilds, the business of whose members had been to produce the goods which the traders marketed over too wide an area for the craftsmen to serve direct. It was thus that the London Haberdashers had absorbed the Hatters and the Cappers, and the Leathersellers the Glovers, the Pursers and the Whitawyers.[4] Whatever the origins of the movement, its institutional end-product was always the same, and its essence is to be found in the combination by mercantile interests of institutions which had once been craft associations, but which were rapidly becoming associations of both craftsmen and tradesmen in which the latter, by virtue of their greater command of capital, their control of access to markets – and often raw materials too – both paid the piper and called the tune.

But it would be rash to assume that all who contributed heavily to the payment of the piper necessarily wished to call the same tune. The higher we move up the hierarchy of the greater livery companies, the more prominent become the members of what can be described as the *haute bourgeoisie*. The nature of this business élite has already been examined in the previous chapter, from which it must be clear that its wealth was derived mainly from activity in the sphere of overseas and domestic trade, sometimes associated with the exploitation of government concessions. It was from such persons that the ruling civic class – those who attained to the aldermanry and mayoralty – was primarily recruited; and in their view the

---

[4] Unwin, *Gilds and Companies*, pp. 166–8, 231, and *Industrial Organization*, pp. 44, 82, 128–30.

raison d'être of membership of a livery company was probably radically different from that of those liverymen who sought to use the machinery of the gild to put themselves in a favourable position vis-à-vis the crafts.

It must already be apparent that the centre of gravity of the economic world of many of the members of this *haute bourgeoisie*, institutionally speaking, was not the livery company but the privileged chartered company engaged in foreign trade. This, however, is not quite the same thing as to say that they valued membership solely for the very substantial social facilities it provided and as the essential path to civic honours and influence. It is undeniable, of course, that, then as now, these things were valued for their own sake. But they were also by no means devoid of significance in the narrower economic sense. For it was only via membership of a gild that the custom of London conferred the right to trade within the confines of the City. As far as the *haute bourgeoisie* was concerned, it was an additional advantage that this custom conferred the right to exercise any trade and not simply that trade from which a particular company took its name. Such views were shared by those engaged in overseas commerce and by those larger domestic merchants who dealt in a wide range of enterprises and commodities. They naturally found far greater favour in the greater gilds than in the smaller, since wealthy merchants were obviously more likely to join the large companies because of the greater range of social facilities which they provided, the greater prestige attaching to them and the need to be a member of one of the twelve major companies as a condition of obtaining the highest civic honours. Thus Alderman Edward Barkham found it necessary to secure translation from the Leathersellers to the Drapers before becoming lord mayor in 1621, while Cuthbert Hacket moved from the Dyers to the Drapers before his mayoralty of 1626–7.[5]

III

The struggle between the relatively liberal concept of the custom of London and the traditional principle of one man/one

[5] A. H. Johnson, *Drapers*, III, 9–10, 198n.

trade is a vitally important aspect of London's economic history. We have seen how the ideas embodied in the custom of London were eminently acceptable to the greatest merchants of the City. Equally obviously, they were totally unacceptable to many master craftsmen whose economic conservatism was based upon a firm realization of their true economic interests. What is perhaps less obvious is that the custom of London might be viewed with suspicion by those merchant liverymen who dealt with the craftsmen and sometimes virtually employed them, and who confined themselves to dealings in the products of one craft or group of allied crafts. It has already been suggested that, for such merchants, a primary object of attaining to a position of power within the gild was the opportunity which this afforded of manipulating the gild ordinances as a means of separating the master craftsman from his market. It is obvious that the efficiency of the gild for these purposes will be directly proportionate to the occupational homogeneity of its members. Conversely, the notion of the custom of London was likely to achieve favour among the members of a particular gild in direct proportion to its occupational heterogeneity. A good example is the Drapers' Company. Of the 528 members of the yeomanry paying quarterage in 1624, only 25 are described as drapers, while among the remainder are 116 tailors, 4 clothworkers, 8 mercers, 5 haberdashers, 16 upholsterers, 2 carpenters, 1 bowyer, 4 cutlers, 2 grocers, 2 vintners and a goldsmith. For all of the trades here specified there existed an appropriate company, and if it had not been for the custom of London, none of the persons here enumerated could have been members of the Drapers' Company.[6]

But there was in fact more than one custom of London. The craftsmen who pursued the heterogeneous occupations described above no doubt did so by virtue of the custom with which we are already familiar whereby anyone who was free of any company might pursue any occupation. But how, it may be asked, had they come to be members of the Drapers' Company at all? The answer could well be that they had taken advantage of another custom of London, the right of any person

---

[6] Ibid. III, 94–5n, 198, IV, app. X, 98–102.

to claim membership of any company by patrimony. Thus if the son of the member of one company was apprenticed to a member of another, he could ultimately, if he chose, claim membership of his father's company, in which circumstances his own apprentices would eventually become free of that company too, except insofar as they were able and chose to exercise the same privilege on their own behalf. A gildsman might therefore cite the custom of London as the justification both for pursuing a craft unrelated to that which gave its name to the gild to which he belonged, and for belonging to a gild while not pursuing the craft associated with it.[7]

It should not be surprising therefore that many liverymen of London companies did not view gild membership primarily as a means to secure the insulation of craftsmen from the market. This can be illustrated from the history of the Leathersellers' Company.[8] The ruling body in this company does not seem to have consisted exclusively, or even preponderantly, of dealers in leather. On the other hand, many of the chief leather dealers in London appear to have been prominent members of other companies whose titles suggest no connection with leather. Although the former group dealt in commodities other than leather, it was nevertheless in their interests, as rulers of the Leathersellers' Company, to oppose the break away from the the parent company of craftsmen such as pursers, tawyers and, above all, the glovers. It was in their interest, because the breaking away of subordinate crafts was an infection which was likely to spread rapidly, and which might prove to be the thin end of a wedge driven into the economic freedom and flexibility enshrined in the custom of London. It was, similarly, in the interests of the latter group – for example, of members of the Haberdashers' Company, who took advantage of the custom of London to deal in leather and employ workers in leather – that these workers should be kept in proper subordination to the Leathersellers' Company, even though the employers did not belong to that company. For the alternative might well have been the enforcement of those regulations of the company

---

[7] I am deeply indebted to Professor F. J. Fisher for discussion of the points raised here.

[8] On the Leathersellers see Unwin, *Industrial Organization*, pp. 128–30.

which confined the practice of a trade to members of the appropriate company. Such entrepreneurs worked their wills not positively, by directly manipulating the ordinances of their companies to secure the economic subordination of the craftsmen, but negatively, by ignoring those provisions of the ordinances relating to the search, apprenticeship and similar matters, with the aim of profiting from the economic freedoms conferred by the custom of London.

IV

As the example from the Drapers' Company suggests, occupational heterogeneity was not a phenomenon which was confined to the livery or upper reaches of the livery company. Moreover, quite apart from considerations of diversity of occupation, the yeomanry, or lower sector of the company, was by no means always confined to craftsmen. Certainly the yeomanry organization of most of the major companies contained an important leavening of persons whose interests were more in trade than in manufacture, and who viewed the period which they spent in the subordinate organization as a preliminary to their elevation to the ranks of the livery. They presented an important obstacle to the use of the yeomanry organization as an economically homogeneous pressure group. Their significance is out of all proportion to their numbers, since, as a consequence of the subordination of the yeomanry organization to the ruling elements in the company, they usually obtained far more than their fair share of the offices in the lower organization.

The aspirations of many of the more influential members of the yeomanry were therefore more closely aligned with those of the merchant liverymen than with those of the craftsmen who made up the vast majority of this lower part of the livery company.[9] To these latter the old craft-gild idea, or something closely resembling it, while bearing ever less correspondence to the realities of economic life, was still a profoundly influential

---

[9] For a good example see C. Welch, *History of the Cutlers' Company of London and the Minor Cutlery Crafts*, 2 vols. (1916–23), II, 79.

C

force. In their view gilds ought to be associations to protect standards of quality, to organize technical training, and to ensure a decent livelihood for all of their members. Monopolistic as to their privileges in relation to the practice of a craft within a particular community, their rules and ordinances should be directed, *inter alia*, to the preservation of rough economic equality between members. Reflecting as they did the conditions of a simpler bygone age when the division of labour had been rudimentary, when the simple tools and other items of fixed capital required for independent production had been relatively easy to acquire, and when the market served by the crafts had been smaller and to that extent less subject to the violent economic fluctuations which are the bane of the small independent producer, such conceptions had originally denoted a wide area of community of economic interest between master and journeyman based upon the ample opportunities afforded to the latter of rising to the mastership.

But this state of affairs was not to last, for in later medieval and Tudor towns journeymen were increasingly being excluded from membership of the craft gilds and were forming their own associations – Yeomen or Bachelor gilds, the only institutions of pre-industrial society which are in any way analogous with modern trade unions. Here was a clear sign that the old community of interest between master and journeymen was wearing very thin. In this development, ownership of shop sites seems to have been more important than ownership of tools, and, as a result of the limited supply of shop sites, back-street artisans tended increasingly to work for front-street shopkeepers.[10] Moreover, in London the depression of the status and condition of the journeymen was paralleled by a similar depression of many master craftsmen, a tendency which is reflected in the composition of the greater livery companies, many of which had owed their origins to the amalgamation of craft and other gilds. Despite the presence of tradesmen within the yeomanries of these companies, the bulk of the members of the yeomanry were craftsmen and, moreover, master craftsmen, not journeymen. For instance, out of the 777 members of the Drapers'

---

[10] I owe this information to Professor Fisher.

Company in 1641 whose occupations were specified, only 37 were journeymen.[11] The Drapers' Company was, of course, one of the largest of the London livery companies, whose livery was dominated by merchants, and in which a parallel exclusivism within the ranks of the yeomanry was correspondingly highly developed. It has already been shown that only a relatively small minority of the yeomanry of this company consisted of practising drapers, and, as such, these would, of course, be retailers rather than craftsmen. Of the remainder it would probably be true to say that, even if they were handicraftsmen, exclusion from the livery of a company which had nothing to do with the regulation of the crafts which they practised could hardly be a matter of great moment to them. This situation is therefore notably different from that prevailing in other companies, such as the Leathersellers and the Cutlers, which were characterized both by a greater degree of occupational homogeneity and by liveries consisting primarily of tradesmen and yeomanries primarily of master craftsmen. In yet other lesser companies the distinction between livery and yeomanry was not simply a distinction between trades and master crafts-men, for the yeomanry contained quite a large number of journeymen. Thus in the Coopers' Company in 1622, out of 588 members of the yeomanry as many as 273 were journeymen free of the company.[12]

It follows therefore that internecine disputes within livery companies might take many forms. Some of the causes of disputes among liverymen have already been treated. It is now time to turn to an analysis of the nature of the disputes between the livery and the yeomanry, from which it will emerge that by no means all of these disputes are explicable in terms of an Unwinesque divergence of interest between traders and crafts-men. Nevertheless a common cause of complaint was the domin-ation of the company as a whole by non-craftsmen. Such complaints were directed against two distinct types of person: the trader who dealt primarily, if not exclusively, in the product from which the gild derived its name, but played no part in their

---

[11] A. H. Johnson, *Drapers*, IV, 161–2.
[12] London Guildhall MSS., 5614/1 (Coopers' Quarterage Book, 1622–8).

manufacture; and the trader who did not even deal in these products. Bitter complaints against both types were a prominent feature of the recurrent crises in the Goldsmiths' Company in the 1620s.[13] The trouble in the Cutlers' Company in 1606 and again in 1609–10 was connected with craft complaints against 'sundrye persons free of the Companie . . . but not being working Cutlers', which could refer to either or both types of situation.[14] Less equivocal is the evidence relating to the complaints of the artisan skinners in 1606 that the master and wardens of the Skinners' Company

ought to be men of the misterye or Art for vndergoing and supporting of other the members of the said Companye. They of late yeres for the most part have bene, and nowe all fyve are, men vsing other professions, whereby they have noe compassionate feeling of the abuses in the sayd Art or misterye, to the vtter overthrowe of the sayd Art in verye short tyme.

To men brought up in the gild tradition it was outrageous for the company 'to be governed by men altogether vnskilfull'. They claimed that representation of the craft element on the governing body of the company had been almost entirely whittled away

Soe that in verye few yeares by this their plott there shold scarcely sitt a man of the misterye in Counsell with them in the governing of ther owne Art & birthright.[15]

Similar complaints were made within the Fishmongers' Company in 1636 that it was dominated by men of other trades who knew nothing and cared nothing about fish.[16]

At this point it needs to be emphasized that by no means all of the grievances of the yeomen related to the domination of the gilds by commerce, whether from inside or outside the ranks of those dealing in the products of the crafts. In many of

---

[13] P.R.O., S.P. James I, cxviii/119, clxiii/10, 11; C.L.R.O., Rep. xxxiv, fo. 133; Rep. xliii, fo. 64; Rep. xliv, fos. 15–15(b), 84(b)–85.

[14] C.L.R.O., Rep. xxvii, fos. 213(b), 218(b), 225(b)–226; Rep. xxix, fos. 60–60(b), 232–232(b); Welch, *Cutlers*, ii, 198–206.

[15] C.L.R.O., Rep. xxvii, fos. 321(b), 351; Rep. xxviii, fos. 21(b)–27; Remembrancia, ii, 282; J. J. Lambert (ed.), *Records of the Skinners of London: Edward I to James I* (1933), pp. 341–3.

[16] *Cal. S.P.D. 1636–7*, p. 26.

the smaller companies, in which a much higher proportion of the liverymen and officials were master craftsmen, the criticism was quite different. In the Weavers' Company, for instance, the complaints which were directed against the bailiff, wardens and court of assistants during the reign of Charles I related not to the dominance of a trading element which stood outside production, but to the more old-fashioned type of grievance of journeyman employees against master craftsmen.[17]

One of the consequences of all these varied forms of domination of the livery company by one exclusive group or another was the lapsing of the 'search'. It was only via the stringent application of the duty of the gild to inspect the products over which it exercised supervision that the interests of the skilled craftsmen who had served their apprenticeship could be safeguarded. The search could be efficiently prosecuted only by 'manuell tradesmen of exquisit skill & knowledge', but too often its execution was in the hands of company officers whose ignorance of the craft made them incapable of discovering 'such deceipt as [is] dayly practised by lewde persones, plate-workers and otheres ... which ... falcehood the best experience can hardly be able to discover'.[18] So argued the working goldsmiths in complaints made during the early 1620s, and their views were echoed by dozens of craftsmen in other companies. They sometimes evoked sharp and spirited replies from the company officials. Thus in 1606 the master and wardens of the Skinners' Company, while admitting that they had no knowledge of the intricacies of the craft, argued that this need not prevent the efficient execution of the search. Skilled craftsmen might be deputed to aid and advise the officers of the company, with results – so the latter claimed – which would be far more satisfactory than if the conduct of the search had been left solely in the hands of the craftsmen, 'for they wold surelye winck one at anothers faultes as heretofore they have done'.[19]

---

[17] C.L.R.O., Rep. xli, fos. 148, 287(b)–289; Rep. xliv, fos. 364(b)–365; Rep. xlv, fos. 74–79(b); Rep. xlvii, fos. 43(b), 265(b), 392(b), 398(b); Rep. xlviii, fos. 76(b)–78(b).
[18] P.R.O., S.P. James I, cxviii/119, clxiii/10.
[19] C.L.R.O., Rep. xxviii, fos. 24–24(b).

The controversies arising out of the conduct of the search might on occasions be more complex than the foregoing account suggests. In 1641, in the course of their long-drawn-out struggle to free themselves from the domination of the leathersellers within the company of that name, the London glovers specified two main abuses to which the search was subject when conducted by the leathersellers. The first was the now familiar one that the leathersellers, being purely tradesmen and 'not being skilled in making gloves, cannot iudge of workemanshipp therein'. But the second abuse was more singular, for the leathersellers were not simply dealers in gloves and, as such, controllers of the outlets for the products of the glovers' labour. They also sold to the glovers dressed leather, the basic material of their craft, and 'in regard the leather is bought of them, they wilbe willing to passe by faultes in ye same'.[20]

The lapsing of the search might equally be a cause of complaint in cases where the company was dominated by small master craftsmen rather than by traders, and where the yeomanry consisted mainly of journeymen. For although the master craftsman might appear as the champion of gild standards when it suited his book to do so, he was not always quite so particular when it was he and not the trader who dominated the gild, and might employ cheap unapprenticed labour – or even aliens – producing shoddy goods. It was such practices which produced a crop of complaints against certain masters in the Weavers' Company during the early years of the reign of Charles I.[21]

The disregarding of the apprenticeship regulations – and therefore of the provisions of the famous Statute of 1563 – was obviously closely connected with the lapsing of the efficiency of the search. Complaints against gild officials for their failure to see that only properly apprenticed workers were employed were made by, for example, working basketmakers in 1610, spectaclemakers in 1628, and goldsmiths and printers during the 1620s and 1630s.[22] But if the employment of cheap unapprenticed

[20] C.L.R.O., Rep. LV, fo. 226.
[21] C.L.R.O., Rep. XLI, fos. 287(b)–288; Rep. XLV, fos. 74–79(b).
[22] C.L.R.O., Rep. XXIX, fo. 169; Rep. XLIV, fos. 84(b)–85; *Cal. S.P.D. 1628–9*, p. 200; *Cal. S.P.D. 1635*, pp. 483–4.

labour was one source of grievance, another method of utilizing sources of cheap labour was to fail to observe the stipulated ratio between the numbers of apprentices and journeymen, to the detriment of the latter. In April 1611 the common council of London appointed a committee to look into the matter and suggest ways of preventing abuses.[23]

What, in fact, the rank and file of the companies were complaining about was the disregard of the gild ordinances by the dominant element within the company, so as to make the livelihood of the former more precarious and to increase their economic dependence upon the latter. Among the complaints of the London weavers against the ruling body of the Weavers' Company was their engrossing of looms, a practice which was bound to result in tighter entrepreneurial control of journeyman weavers.[24] Sometimes the dominant element whose practices provoked protests was a class of relatively small-scale master craftsmen who employed journeymen and apprentices; at other times it was traders who dealt in the products of the gild, and at others it was traders who dominated the gild but had no connection with its products. In most of the larger companies formidable barriers had been raised against the accession of handicraftsmen to company office and influence. The master and wardens of the Skinners' Company may have been correct in their assertion of 1606 that places on the court of assistants had been offered from time to time to handicraftsmen, but 'there was not above one of the Art that found himself hable to take the charge vppon him'.[25] But even if this was true, the most significant feature of their argument is the fact that it reflects those basic characteristics of the livery company which were so strongly stressed by Unwin – that it was a far grander and more magnificent form of corporate organization than the old gild out of which it had grown. As such, it was bound to give to those of its members who commanded considerable capital resources substantial advantages over the handicraftsmen, whose interests were to that extent likely to be less favour-

---

[23] C.L.R.O., Jor. xxviii, fo. 186(b).
[24] C.L.R.O., Rep. xlv, fos. 76(b)–77.
[25] C.L.R.O., Rep. xxviii, fo. 24. See also ibid. fo. 25, where the same point is made, even more disingenuously, about the offices of master and warden.

ably regarded by the livery company than they had been by the craft gild. In such circumstances complaints against those who purchased company office, like those against one Richard Fisher who paid forty marks to become a warden of the Plasterers' Company in 1611, and had on that account been preferred above some of his more senior colleagues, may not have been uncommon.[26]

Such were the main issues at stake in the internal disputes of the gilds and companies of London in the early seventeenth century. Many of these issues were to find expression in one of the most characteristic and important of the movements of the period, the formation of breakaway craft institutions, which is treated elsewhere.[27] But it is not only in internal disputes that the discontent against gild oligarchy and plutocracy manifested itself. It is also apparent in the intergild disputes of the period and it is to these that we must now turn.

V

In January 1607 the court of aldermen of the City of London appointed a sub-committee to

consider of the requestes made to this Court by certein of the inferior Companies of this cittye, That such handicraftsmen as are free of other Companies maye be translated to those Companies whose trade or art they use, as fittest to governe them, and to search and judge of their workmanships.[28]

In the case of those lesser companies whose affairs were still conducted more or less in conformity with the old gild tradition, the practice of the craft by persons who were free of other companies obviously imposed crucial difficulties in the way of efficient enforcement of craft regulations. According to the so-called custom of London, the acquisition of the freedom, whether by apprenticeship, patrimony or redemption,[29] carried with it

---

[26] C.L.R.O., Rep. xxx, fos. 97(b), 116(b)–117, 179(b)–180, 194–194(b), 200(b)–201.
[27] See below, pp. 71–82.
[28] C.L.R.O., Rep. xxvii, fos. 326(b)–327.
[29] I.e. purchase.

the right to practise any craft or trade. Once a few persons had taken advantage of the custom, the practice was bound to spread, for their apprentices would succeed to the freedom in the company of which their master was a member, and not necessarily in the company appropriate to the craft which they pursued. So much for freedom by apprenticeship. As to patrimony, as the occupational structure of the City became more fluid and the range of economic opportunities widened, there was a diminished likelihood that the pursuit of a craft would be endogamous. Sons often prefer not to enter the occupations of their fathers if afforded a sufficient opportunity not to do so. Thus, as has already been remarked, there was no guarantee that those who attained to the freedom by patrimony would pursue the craft appropriate to the companies of which they became members. In the case of those who obtained the freedom by redemption, the obstacles to taking advantage of the custom of London were greater, for it was customary for the City to demand a recognizance in penalty of £100 from anyone who proceeded to the freedom by redemption, that he would engage, principally, if not exclusively, in the craft of the company in which he had been made free. This made such individuals somewhat more vulnerable than those who had attained the freedom by other means, for the recognizances might be sued by an individual or company if their conditions were broken. This happened in 1628 to one Josias Elmer, 'who obteyned his freedome of this Cittie by redemption in the Company of Bricklayers', but 'vseth the trade of an Iremonger [*sic*] and not the trade of Bricklayer, contrary to the Condicion of his Recognizance'. Whether the recognizances were interpreted strictly or liberally depended largely on the attitude of the municipal authorities. In the mid 1630s there was for a time a danger that an extremely illiberal interpretation might be put upon them, when Lady Elizabeth Savage, an impecunious but ingenious courtier on the make, petitioned the king for a grant of the penalties of these recognizances. To have given to a private person a financial interest in prosecuting such recognizances would unquestionably have resulted in a far more energetic harrying of redemptioners who were practising crafts other than those connected with the companies in which they had taken the freedom. Fortunately for them, these penalties were not the king's to grant.[30]

Nevertheless the civic authorities, yielding to pressure not only from below, but also from the government, had from time to time at least to give the impression that they were doing something about the problem. In December 1620 the court of aldermen called for a bill to be drawn up 'for explanacion of the custome of this Cittie touching such as are made free by redempcion and vse other trades then they take their freedome for'. In the following month the aldermen were probably overjoyed to receive – if indeed they had not had a hand in instigating – a petition from

> a greate nomber of poore freemen . . . that a bill may be preferred at the Parliament for a tolleracion or some other course to be taken for releife of the peticioners against a statute made quinto Elizabeth, in regard they vse and exercise the arte and trades whereunto they haue not bene brought vpp as Apprentice for the space of Seaven yeares.

The apprenticeship clauses of the Statute of 1563 with their insistence on seven years' apprenticeship in a craft which the erstwhile apprentice should pursue thereafter fitted in very well with the notion that there should be an identity between membership of a gild and pursuit of the appropriate craft. It was, however, naturally unpopular with those who favoured the more liberal and flexible arrangements which were enshrined in the custom of London. Such a person was John Bagshaw, a member of the Cordwainers' Company who in 1634 pleaded the custom of London as his defence against the charge of exercising the craft of a goldsmith to which he had never been apprenticed. He was, however, a trifle out of date, for earlier in the same year a committee of the court of aldermen had produced a report which cleared up the apparent contradiction between the custom of London and the apprenticeship provisions of the Statute of 1563, though it was careful to do so without detracting unduly from the value of the former to the commercial bigwigs who ruled the City. The committee's

[30] C.L.R.O., Rep. xlii, fo. 129; Rep. l, fos. 67, 110–11; *Cal. S.P.D. 1635*, p. 536; *Cal. S.P.D. 1635–6*, pp. 194–5.

findings were that the custom of London was applicable only to 'marchandizing and trades' and not to crafts.[31]

Most of the pressure came from the smaller companies where master craftsmen rather than traders were the dominant force. What these companies particularly desired was the translation to them of all members of other companies who pursued their crafts. During the reign of Charles I there were fifteen such translations from the Drapers' Company, all but one being to lesser companies of the City. To the latter the advantages of translation were many. Most of them probably stood to make a net gain in membership out of it. Moreover, the practitioners of a craft who were not members of the company connected with that craft could the more easily evade regulations about the numbers of apprentices and journeymen employed, more especially if, as was often the case, the regulations of the company to which they belonged were more generous on this point; they could more easily employ cheap untrained labour and were therefore the more likely – or so it was claimed – to produce shoddy work. In the view of those who sought to use translation as a device to bring about an identity between the practitioners of a particular craft and the members of the appropriate gild or company, the tendency for the two to diverge was encouraged by the unfair advantages which membership of another gild brought about. Thus the Farriers' Company complained in 1609 that the number of farriers who were free of the Painter–Stainers' Company was growing at such an alarming rate that it would lead to 'the vtter overthrow and vndoeing of the peticioners poor Companie which had bin a Companie of ccc yeres continuance or thereaboutes'. They succeeded in obtaining the required translations, and, in the following year, though with some difficulty, the translation of three members of the Blacksmiths' Company.[32]

Before and even after the decision of 1634 the attitude of the municipal government to translation had varied from case to case. In most cases it seems to have preferred to attempt to stem the tide of complaint by making concessions which

---

[31] C.L.R.O., Rep. xxxv, fos. 42, 80; Rep. xlviii, fos. 66–66(b), 304(b)–305.
[32] C.L.R.O., Rep. xxix, fos. 28, 63–63(b); Rep. xxx, fos. 47(b)–48, 55(b), 70; A. H. Johnson, *Drapers*, iii, 199–200.

amounted to less than wholesale translation of all the practitioners of a craft to the appropriate company. Sometimes,
however, the need for control was so urgent that the municipal
authorities were obliged to throw themselves completely
behind attempts to get all the practitioners of a craft translated
to one company in the interests of efficient control. Down to
1606 the control of carters, or carmen, had been nominally in
the hands of a Carmen's Company which had been founded in
1516, but the familiar process had taken place whereby large
numbers of carmen had become free of other companies, and
the original parent company had been too weak to exercise
efficient control of a problem which was attaining the dimen-
sions of a massive public nuisance. The official answer to the
problem was the absorption of the carmen by the recently
formed Woodmongers' Company, presumably on the grounds
that the Woodmongers were the most regular employers of the
carmen's services. For once the policy was energetically pursued
by the City government. It was, however, no less energetically
resisted, since the new arrangement put the carmen at the
mercy of the Woodmongers. In 1606 John Atkins, a dissident
carman, was committed to Newgate prison for describing the
ordinance for translation as 'noe better then Jack Strawes
lawe'. At the same time recalcitrant carmen, members of other
companies who resisted translation, were either committed or
refused permission to operate or both. In 1611 a bill of complaint brought by two carmen against the Woodmongers'
Company was referred by star chamber to the court of aldermen, which rejected it. On the other hand, a counter-bill by
the master and wardens of the Woodmongers' Company against
other carmen 'for maintenance and vnlawfull contribution &
assemblies to overthrowe the . . . ordinances & goverment of
the said Company' was declared to be just, though the plain-
tiffs were persuaded not to press it further. However, strife by no
means ended here, and dissident carmen continued to give
trouble by resisting translation.[33]

---

[33] C.L.R.O., Jor. xxx, fos. 230(b)–231(b), 339; Rep. xxvii, fos. 153, 158–158(b),
271(b)–272; Rep. xxviii, fo. 192; Rep. xxx, fos. 190(b)–191(b); Rep. xxxiv,
fos. 366(b)–367, 429(b)–430; Rep. xxxvi, fos. 110–11, 127–127(b); Unwin,
Gilds and Companies, pp. 355–7; H. B. Dale, *The Fellowship of Woodmongers* (1924),
pp. 9–11.

The Cooks and the Brewers were even less successful than the Woodmongers. In 1605 the Company of Cooks succeeded in obtaining an act of common council ordering the translation of all cooks who were free of other companies. But this triumph was relatively short-lived, for the ordinance was repealed a decade later. The municipal authorities doubtless felt that a dangerous precedent had been created, and their concern that the movement for wholesale translation might get out of hand was reflected in a notable stiffening of their attitude. At all events, a determined attempt by the Brewers to secure the wholesale translation of brewers during the early 1630s seems to have been effectively foiled. The Brewers were among the most substantial of the minor companies, but they would have been enormously more substantial if they could have forced all the practising brewers of London into their ranks. Their failure to do so is all the more surprising in view of the strong support which they received from the crown. The royal motives were a familiar mixture of paternalism and fiscalism. Brewers who were not members of the Brewers' Company were, it was claimed, likely to brew beer of excessive and dangerous potency. But of at least equal importance was the diminished yield of the composition paid by the Brewers' Company to the crown in lieu of purveyance for the royal household, a decline of revenue which can be ascribed to the fact that the company contained within its ranks an ever diminishing proportion of the practising brewers of the City.[34]

There was, of course, a variety of stratagems open to a company which desired to bring about the translation to itself of all practitioners of its craft who were free of other companies. It was not confined to petitioning the City authorities for their unlikely, or at best, lukewarm, support. By pressing rights of search and even by exacting quarterage from non-members who pursued the craft – which often meant that they were paying quarterage to two companies – their lives could be

[34] C.L.R.O., Jor. xxvi, fos. 339(b)–340; Jor. xxix, fos. 299–299(b); Rep. xxxi, pt ii, fo. 335(b); Rep. xliv, fos. 322(b)–323; Remembrancia, vii, 61; *Cal. S.P.D. 1629–31*, pp. 420, 440–1, 488; *Cal. S.P.D. Addenda 1625–49*, p. 404; *A.P.C. 1621–3*, pp. 385–6; *A.P.C. 1630–1*, pp. 31–2, 206, 273–4; Ashton, 'Charles I and the City', pp. 145–6.

made intolerable. The Drapers' Company appears to have recognized the difficult situation arising out of such practices which was faced by some of its members who practised other crafts. In 1603 the company paid half the fine imposed on one of its members, Leonard Gale, by the Painter–Stainers' Company, because he exercised the craft of painting without being a member of the appropriate company. In addition the Drapers appear to have put no obstacles in the way of members of their company when the latter decided that they could resist outside pressure no longer and would have to yield to translation. Members of other companies in the same plight were not always so fortunate. William Siddon, a member of the Cutlers' Company who received permission to be translated to the Barber–Surgeons in 1609, had to pay a fine of £10 to the Cutlers, to give new gloves to each member of the court of assistants and a dinner to the six cutlers who were deputed to attend the formalities in Guildhall associated with his translation. In 1604 Walter King, a practising dyer and member of the Skinners' Company, had to provide a piece of plate of the value of at least £4 before that company allowed him to translate to the Dyers' Company, even though he had requested translation on account of his being 'greatly molested in law' by the Dyers.[35]

Legal actions of this type were not infrequent, even though the expense was often considerable and the outcome always uncertain. Preserved in the Guildhall Library is a book of informations against non-freemen of the Whitebakers' Company for exercising the craft of baking white bread. The details begin in 1631 and peter out in 1634. From 1631 until some time in 1633 there are full details of twenty-one informations, not counting three against persons who were sued on more than one occasion. Of these cases, fourteen persons were bakers who were members of other companies – of the Mercers', Clothworkers', Blacksmiths' and Lorimers' companies (two each); and of the Drapers', Haberdashers', Pewterers', Vintners', Innholders' and Woodmongers' companies (one each).

---

[35] A. H. Johnson, *Drapers*, iii, 98; Welch, *Cutlers*, ii, 212; Lambert (ed.), *Records of Skinners*, pp. 294–5.

The list is eloquent testimony of growing lack of identity between the practice of a craft and membership of the appropriate gild – the situation which the translation movement was designed to cure. But another interesting feature of the list relates to those seven offenders who either were not free of any company or the nature of whose gild affiliation is not disclosed. Of these, four were persons such as millers, chandlers, badgers and mealmen, who were clearly engaged in the metropolitan grain trade. In the first two years after 1631 the searching out and prosecution of offenders appears to have been vigorously conducted and was attended with considerable success. Some of the offenders were successfully translated to the Whitebakers while others left off baking bread completely. Sometimes those who were prosecuted pleaded the opposition of their company rather than of themselves to translation, while one was excused from translation only on account of the fact that he was about to obtain high office in the Drapers' Company. Another person, 'an Ancient and a very poore lame man vseing the trade of Bakeing', was allowed to continue, though only under extremely stringent conditions. From 1632 onwards, however, there is increasing evidence of offenders obtaining licences under the great seal which allowed them to continue unmolested, while in the following year a number of crucial prosecutions seem to have been unsuccessful. The last entry in the book for 1634, an information against a Holborn victualler, carries with it the ominous comment that 'wee durst not yett goe to triall vpon this Informacion, haueing such ill success in the former suite'.[36]

The Whitebakers had to contend not only with competition from other bakers who were members of companies in no way connected with baking, but also with the complaints made against them by the Brownbakers' Company. Here we approach more nearly the familiar modern type of demarcation dispute between closely related crafts, which because of their similarity can poach the more easily upon each other's preserves. This can also be illustrated by the complaints which the Brownbakers made in 1622–3 against a member of the Tallowchandlers' Company who was engaged in baking. What is interesting about these complaints is that they were not so much concerned with the fact that the offender was a tallowchandler exercising the craft of a baker, as that he was a person who normally baked white bread but was also baking brown. A member of the Whitebakers' Company who baked brown bread would have incurred similar censure by the Brownbakers' Company, and in the spring of 1640 the court of aldermen reaffirmed the traditional ruling that the two crafts should be kept separate.[37]

Such demarcation disputes between similar crafts were often concerned more with the strict delimitation of the province of each than with the problem of translation of members from one company to another. The disputes between the Carpenters' and Joiners', and the Joiners' and Turners' companies in the early years of the reign of Charles I provide excellent examples, as indeed do the Plasterers' disputes with the Painter–Stainers in the dying years of Elizabeth I and under the early Stuarts, with the Bricklayers in 1613 and 1619, and with the Masons in 1637. But such companies, like modern craft unions, were also fully aware of the advantages of the 'closed shop', and the Painter–Stainers, for example, were not averse from trying to secure the compulsory translation of all working painter–stainers who were not already free of their company. The common council, while not prepared to concede all that the company desired, did go some of the way with the company in insisting that such persons should be subject to its search and to the ordinances of the craft, and that they should formally bind their apprentices to members of the Painter–Stainers' Company, so that they would attain to the freedom as members of that company.[38]

The Poulters' quarrel with members of the Butchers'

[37] C.L.R.O., Rep. xxxvi, fos. 170(b)–171; Rep. xxxvii, fo. 70(b); Rep. liv, fos. 125(b)–126, 160–160(b); Remembrancia, iii, 23, v, 68–70.

[38] B.L., Lansdowne MSS., 106, fos. 224, 226; ibid. 487, fos. 222–223(b); P.R.O., S.P. James I, lxxiv/51, lxxv/77; C.L.R.O., Jor. xxv, fo. 106(b); Jor. xxviii, fos. 240(b)–241, 318–318(b); Rep. xxxiv, fos. 195–195(b), 260, 271–2; Rep. xl, fos. 302(b)–303; Rep. xliii, fo. 270(b); Rep. xlvi, fos. 133(b), 207(b)–208, 221–221(b), 382(b)–385(b); Rep. xlviii, fos. 111(b), 241(b)–243; Rep. l, fo. 128; *Cal. S.P.D. 1611–18*, p. 186; *Cal. S.P.D. 1637*, p. 421; *A.P.C. 1613–14*, pp. 372–3; Tawney and Power (eds.), *Tudor Economic Documents*, i, 136–40; W. A. D. Englefield, *The History of the Painter–Stainers' Company of London* (1923), pp. 74–6.

Company who dealt in poultry as a sideline was another demarcation dispute which gave rise in 1607 and 1635 to demands for the translation of such persons to the Poulters' Company. The civic authorities, however, seem to have successfully resisted any attempt to go beyond their decision of 1606 that only those poulters who had obtained the freedom in other companies by redemption should be translated. In spite of intermittent pressure both from the crown and the company, they seem to have been successful in preventing the extension of this ruling to those who had become free by patrimony or apprenticeship. This apart, they appear to have been unwilling to do more than to make certain ordinances of the Poulters' Company for the regulation of the trade applicable to those who dealt in poultry but were not free of the company. Even this, however, might be very irksome to the latter, one of whom, Robert White, obstinately refused to submit to the ordinances over the years 1628–30. According to an affidavit sworn by a member of the Poulters' Company, White had replied to the threat that the lord mayor might shut up his shop if he failed to conform by asserting 'That if any man (except the kinge) should shutt vpp his shopp on the one daie, he would be gladd to open it on the other. And that he was as readie to goe to lawe with the Citie as with a private man.'[39]

From the early years of the century down to 1640, when its efforts were at last crowned with success, the Weavers' Company struggled to obtain the translation to it of weavers who were free of other companies. While its efforts were directed against a wide variety of companies, among them the Joiners, the Waxchandlers and the Tallowchandlers, there can be no doubt that the real struggle was with three of the greater companies, the Clothworkers, the Drapers and the Merchant Tailors, which had a direct interest in weaving. As early as January 1617 the Weavers appeared to have gained their objective, but the City later went back on its decision that all weavers who were not free of the company should be translated to it, and the company had to be content with a *pis aller*

[39] C.L.R.O., Rep. XLIII, fo. 43(b); Rep. XLIV, fos. 256–8, 300–300(b); Remembrancia, VII, 137, 145; *Cal. S.P.D. 1603–10*, p. 392; P. E. Jones, *The Worshipful Company of Poulters of the City of London* (1939), pp. 54–8.

whereby it was allowed to exercise certain controls over the operations of such weavers. The fact that the City governors revoked their earlier decision in the face of severe opposition from the privy council is eloquent testimony both to the influence which was exerted upon civic policy by major companies, like the Drapers, Merchant Tailors and Clothworkers, and to the dislike of the aldermanry for any measure which threatened, however remotely, the freedoms enshrined in the custom of London. On further complaints from the Weavers in 1622, they were given the choice between taking their case to common law and accepting the judgment of the court of aldermen on the matter. Given, on the one hand, the well-known hostility of so many common-law judges to restrictions on freedom of enterprise, and, on the other, the aldermen's dislike of anything that tended to limit the freedoms of the custom of London, it is hardly surprising that the Weavers requested that their case be referred to a decision of the privy council instead. Despite the fact that the next few years saw a number of interventions by the privy council on behalf of the Weavers, their wish does not seem to have been granted, and in 1629 they put forward a modest new set of proposals, which was accepted by the common council. These were that all apprentices of weavers who were not free of the Weavers' Company should be formally bound to members of that company, though they might afterwards be turned over to their original masters. The object was obviously to secure the translation in the long term of those who obtained the freedom by apprenticeship, who would become members of the Weavers' Company on attaining the freedom, and yet to avoid the disruption and inconvenience which would be caused to practising masters by insisting on the immediate translation of their apprentices in anything but purely formal terms. It was more acceptable to the City authorities, since it left out of consideration not only those practising weavers who were free of other companies, but also those who attained the freedom by patrimony and redemption, as well as those who changed their trade to weaving after having been apprenticed to another craft. Limited concessions of this sort had already been accorded to the Painter–Stainers in 1611, the Broderers in 1613, the Whitebakers in 1618 and the Clothworkers in 1619. Far from being placated permanently by this concession, however, the Weavers were back on the offensive again in 1640 and this time their pertinacity received its due reward, their demands for complete and unattenuated translation being at last accepted by the court of aldermen.[40]

Although such complete success was rare, it is important not to discount the significance of the partial successes which were achieved, for example, in the cases of those individuals who, yielding to varied forms of pressure, consented to their translation to other companies. Other compromise solutions might fall far short of achieving complete identity between the practice of a craft and the membership of a gild, but they are none the less indicative of the pressures to which the municipal government was subject and the unwilling concessions which it had to make. Even if concessions such as the insistence that in future apprentices of non-members practising the craft should be formally bound to members of the appropriate company offered less than the companies in question were demanding, they represented a substantial advance on the previous situation. The same is true of the tightening of the regulations imposed on non-freemen in matters such as the control of quality, the numbers of journeymen and apprentices whom they could employ and their subjection to the search. Needless to say, the constitutional concessions which were made by the municipality were often difficult to enforce. It was obviously much easier for a company to exercise control over its own members than over outsiders, a fact which was brought home forcefully in 1628 to

[40] On the Weavers, C.L.R.O., Jor. xxxv, fos. 63(b)–64; Rep. xxxiii, fo. 258(b); Rep. xxxiv, fos. 335, 412, 456, 526–526(b); Rep. xxxv, fos. 11(b)–12, 128(b); Rep. xxxvi, fos. 25, 276(b), 279(b)–280; Rep. xlii, fos. 323(b)–324; Rep. xlvii, fos. 315–315(b); Rep. liii, fo. 209(b); Rep. liv, fos. 51(b), 147–150(b); Remembrancia, v, 137; *Cal. S.P.D. 1619–23*, pp. 412, 434, 457; *Cal. S.P.D. Addenda 1625–49*, pp. 411–12; *A.P.C. 1621–3*, pp. 262–3; *A.P.C. 1630–1*, pp. 70–1, 87. On the Painter–Stainers, C.L.R.O., Jor. xxviii, fos. 240(b)–241, 318–318(b); Englefield, *Painter–Stainers*, pp. 75–6. On the Broderers, C.L.R.O., Rep. xxxi, pt i, fos. 90–90(b). On the Glaziers, C.L.R.O., Jor. xxx, fos. 132–3, 339; Rep. xxxii, fo. 259(b). On the Whitebakers, C.L.R.O., Rep. xxxiii, fos. 254–254(b), 350–350(b), 359–359(b), 371(b)–372. On the Clothworkers, *A.P.C. 1619–21*, pp. 38–9. For similar requests from the Paviours and the Upholders and Glaziers, see C.L.R.O., Rep. xxxii, fo. 259(b); Rep. xlv, fo. 456; Rep. li, fos. 54(b)–55, 268(b).

members of the Dyers' Company who, when searching among non-members for 'deceitful work appertaining to the same mystery', found workshop doors locked against them and were set upon by mastiffs.[41] Nor should it be forgotten that those whose translation was demanded were themselves craftsmen, who had become members of other companies as a result of the growth of economic opportunities afforded by the developments of the preceding century and the freedom of movement allowed by the so-called custom of London. Some of the most notable victims of this attempt of the crafts to secure that strength which comes from unity were themselves craftsmen.

VI

Although the municipal government had from time to time to make concessions to the crafts and to pursue policies with which the City bigwigs had little sympathy, it is probable that, on balance, the intercompany disputes which have been described in this chapter were a factor which helped to underline the importance of the municipal authorities vis-à-vis the gilds. Indeed it was during the reign of James I that the lord mayor first put forward the claim that he was, *ex officio*, the master of all of the livery companies. The latter might receive their charters from the crown, but the municipality was to insist that they held them in a quasi-feudal manner in direct subordination to itself, and that companies might not sue for new charters without its permission. Another factor working in the same direction was the City's use of the companies in furtherance of both municipal and royal policies. The crown was an increasingly frequent suitor to the City for loans, and in such cases, as well as in the raising of compulsory levies such as benevolences and ship money, the burden of raising the money was often passed on to the livery companies by the municipality.[42] Similarly, the companies were used by the crown, again working through the municipal government, in con-

---

[41] *Cal. S.P.D. 1628–9*, p. 238.
[42] See Ashton, *The Crown and the Money Market*, pp. 26–7, 114–17, 135–8, 140–1, 181–2; M. C. Wren, 'London and the Twenty Ships', *Amer. Hist. Rev.*, LV (1950), 321–35.

nection with the resettlement of the lands of the Irish rebels in Ulster in 1610.[43] All of these things were to become important sources of contention between crown and City in the 1630s,[44] but in the present context they are significant as factors which helped to increase the latter's power over the companies. The use of the companies in connection with the provision of municipal corn supplies provides a further example of the same tendency.[45] And while the assertion of municipal power sometimes brought the City into conflict with the lesser gilds, the divergence of interest between the municipality and the greater gilds, from which the City élite itself was drawn, was minimal.

Nowhere is the alignment of municipality and major companies more apparent than in the attitude of both to the formation of breakaway associations by groups of handicraftsmen. This subject has a further interest for us as providing a major example of a genuine and highly important area of dispute between the crown and the municipal government, even more significant than the aldermanic disquiet at royal support for translation, irritating though this was to the City fathers. The history of the incorporations of small handicraft masters has been well told by George Unwin,[46] in which circumstances it will be convenient to concentrate our attentions on the issue as it affected relations between the crown and the municipal governors.

The reasons which lay behind the governors' opposition to a multiplicity of new incorporations are not far to seek. They emerge clearly enough, for example, in connection with the Artisan Skinners' bid in 1606–7 to obtain independence from their parent company, which they believed to be dominated by men who knew nothing about the craft. Appealing to the government without the knowledge of their superiors in the company, they came dangerously close to success, and obtained royal approval of their request for a charter of incorporation. This development provoked vigorous counteraction from the out-

[43] See T. W. Moody, *The Londonderry Plantation 1609–1641* (Belfast, 1939), *passim*.
[44] See below, pp. 158–60.
[45] See N. S. B. Gras, *The Evolution of the English Corn Market from the Twelfth to the Eighteenth Century* (Cambridge, Mass., 1915), pp. 77–94.
[46] Unwin, *Industrial Organization*, pp. 126–69, and *Gilds and Companies*, pp. 297–317, 319–20.

raged rulers of the Skinners' Company. Since the lord mayor and aldermen were themselves members of the governing élites of the London livery companies, the élite Skinners felt confident that they could count on a favourable response to their urging on the City fathers the need to consider 'whether these men that geve soe scornfull wordes beare not also mutinous mindes, and what it maye work in tradesmen thus to be imboldened against the auncientes and governors of their Companie'. They were not disappointed. The aldermen recoiled with predictable horror from this plot on the part of presumptuous craftsmen to acquire power under the specious pretext of the common good.

But the artizan skynners pretending the good of their art, seke principally rule and auchthoritye in their Companie, which end of theirs tending to disturbe a well settled and governed Companie wee find is not to be suffered.

And, of course, it did not stop here. Order and due subordination were indivisible, and it was no doubt such considerations, strongly urged by the aldermen, which persuaded the privy council to have second thoughts and to cancel the bill for the Artisan Skinners' patent, whose effect would surely have been 'to authorise the government of the inferior sort to the great daunger and preiudice of government of this Cittye'.[47]

But a great deal more often than not the City did not find the government so obliging. Indeed in no sphere of activity is the opposition of the City fathers to royal policies more apparent than in their foot-dragging over their formal recognition of such grants of incorporation made by the crown. The incorporation of the Glovers is a case in point, and one which is crucially different from the case of the Artisan Skinners, since the Glovers had previously enjoyed an independent existence as a gild before being absorbed by the Leathersellers as part of a process of gild amalgamation. Their attempt to secure independence from the Leathersellers had been frustrated in 1619, and it was not until 1638 that they succeeded in obtaining incorporation.

---

[47] C.L.R.O., Rep. xxvii, fos. 321(b), 351; Rep. xxviii, fos. 21(b)–27; Remembrancia, ii, 282; H.M.C., *Salisbury MSS.*, xix, 492; Lambert (ed.), *Records of Skinners*, pp. 341–3; J. F. Wadmore, *Some Account of the Worshipful Company of Skinners of London* (1902), p. 20; Unwin, *Industrial Organization*, pp. 202–3, and *Gilds and Companies*, p. 237. And see above, p. 54.

But this only set the seal of royal and not of municipal approval upon their organization, and the company had to endure a further six years of aldermanic delaying tactics before their charter was finally enrolled and they received full civic recognition.[48] The Glaziers' Company had a similar experience. Incorporated in the same year as the Glovers, its members were still complaining three years later of the City's refusal to enrol its charter.[49]

Although the case of the Feltmakers' Company, which was incorporated as early as 1604, is in some respects different from that of the Glovers, since the craftsmen in question were not breaking away from a parent organization which was dominated by mercantile interests, there can be no doubt that the subjection of the working feltmakers to members of the Haberdashers' Company had long been an economic reality even if it lacked the formal institutional expression of the subordination of craftsmen within the framework of a livery company. And for our purposes the most significant point of similarity between the two cases is to be found in the basic pattern of royal support for and unrelenting municipal opposition to the scheme. In fact the City fathers put every conceivable obstacle in the way of the achievement of the royal purpose. Doubtless they feared that incorporation and civic recognition would be the prelude to a drive to force the translation to the new company of all practitioners of the craft who were free of other companies. But among the official reasons which the City fathers gave for their opposition were considerations which, one suspects, were especially designed to touch the nerve of a government which was normally responsive to arguments stressing the need for order and stability. In 1622, for example, it was argued that the granting of incorporation to the feltmakers had resulted in an influx of provincial feltmakers to the metropolis and, since

---

[48] P.R.O., S.P. Charles I, ccclxxvii/38, ccclxxxvi/90–2; P. C. R., P.C. 2., xlix, fo. 149; C.L.R.O., Rep. l, fo. 155; Rep. lv, fos. 150, 225–226(b), 334(b); Rep. lvii, fos. 175–175(b), 180(b)–181, 192, 200, 207(b)–208, 211(b), 223, 232(b), 239–239(b); *Cal. S.P.D. 1635–6*, p. 552; *Cal. S.P.D. 1638–9*, p. 245; Unwin, *Industrial Organization*, pp. 128–9, 143, 211, and *Gilds and Companies*, pp. 263, 309.

[49] *Cal. S.P.D. 1637*, p. 68; *Cal. S.P.D. 1640–1*, p. 368; C. H. Ashdown, *A History of the Worshipful Company of Glaziers of the City of London* (1919), pp. 34–5, 113–21; J. A. Knowles, 'Additional Notes on the History of the Worshipful Company of Glaziers', *Antiquaries Journal*, vii (1927), 282.

food prices and rents were higher in London than in the provinces, a precipitous rise in the price of felt. In addition, the craft was unsavoury, as were its practitioners, poor people who were incapable of bearing municipal and national burdens. The influx of such people would foster the proliferation of slums and aggravate the inmate problem. As to their separate incorporation, such people were made not to govern but to be governed and, even though they could hardly say as much, the lord mayor and aldermen no doubt felt that the government ought to know better than to encourage their independence. It is difficult to imagine a more flagrant defiance of the royal will than the repeated assertion of the court of aldermen that the government of the feltmakers belonged to the Haberdashers' Company; its continued refusal down to 1650 to recognize the Feltmakers' Company; and its offer of the freedom to any feltmakers who were willing to desert this body and join the Haberdashers' Company.[50]

It has long been recognized that the motives which lay behind the social policies of early Stuart governments were very mixed. Royal support for the aspirations of the feltmakers was probably not unconnected with the privilege of sealing felts which had been granted with the aulnage of new and old draperies to a near relative of James I, the duke of Lenox, and which was in the 1630s the subject of bitter dispute between the feltmakers and the persons to whom the duke had assigned his privilege.[51] As the Glovers also discovered at about the same time, it was not easy to enter the protective orbit of crown and court without falling foul of courtiers on the make.[52] Thus royal

---

[50] C.L.R.O., Jor. xxvii, fo. 144(b); Jor. xxviii, fo. 293(b); Jor. xxxii, fos. 77–8, 83(b)–84(b); Rep. xxxiii, fos. 354(b)–355; Rep. xlvi, fo. 401(b); *Cal. S.P.D. 1619–23*, p. 442; *Cal. S.P.D. 1639–40*, pp. 335, 344–5, 370; *Remembrancia Index*, p. 95; Unwin, *Industrial Organization*, pp. 130–5, 156–64, 196–7, 240–5, and *Gilds and Companies*, pp. 237, 254, 304–6.

[51] *Cal. S.P.D. 1636–7*, pp. 65–6; *Cal. S.P.D. 1638–9*, pp. 278, 348.

[52] As early as 1592 the Glovers are found supporting the courtier Edward Darcy's patent for searching and sealing of leather which was opposed by the Leathersellers, while the opportunities presented by the Glovers' proposals of the 1630s which resulted in their incorporation in 1638 were not lost upon Lady Killigrew, who had already received a patent which gave her the right to search and seal leather, and who backed the Glovers strongly at court (*Cal. S.P.D. 1635–6*, p. 552; Unwin, *Industrial Organization*, p. 142, and *Gilds and Companies*, pp. 257–8, 309, 330).

policies towards the gilds, while doubtless inspired in some measure by genuine paternalistic concern, were shot through by ambivalence and inconsistency. For instance, although the crown was eager to help the feltmakers in their struggle against the Haberdashers, this did not prevent it from lending its support in the 1630s to another breakaway organization, the manufacturers of beaver hats, even though the company from which the beavermakers were trying to escape was the crown's former protégé, the Feltmakers. This situation produced an astonishing reversal of alliances, the Feltmakers joining forces with their old enemies the Haberdashers and the City against the Beavermakers and the crown. For once, the latter could not claim to be lending its protection to a group of penurious small craftsmen with a laudable itch to obtain economic independence. As the Feltmakers explained to the parliament, to which, in default of royal sympathy on this issue, they appealed in 1640, the breakaway beavermakers were all substantial manufacturers, and indeed had drawn off some of the wealthiest of the feltmakers into their company. But while considerations of social paternalism played a relatively small part as a determinant of royal policies in this matter, the no less familiar fiscal motives were as prominent as ever, as was the utility of a new corporation as a form of courtly out-relief. The Beavermakers were to pay a duty of 12d. on each hat or cap made, and this, together with half the benefit arising from the confiscated foreign hats whose importation was now prohibited, was demised by the crown to Sir James Cunningham, the later earl of Stirling, with a yearly rent of £500 reserved. Cunningham, who had sunk a good deal of personal capital in the beaver-making business, had been its chief advocate at court. But opposition from the Feltmakers and their unaccustomed allies, the Haberdashers, continued unabated, and, in view of the notorious hostility of the lord mayor and his colleagues to new incorporations, it is rather surprising to find some of the main issues in dispute being referred by the privy council to the lord mayor in January 1639. However, the complaint of the Beavermakers on 1 February that the lord mayor had referred the matter to an aldermanic sub-committee, whose verdict was entirely predictable since a majority of its members were haberdashers, was sufficient to shock the privy council into calling the matter back from the City for the consideration of the attorney-general and Secretary Windebank. Certainly the picture of the crown as the protector and patron of small craftsmen against mercantile exploitation does not show up to advantage in this case, since its former protégés, the small feltmakers, as manufacturers of mixed felt and beaver hats, had everything to lose from the establishment of a Beavermakers' Company.[53]

Another example of the by now familiar alignment of interests in court and City over the issue of new incorporations is provided by the circumstances attending the royal incorporation of the Distillers' Company in August 1638. Among the influential moving spirits behind the formation of the new company were the royal physician, Sir Theodore de Mayerne, and two other eminent physicians, Sir William Brouncker and Dr Cadiman. It was these well-placed and knowledgeable individuals who had successfully pressed upon the crown the need for regulation. The products to be distilled included something which was euphemistically known by the title of 'low wines', which seems in fact to have been the dregs of brewers' vessels, the waste products of beer hogsheads and the droppings from alewives' taps. The idea was to secure efficient enforcement of the wholesome recipes to be drawn up by Mayerne and his colleagues by confining distilling to members of the new company.[54]

The case of the Distillers probably provides the most spectacular example of municipal opposition to the court-backed creation of a new company. Immediately after incorporation the lord mayor and aldermen were confronted by the usual

[53] P.R.O., P.C.R., P.C. 2., xlix, fos. 58–9, l, fos. 28, 40, 623, 630, 656–7; *Cal. S.P.D. 1637*, p. 395; *Cal. S.P.D. 1637–8*, pp. 269, 392, 459–60; *Cal. S.P.D. 1638–9*, pp. 329, 351, 398–9, 411–12; *Cal. S.P.D. 1639*, pp. 471, 486, 488, 499; H.M.C., *Fourth Report*, pt I, p. 29; H.M.C., *House of Lords MSS.*, xi, *Addenda 1514–1714*, 228, 244–5; R. R. Steele (ed.), *Bibliotheca Lindesiana: A Bibliography of Royal Proclamations of the Tudor and Stuart Sovereigns . . . 1485–1714*, 2 vols. (Oxford, 1910), I, nos. 1775, 1810; Unwin, *Industrial Organization*, pp. 145–6, and *Gilds and Companies*, p. 320.

[54] P.R.O., S.P. James I, cxix/113–14; Bodleian Library, Bankes MSS., 6/2, 12/20, 12/23; *Cal. S.P.D. 1637–8*, p. 585; *Cal. S.P.D. 1638–9*, pp. 40, 252; *Cal. S.P.D. 1639–40*, pp. 237–8.

royal request that the charter be enrolled and the members of
the new company made free of the City, and there ensued the
equally familiar exercise of municipal delaying tactics, which
were successful insofar as recognition of the Distillers had still
not been conceded two years later. In none of the other cases
which have been examined was royal pressure so strong and
insistent; in none was the municipality so recalcitrant and its
foot-dragging so accomplished; and in none was the royal
anger at the employment of these tactics so strongly expressed.
The main City objection related to the alleged weakening of
existing companies which would result from the new incorporation, but it is certain that the dangers consequent upon the
admission of large numbers of inferior persons to the freedom
ranked very high among the factors determining the municipal
attitude.[55]

It is ironic that the most prominent of those companies
which opposed the incorporation of the Distillers was the
Apothecaries, whose long struggle to free themselves from the
Grocers' Company had also been achieved in the teeth of
municipal opposition. No doubt once the City had conceded
defeat in the struggle and had accepted a new company,
however reluctantly, the latter became, as it were, a paid-up
member of the privileged club and, far from letting down the
ladder for other less fortunate groups to mount, tended to offer
stern resistance to their aspirations, more especially when the
achievement of these appeared to offer a threat to the value of
new and dearly acquired privileges. Such considerations may
well have influenced the Feltmakers' attitude to the Beavermakers, and they are probably equally applicable to the
Apothecaries. Nor were they alone. The Vintners', Barber-
Surgeons' and Coopers' companies claimed that the incorporation of the Distillers seriously infringed their privileges, while
every company which contained any members who engaged
either in distilling or in the manufacture of vinegar opposed not
only their translation to the Distillers but also the compulsory
binding of apprentices to members of that company which, as

[55] C.L.R.O., Jor. xxxix, fos. 36(b), 62, 66–8; Rep. LIV, fo. 3; *Cal. S.P.D. 1638–9*,
pp. 153, 422–3, 480; *Cal. S.P.D. 1639–40*, pp. 237–8; *Remembrancia Index*, pp.
111–12.

was shown earlier,[56] was an equally sure, if somewhat slower, way of achieving the same end. Such measures were the more inappropriate emanating as they did from a new company whose members, the objecting companies claimed and the common council itself affirmed in March 1640,

are for the most parte men illiterate and doe vse such vnsound materialls as that their waters being transported beyond Sea become weake and loose [*sic*] their virtue when they should be most vsefull, to the daunger of his Majesties Subiectes and others in amity with his Majesty in partes beyond the Seas.

Backed by the expert advice of Mayerne and his colleagues, the Distillers would have scornfully repudiated such allegations and, indeed, in a reply which they made in September 1638 to another set of objections to their charter, they made it clear that the Apothecaries, from whom the objections emanated, were meddling in matters beyond their understanding, and that it behoved them to remain content with their lot and to acknowledge respectfully the superior knowledge of the learned members of the College of Physicians whose expert opinions the new company was able to cite to such good effect.[57]

Yet two decades earlier this same College of Physicians had, in conjunction with James I, backed the Apothecaries in their successful attempt to free themselves from the Grocers which they finally achieved in 1617. The Grocers were one of the most powerful of the twelve livery companies, and it is therefore hardly surprising that the lord mayor and his colleagues offered stiff opposition to the Apothecaries both before and after their incorporation; and the case presents yet another example of a sharp clash between the crown and the lord mayor over the latter's refusal to enrol the new charter. The new company tried unsuccessfully to obtain statutory sanctions for its charter from the parliaments of 1621 and 1624. Far from granting its request, the latter parliament declared the charter to be a grievance. The 1620s also provide abundant examples of the

[56] See above, pp. 68–9.
[57] P.R.O., P.C.R., P.C. 2, XLIX, fo. 514; C.L.R.O., Jor. XXXIX, fos. 66–8; *Cal. S.P.D. 1638–9*, pp. 40, 422–3; *Cal. S.P.D. 1639–40*, pp. 237–8; C. Wall, H. C. Cameron and E. A. Underwood, *A History of the Worshipful Society of Apothecaries of London*, I, *1617–1815* (1963), pp. 55–7.

resentment of the Apothecaries at what they deemed to be a number of petty slights administered by the municipal authorities. Between the early 1620s and the mid 1630s the Apothecaries seem to have forfeited the support of the College of Physicians, partly, it would seem, as a result of their refusal to confine themselves to the dispensing of medicines prescribed by physicians and to desist from proffering medical advice to their customers. This is the background to the Physicians' enthusiastic support for the incorporation of the Distillers, and the determined support of the municipal authorities for the Apothecaries towards whom they had formerly been lukewarm. The City fathers' attitude was to be an important irritant in the relations between crown and City in the later 1630s.[58]

The cases which have been dealt with up to now are all variations on a single theme whose essence is royal support for breakaway craft associations, whose separate existence was bitterly opposed not only by the parent group from whose control independence was sought, but also by the municipality itself. Since the case of the incorporation of the Pinmakers will be familiar to many readers through the work of Unwin,[59] it will not be necessary to recount all the tortuous details here. It will be enough for us to notice that while this case has a number of features in common with those already discussed, there are also some very significant differences.

The history of the pinmaking projects falls into two distinct phases, the first of which ends in the early 1620s with the collapse of the Jacobean scheme. Dragged down in the ruins was the courtly sponsor, Sir Thomas Bartlett, a servant of the queen. Powerful friends at court were in this case insufficient to secure

---

[58] B.L., Lansdowne MSS., 487, fos. 196(b)–198; P.R.O., S.P. James I, xcIV/95, cxIx/113–14, 135; C.L.R.O., Jor. xxx, fos. 299–306; Jor. xxxI, fo. 121(b); Jor. xxxv, fo. 152(b); Rep. xxxII, fo. 36(b); Rep. xxxIII, fos. 268(b)–269, 280; Rep. xlI, fos. 362–362(b); Rep. xlII, fos. 206(b)–207, 256(b); Rep. xlIX, fo. 11; Remembrancia, vIII, 26; Grocers' Hall, Orders of Court of Assistants 1616–39, fos. 161, 164, 188; *Cal. S.P.D. 1611–18*, p. 507; *Cal. S.P.D. 1619–23*, p. 171; *Cal. S.P.D. 1639–40*, p. 394; *A.P.C. 1613–14*, pp. 450–1; *Remembrancia Index*, pp. 96–7, 526; *H. of C. J.*, I, 706, 756; *C.D. 1621*, v, 259, vII, 77–85, 324–7; Steele (ed.), *Bibliotheca Lindesiana*, I, no. 1289; Wall, Cameron and Underwood, *Apothecaries*, pp. 5–6, 8–25, 28–31, 35–9, 41–57; C. R. B. Barrett, *History of the Society of Apothecaries of London* (1905), pp. xix–xxix, 1–29.

[59] Unwin, *Industrial Organization*, pp. 79, 164–9, and *Gilds and Companies*, pp. 306, 315, 319, 328.

the success of the project, and for once the government showed
an unwonted sensitivity to opposition to the scheme in the City
and abroad. This came from the English importers of pins, the
haberdashers who sold them on the home market and the
Dutch merchants who brought pins to England and who
hinted at the likelihood of drastic retaliatory action from the
Dutch government in the form of a ban on the importation of
English cloth. The net result was that the privy council showed
an unusual willingness to take heed of mercantile pressures and
to adopt the sensible compromise suggestion of the City fathers
that the haberdashers should undertake to take off all the pins
produced by the Pinmakers' Company and to govern their
purchases of imported pins in the future with reference to the
difference between the total amount of domestic pins produced
and the total domestic demand for pins.[60] The collapse of the
project, of course, prevented this agreement from taking
permanent effect.[61]

The unwonted harmony between crown and City over pinmaking did not, however, survive the second phase of the
history of the project during the 1630s, when the court of
aldermen came down heavily against the schemes of one James
Lydsey, who aspired to a rôle similar to that of Bartlett in the
previous reign, though, in Lydsey's case, in more propitious
circumstances, which he had endeavoured to make still more
favourable by settling an annuity of £500 on the queen.
Lydsey's scheme in fact outraged almost every deep-rooted
City interest about the proper ordering of trade. It was felt to
be outrageous that one man should perform the dual functions
of sole supplier of wire to the Pinmakers and sole exporter of
their products; the more so since 'whereas the said James
Lidsey . . . affirmeth himselfe to bee a Marchant . . . it appeareth
vnto vs that he is a Haberdasher and a sole shoppkeeper

---

[60] This is not quite true, since the Pinmakers' monopoly extended only to London
at this time.
[61] B.L., Cottonian MSS., Titus Bv, fo. 287; P.R.O., S.P. James I, xxvi/23, 100,
lxxviii/81, lxxxvi/146; S.P. Charles I, ccccxxxviii/54; *Cal. S.P.D. 1603–10*,
p. 211; *Cal. S.P.D. 1611–18*, pp. 532, 557; *A.P.C. 1619–21*, pp. 6, 162; *Remembrancia Index*, pp. 97, 521–6; L. M. Hill (ed.), 'Sir Julius Caesar's Journal of
Salisbury's First Two Months and Twenty Days as Lord Treasurer, 1608', *Bull.
Inst. Hist. Res.*, xlv (1972), 323.

altogeather vnfitt to vndertake and manage soe greate an ymployment'. The aldermen urged the government to take a leaf out of the book of continental mercantilism and encourage the manufacture in places remote from the metropolis. Instead, by doing the opposite, it was upsetting established interests, creating dangerous precedents, and violating that quintessential feature of the City élite's notions of the proper ordering of economic life: that foreign trade must be kept in the hands of 'mere merchants.'[62]

Other cases could be cited of municipal opposition to new incorporations which were backed by the crown, but this would serve no useful purpose. It was the threat which such organizations offered to the prevailing *status quo* in the City which lay at the bottom of municipal anxiety in such matters. In this, as in so much else before 1640, the crown was seen as an innovator, and those who disagreed with its policies and attempted to obstruct their implementation felt themselves to be acting not in the spirit of factious opposition but from the most respectable and conservative of motives. Fortified by this belief they were decidedly in no mood to be convinced by the verdict of the crown's legal advisers, given at some time during the 1630s in connection with a particular case under consideration, but nevertheless intended to have a more general significance. This was that 'his Majestie may incorporat the said parties into a company by his charter and comaunde them to be admitted into the freedome of the saide Citty without impeachment to their [viz. the City's] liberties'.[63]

The history of the City fathers' attitude to new incorporations of craftsmen is the tale of bitter opposition to royal policies, defiance of royal commands and determined attempts to hold out against them for as long as possible. It provides the

---

[62] B.L., Cottonian MSS., Titus Bv, fo. 314; P.R.O., S.P. Charles I, cccxxviii/76, cccxxxvi/1, cccxxxviii/54; C.L.R.O., Rep. xlix, fos. 205(b), 218–221(b); Rep. li, fos. 304(b)–305(b); Rep. lii, fo. 60(b); *Cal. S.P.D. 1635*, pp. 513–14; *Cal. S.P.D. 1635–6*, p. 245; *Cal. S.P.D. 1637*, pp. 360–1, 456; *Cal. S.P.D. 1637–8*, pp. 107, 589; *Cal. S.P.D. 1638–9*, pp. 71, 247, 531–2; *Cal. S.P.D. 1639–40*, pp. 232–3; *H. of C. J.*, ii, 35; H.M.C., *Fourth Report*, pt i, p. 29; Unwin, *Industrial Organization*, pp. 168–9, 236–40.

[63] P.R.O., S.P. Charles I, ccxxx/59. The proposed incorporation was of a company for 'the smelting of brasse and conuerting the same into copper'.

first of our major examples of a conflict of interest between the crown and the City. Although in tracing this conflict it is the concept of the City as a civic rather than as a business élite with which we have been especially concerned, this is an area of municipal activity where it is both peculiarly difficult and not especially rewarding to try to separate the two connotations in terms of the motive forces of civic action. In the two chapters which follow we will be exclusively concerned with the business élite *per se*, before turning in the remaining chapters to examine the general relations between the crown and the municipality.

3

Big business and politics under James I

I

It was a central theme of the first chapter of this book that concessionaires of one sort or another formed a significant part of the business élite of London. During the last two parliaments of Elizabeth's reign one type of concessionaire, holders of internal patents of monopoly, had been the object of bitter attacks, and, as the debate on monopolies in 1601 had made abundantly clear, monopolies raised issues which transcended considerations of economics. For, as Francis Bacon put it in a speech which was to become justly celebrated, the question of monopolies was intimately bound up with that of the royal prerogative.

The Queen, as She is our Sovereign, hath both an Inlarging and Restraining Liberty of Her Prerogative; that is, She hath Power by Her Patents, to set at liberty Things restrained by Statute-Law, or otherwise: And by Her Prerogative, She may restrain Things that are at Liberty.[1]

The debate on monopolies in 1601 thus highlighted the fact that concessionaires of the crown had everything to gain from the maintenance of the royal prerogative intact, and everything to fear from determined parliamentary assaults upon it. And this attitude was common to a much wider variety of concessionaires than the actual patentees who came under attack in 1601 and the business men to whom they sublet their concessions. Quite apart from the holders of those royal concessions which were showered upon the London business world in the opening years of the reign of James I, and of which the great farm of the royal customs was only the most glittering example, old-

---

[1] Tawney and Power (eds.), *Tudor Economic Documents*, II, 271.

D

established and more reputable interests were hardly less threatened. Bacon's arguments about the enlarging and restraining powers of the crown were equally applicable to the privileges of those great chartered companies which dominated foreign trade. For instance, the privileges of the Merchant Adventurers' Company, whereby English commodity trade to the coast of Europe between the Scaw and the Somme was confined to a restricted number of merchants, were as obvious an example of the use of the royal restraining power as that provided by any of the patents of monopoly which had been questioned in 1601; while the one concession which made these privileges of value to that company, the licences *non obstante* statutes passed by parliament against the export of undressed cloth, whether these licences were obtained direct from the crown or through grantees of first instance who resold their concessions to the company, present a classic example of the use of the royal enlarging power.[2] Members of the great privileged chartered companies had, therefore, every reason to watch anxiously the developing attack on monopolies in the closing years of Elizabeth, and can hardly have been surprised when, in the first parliament of her successor's reign, the front was widened and they themselves came under fire.

The peace which was finally concluded between England and Spain in August 1604 opened up the prospect of the revival of English trade with the Iberian peninsula. But the problem of what sort of trade this was to be still remained to be solved. Was it to be a strictly controlled and limited trade in the hands of a regulated company such as the Spanish Company which had been founded in 1577, but which the advent of war with Spain had forced into effective dissolution? Powerful commercial interests in London were already at work reviving the old company and canvassing statesmen such as Robert Cecil for their support. Or was the trade to be open to all, a course of action which was vigorously advocated by the merchants of the south-western ports, who feared that any chartered company for trade with Spain would be dominated by Londoners? It was almost inevitable that the issue would be generalized

[2] See above, pp. 18–20, 29, 33–4.

into a discussion of the respective merits of free versus restricted trade, since the arguments of both sides were bound to draw heavily upon recent commercial experience. In these circumstances the protagonists of free trade were bound to attempt to extend the principle from the Spanish trade to overseas trade in general.

On 21 May 1604, the report of the committee appointed by the House of Commons for the consideration of two bills for free trade was presented to the House by Sir Edwin Sandys.[3] The Journal of the House of Commons prints a version of the report by Sandys himself, entitled 'Instructions touching the Bill for free trade'. This tells us that

all the Clothiers, and, in effect, all the Merchants of *England*, complained grievously of the Engrossing and Restraint of Trade by the rich Merchants of *London*, as being the Undoing, or great Hindrance, of all the rest; and of *London* Merchants, Three Parts joined in the same Complaint against a fourth Part; and of that fourth Part, some standing stiffly for their own Company, yet repined at other Companies. Divers Writings and Informations were exhibited on both Parts; learned Counsel was heard for the Bill, and divers principal Aldermen of *London* against it.

Both provincial merchants and manufacturers were alike resentful of the commercial stranglehold which Londoners were exercising on the trade of the nation. The connection between greater freedom of entry into foreign trade and the interests of the outports vis-à-vis those of London is made clear by the statement that the achievement of the former would produce a more equal distribution of trade and wealth between the metropolis and the outports,

which is a great Stability and Strength to the Realm, even as the equal Distributing of the Nourishment in a Man's Body: the contrary wherof is inconvenient in all Estates, and oftentimes breaks

---

[3] The view of the free-trade movement which I take here comes nearer to that of Friis, *Cockayne's Project*, pp. 149–56, than to that of T. K. Rabb, 'Sir Edwin Sandys and the Parliament of 1604', *Amer. Hist. Rev.*, LXIX (1964), 661–9, and 'Free Trade and the Gentry in the Parliament of 1604', *P. & P.*, no. 40 (1968), 165–73. I give in detail my reasons for disagreeing with Rabb's views in my articles 'The Parliamentary Agitation for Free Trade in the Opening Years of the Reign of James I', *P. & P.*, no. 38 (1967), 40–55, and 'Jacobean Free Trade Again', *P. & P.*, no. 43 (1969), 151–7.

out into Mischief, when too much Fulness doth puff up some by Presumption, and too much Emptiness leaves them in perpetual Discontent, the Mother of Desire of Innovations and Troubles: And this is the proper Fruit of Monopolies. Example may be in *London,* and the rest of the Realm: The Custom and Impost of *London* come to a Hundred and Ten Thousand Pound a Year, and of the rest of the whole Realm but to Seventeen Thousand Pound.

It was not that provincial merchants were against trading in companies as such, or that they favoured extensive trading by those who were not professional full-time merchants. What they were clearly against was trading in national companies whose restrictive membership was a factor ensuring the continued domination of London.[4]

Apart from the struggle between London and the provinces, the report also mentions differences between the ranks of the Londoners themselves. The 'three parts' who complained against a fourth part were, of course, the actual or would-be interlopers who were excluded from the right to trade by the privileged members of chartered companies. Moreover, as the report goes on to say, even the latter were by no means a united force, for 'of that fourth Part, some stand[ing] stiffly for their own Company, yet repined at other Companies'. To the top-ranking members of the commercial élite, merchant princes with directive interests in several privileged companies, such intercompany disputes might be a source of considerable embarrassment. But there was abundant scope for privileged commercial groups to tread upon each other's toes.[5]

At first sight this may seem surprising, when one considers the mutually exclusive area monopolies of trade that were enjoyed by the companies. But the conception of area monopoly unquestionably suited some companies better than others. The early charters of the Levant Company, for example, had gone some way towards extending the concept of monopoly of trade with a region in the direction of monopoly of trade in the commodities of a region. The charter of 1592 had given to the company the sole right to import currants from any land and not simply the sole right to import them from the countries of

[4] *H. of C. J.*, I, 218.
[5] Ibid.

their origin, and the charter of 1600 had extended this concession to the oils of Greece and Crete. The charter which the reconstituted company was to obtain in 1605, however, was to see a reversion to the principle of area rather than commodity monopoly. The disadvantages of this to the Levant Company were obvious. The grant of the sole right to trade with specified areas of the eastern Mediterranean was no protection to the company against the competition of the Dutch, nor did it preclude another privileged company with an area monopoly of trade to the Netherlands from importing from its privileges commodities which the Dutch had brought back from the eastern Mediterranean. This commerce, regularly indulged in by members of the Merchant Adventurers' Company, remained a bone of contention between that company and the Levant Company down to 1617, when the issue was settled in favour of the latter. And precisely similar arguments applied to the import trade in Baltic commodities which bred antagonism between the Merchant Adventurers and the Eastland Company.[6]

The free traders in the House of Commons were quick to exploit this situation. Their attack on the companies was selective rather than indiscriminate, some companies being singled out for particular condemnation, while others were ignored and still others actually praised by the committee on free trade. From the first the Merchant Adventurers came in for particularly severe criticism, and at one time the dissolution of the company seemed imminent. There had, of course, been a continuous history of opposition to the company throughout the Tudor period, but it was in a more vulnerable position in 1603–4 than it had occupied during the early Elizabethan period. Economic depression and the foundation of new companies both may have contributed to the eroding of its traditional commercial supremacy since the 1580s. In addition, Merchant Adventurers certainly figured much less prominently in municipal government than they had done in the company's early Elizabethan heyday.[7] Even though, as was emphasized

---

[6] Friis, *Cockayne's Project*, pp. 181–3; Wood, *Levant Company*, p. 51; Hinton, *Eastland Trade*, p. 25.
[7] Dr G. D. Ramsay informs me that in the 1560s about three-quarters of the

earlier, involvement in municipal affairs and membership of the aldermanic élite are not reliable indexes of economic position, such involvement might well be a significant factor in times when pressure needed to be brought to bear on government or parliament in the face of an attack on the privileges of the company. A number of factors made it an obvious target for criticism. In the first place, although the company had branches in both London and the provinces, nowhere was the predominance of London merchants more pronounced, and the numerous attempts by provincial branches to break away from the parent organization were successfully resisted in this period. Thus the complaint of the report of the committee on free trade against the restrictive practices of the company – 'the Company of Merchant Adventurers . . . in effect not above Two hundred, have the Managing of the Two third Parts of the Clothing of this Realm, which might well maintain many thousands Merchants more' – was to elicit a sympathetic response not only from those merchants who were actually excluded from the company, but also from many of its provincial members who chafed at the metropolitan domination. Moreover, the life-blood of the company's trade – the export of unfinished cloth – made the company numerous enemies among the cloth-finishing interests at home and came to acquire an importance in relation to what was to become one of the outstanding constitutional issues of the reign, since it was based on a *non obstante*, that is, the exercise of the royal prerogative right to dispense with the operation of a parliamentary statute. In the case of the Merchant Adventurers, therefore, the links with the crown and – via the company's purchase of export licences from highborn grantees such as the earl of Cumberland – with the court were plain for all to see, and the hostility of the more determined free traders in the House of Commons was hardly likely to be assuaged by fears that the throwing open of trade might well have disastrous results, since the Merchant Adventurers were likely to respond by boycotting trade, as they had done when the government had taken similar action in the 1580s. Such

---

aldermen had been Merchant Adventurers. I can identify with certainty less than a third of the aldermen of 1603 as connected with the company.

retaliation would be bound to have ruinous consequences for the clothing industry, but considerations of this nature were dismissed as unworthy by the more forthright free traders on the grounds that 'it doth not stand with the Dignity of Parliament, either to fear or favour the Frowardness of any Subject'.[8]

Provincial jealousy of London was also a factor in the Commons' decision to single out the Muscovy Company – 'a strong and a shameful Monopoly, a Monopoly in a Monopoly' – for no less severe condemnation. The whaling expeditions to Spitzbergen, a profitable sideline of the company from 1603 onwards, had aroused the hostility of fishermen in a number of east-coast ports, and notably in Hull and King's Lynn. But while the joint-stock arrangements and monopolistic activities of the Muscovy Company came in for special opprobrium in the parliament of 1604, the newest and most spectacular of the Elizabethan joint-stock companies, the East India Company, met with more general approval, even though it was lumped together with other restrictive organizations in the text of the free-trade bill itself. The Commons were quick to recognize both the necessity of joint-stock organization for this long-distance trade and the opportunities for profitable investment which it opened up. At the same time it was obvious that capital sufficient to finance the trade could be mobilized only in London. In these circumstances the East India Company outraged none of the basic interests of the outports, and the joint-stock organization which had been a main cause of the Commons' criticism of the Muscovy Company was considered entirely appropriate to the needs of the East India trade.[9]

On the whole the East India Company continued to enjoy the approval of both crown and Commons throughout the period of James I's first parliament. The company's relations with the crown culminated satisfactorily enough in 1609 with the obtaining of the new charter which made its exclusive commercial privileges in the orient unequivocally clear. However, the reasons why the company felt the need for a new

---

[8] B.L., Lansdowne MSS., 487, fos. 146(b)–182; *H. of C. J.*, I, 218–20.
[9] P.R.O., S.P. James I, VIII/59; *H. of C. J.*, I, 220; Scott, *Joint-Stock Companies*, I, 123, II, 50–1; Friis, *Cockayne's Project*, p. 155; E. Lipson, *The Economic History of England*, 3 vols., II (4th edn, 1947), 329–30.

charter betray the existence of doubts as to the certainty of royal support under the terms of its Elizabethan charter. Two incidents make this clear. The first is the royal licence granted in 1604 to Sir Edward Michelborne to trade with China, irrespective of any rights which the charter of 1600 conveyed to the East India Company. The simple fact of the technical infringement of the monopoly by Michelborne, who had been expelled from the East India Company in 1601, was less important than the doubts as to the crown's attitude to which the incident gave rise, and the consequent fear that there might be a proliferation of such licences to unscrupulous adventurers whose activities could only redound to the discredit of the company and impose serious obstacles in the way of its painful attempts to build up permanent economic relations with the orient. The second incident, the royal grant in 1607 to Richard Penkewell and a group of adventurers of the right to pursue trade with China, was even less of a menace *per se* to the interests of the company. Nevertheless, like the Michelborne incident, it helped to underline the somewhat precarious position of the East India Company vis-à-vis the crown, and, indeed, it foreshadowed far more serious developments which were to blight the company's relations with the crown in the next reign. Incidents of this type enormously strengthened the case for a new charter. However, the events of the decade following the charter of 1609 were to offer convincing proof that not even this charter provided the company with a completely watertight defence against further infringement of its rights.[10]

At the time of the debates on free trade in 1604 the future of English trade with the eastern Mediterranean was very uncertain. On the death of Queen Elizabeth the Levant Company had renounced its privileges on the grounds that it was no longer capable of paying the annual rent of £4,000 which had been agreed with the crown as the price of the new charter of 1600.[11] As a result, the trade had been thrown open and the

[10] *Cal. S.P.D. 1603–10*, p. 512; *Cal. S.P. East Indies 1513–1616*, pp. 127, 141, 146, 156, 184; Scott, *Joint-Stock Companies*, II, 98–9, 100; Chaudhuri, *East India Company*, pp. 40–1. Michelborne seems to have been readmitted to the East India Company later and advised it on the prospects of the Indian trade in 1608.

[11] The passage which follows on the Levant Company is based on P.R.O., S.P. James I, VI/68–71, X/9, 23, 26, 27, 29, 30–4, XV/3, 4, 54, XVIII/127–8, XX/25–7;

crown had recouped itself for the loss of its rent by levying impositions on the traffic. This state of affairs, claimed the former merchants of the dissolved company, was grossly unfair to them, since 'much more trade hath bin vsed by others then by the Late Company of the Levant, all which personns have vsed theire trade freely without any Charge, either for maintenance of the Embassador & Consull [at Constantinople], but all the same hath bin borne by the levant Company, whereby wee are in effect halfe vndon'. The years 1603–4 were a time of exceedingly delicate negotiations, of jockeying for position, and of intrigues with powerful personages at court on the part of London bigwigs of the former company, such as John Eldred and Richard Stapers. The problem for the Londoners who wished to reconstitute the old company was how to do so without antagonizing the provincial merchants whose voice was so prominent in parliament during these years. A number of alternative solutions were canvassed, and ultimately, as a result of a carefully planned campaign, the Levant Company was reconstituted with a new charter in 1605. However, there can be little doubt that this charter was far more liberal in its provision as to entry fines and membership than might otherwise have been the case had it not been for the need to placate the free-trading and outport interests in parliament. This is attested by the declaration in the charter itself that there was no intention of limiting trade 'to any limited number of merchants nor to any one city or place . . . but to lay open the same to all our loving subjects using only the trade of merchandise, who are willing to enter into the same trade upon such reasonable terms and conditions as shall necessarily belong to the support of the same'. On the whole, however, it may be said that the Levant Company emerged from the crisis of 1604–5 without any special reason for resentment at its treatment at the hands of the House of Commons. Nor, despite the reconstitution of

---

Cal. S.P.D. 1603–10, pp. 51, 136; *H. of C. J.*, I, 220, 297, 466–7; H.M.C., *Salisbury MSS.*, XVI, 380–1, XVII, 16–17, 20, 208, 418, 419, 467–8, XVIII, 16, XIX, 266, 287–8; S. R. Gardiner, *History of England from the Accession of James I to the Outbreak of the Civil War, 1603–1642*, 10 vols. (1883–4), II, 1–7; Friis, *Cockayne's Project*, pp. 158–60; Lipson, *Economic History of England*, II, 340–1; Wood, *Levant Company*, pp. 35–41.

the company in 1605, did it have any reason to feel especial gratitude to the crown. It is true that the new charter of 1605 waived the royal right to the annual rent of £4,000, but the crown was to recoup itself for this by continuing to levy impositions as it had done since the original company's surrender of its privileges in 1603. It was these impositions which, so the Levant merchants claimed, were likely to ruin the English trade in currants, since they put English merchants at an impossible disadvantage vis-à-vis the Venetians, who at least were exempt from the payment of duties which the Venetian state had imposed upon foreign exporters of currants. And it was, of course, these same impositions which became one of the primary grievances of the House of Commons against the crown in the early years of the reign of James I, a situation which afforded some scope for the alignment of the interests of the Levant merchants – of whom the celebrated John Bate was one – with those of the parliamentary opposition.

Another cause for resentment was the royal refusal, despite the crown's appropriation of the impositions to itself, to contribute to the charges of the English ambassador at Constantinople, which continued to fall upon the Levant Company. Many members of that company may well have weighed such grievances against the need to maintain the good will of the crown, and in addition, the parliamentary hostility to impositions against the parliamentary dislike of London-based companies. A further factor in the company's opposition to impositions was the failure of fourteen of its most prominent members, including William Garway and Nicholas Salter, the farmers of the great customs, to obtain the farm of the duties on currants. In these circumstances there was something in the contemporary criticism of the Levant merchants that they had no grounds to quarrel with impositions, since, in the period before 1603, 'they themselfes tooke the saide impositions of a nomber of his Majesties Subiecttes which were not of their company'; or, as another critic put it, 'they deale not sincerely with his Majestie, but . . . would indirectly draw from his Majestie the benefytt of iiii *m.li* per annum ariseing by an imposition layd vppon all corinthes [viz. currants] brought into this Realme'. The issue disclosed the potentialities of a split between different elements in the London concessionary interest. The hostility of the Levant merchants to the earl of Suffolk and his city sublessees of the farm of the currant duties meant that in the periodic attacks upon both the impositions and the customs farms, the farmers could not count on the support of other concessionaires and least of all on the members of the Levant Company, who, besides opposing the impositions on economic grounds, claimed disingenuously that 'the benefitt of ryseing of Customes [and] Impositions . . . farmed to Subiectes is exceeding greate and too much to be withdrawne from the Kinge'. This provoked the obvious retort from the government that impositions were clearly not a just grievance of the Levant merchants 'vnlesse it be a grievance that they are not the ffarmers thereof, as they were before'. The issue was not shelved until Suffolk's abandonment of the currant farm in 1613, and its acquisition by members of the syndicate which farmed the great customs, of which the Levant merchants Garway and Salter were the two most prominent operators. But it was to be revived to much greater effect in the early years of the next reign.[12]

One of the great surviving Tudor companies, the Eastland Company, remains to be treated. At this time less than half of English trade with the Baltic countries went via London, and in these circumstances the Eastland Company did not present an obvious target for outport attack. It is, however, true that the constitutional arrangements of the company, whereby policy formulation was firmly in the hands of the Londoners, a minority of the total membership, were a source of discontent to provincial members which was to come to a head later in the reign. However, it could not be said of the company, as it could of the Merchant Adventurers', Muscovy or even the Levant companies, that it was effectively a metropolitan organization, and it seems to have been relatively untroubled by attacks in parliament in the early years of the reign.[13]

In general, the attacks which were mounted by the free traders in parliament on the chartered companies cannot be said to have been attended with great success, except insofar as they resulted in more liberal provisions in the new charter of

[12] See below, pp. 129–35.
[13] Friis, *Cockayne's Project*, pp. 172–4; Hinton, *Eastland Trade*, p. 56.

the Levant Company than might otherwise have been the case. And even here there was a notable difference between principle and practice. However, it would be a mistake to regard the fact that the free-trade bill of 1604 did not become law as proof that the crown, the chartered companies and the metropolis gained a complete victory over the free traders and the outports. At best the victory was only partial. For the practices and fate of the existing chartered companies was only one of the issues at stake. Equally important was the desire of the outports and the free traders in parliament to prevent the formation of companies in those branches of commerce which were reviving as a result of the Peace of 1604, and for which it was feared – not without justice – that organization on the basis of national companies would inevitably produce the all-too-familiar pattern of metropolitan domination. The most crucial issues here were the fate of the French and Spanish trades. With regard to the latter, Pauline Croft has recently demonstrated conclusively that the agitation for free trade to Spain was a good deal more than the mere tail-end of an otherwise unsuccessful Commons campaign for free trade in general; and that among the reasons for its success was that it commanded powerful support within the House from west-country gentlemen who were interested, as growers of corn, in the grain export trade to Spain in which some of them participated directly. The prospect of the domination of the Spanish trade by a London-based regulated company was anathema to such people, many of whom entertained similar disquiet about the prospect for the profitable trade of west-country ports with Newfoundland and, in Newfoundland cod, direct to the Iberian peninsula. The confirmation of the charter of the Spanish Company in 1604 and the issue of a new patent of incorporation in the following year appeared to confirm their worst fears, not to speak of those of the independent merchants of the south-western outports, even though the terms of the patent of 1605 were more liberal than those which had originally been envisaged in 1604. In a report delivered to the earl of Salisbury in September 1605, Lord Chief Justice Popham expressed the view that the incorporation of a Spanish Company 'will overthrow all the towns, shipping and mariners of the West parts', and stressed the incompatibility of the tightly controlled trade of a London-based regulated company with the quick-turnover trade of young west-country merchants. He admitted that a newly revived Spanish Company might have certain superficial attractions for that small minority of large-scale professional merchants of the ports of the south-west, but they in turn should recall the experience of their Elizabethan predecessors, when the Spanish Company 'was no sooner put in practice, but both they and all the rest of the western merchants found out the drift of the merchants of London that followed it'. Popham was thus in broad agreement with the view of the merchants of the south-western ports that, thanks to free trade, English commerce with the Iberian peninsula and France was the most significant area of European commerce where the outports still held their own with the Londoners.

The trade[s] into ffrance and Spaine are the onely trades which are left to maintaine the outports of this Realme, the Londiners haveing ingrost all others into their handes, and therefore no reason that that should allso be brought into their and a fewe other mens hands to enrich them and impoverish all others.

To such merchants it seemed certain that the fate of other provincial interests at the hands of national chartered companies would be repeated in the case of the ports of the south-west as a result of the establishment of the Spanish Company, by whose constitution 'their goverment is limited to the President and 61 assistants, whereof 31 are to be in London, and that whatsoeuer the greatest of those 61 do conclude, all other men must obay; so that the greatest part beinge in London, bie consequence whatsoeuer the Londiners conclude, all must obay, though it be to the cutting of their owne throtes'.[14]

In 1606, after two years of intense agitation, a bill for free trade with Spain, Portugal and France passed both houses of parliament. The protests of the London Spanish and French lobbies were unavailing. In vain, they ridiculed the efforts of

[14] P.R.O., S.P. James I, xii/63, 64; *H. of C. J.*, i, 256; H.M.C., *Salisbury MSS.*, xvii, 79–80, 301, 418–19; Gardiner, *History*, i, 347–8; Friis, *Cockayne's Project*, pp. 150–1, 156–8, 160–3; Ashton, *P. & P.*, no. 38 (1967), 42, 45–6; P. Croft, 'Free Trade and the House of Commons 1605–6', *Econ. Hist. Rev.*, 2nd ser., xxviii (1975), 17–27.

Sir George Somers in the west country to procure the signatures of 'tapsters, Dyers, Tuckers [viz. fullers] & Weavers & of diverse mecanicall fellowes' to petitions for free trade. In vain they prophesied economic disaster if the bill went through. The professional merchants of London were later to claim that these gloomy prophecies were amply borne out by the events of the succeeding decades. They complained of the 'greater disorder in the generall course now holden by all the traders', arguing that the *status quo post* 1606 put the expert, sober, professional 'mere merchants' at an impossible disadvantage. One such complaint in 1617 inveighs bitterly against the incursion into the Spanish trade of a variety of irresponsible interests, which proper control of the trade by a regulated company would have kept out; among them linen drapers, the northern and west-country manufacturers of cloth and hosiery, spilling over from manufacture into the sacrosanct precinct of commerce, and dealers in tobacco. On account of the high price fetched by tobacco, 'a nedeles yf not a hurtfull Comoditie', the latter were able to undersell honest 'mere merchants' in the 'perpetuanoes, bayes and other the best and most vendible Comodities of this Kingdome', which they exported in competition with them. The benefits of free trade, of course, extended to Londoners as well as to the merchants of the outports, but this advantage was hardly likely to commend itself to the commercial élite of the metropolis, whose complaints against the practices of both metropolitan and provincial retailers and manufacturers engaging in foreign trade were a notable feature of the commercial history of the two decades which followed the decision of 1606. There were, indeed, powerful arguments which could be advanced in favour of the conduct of Anglo-Spanish trade by a regulated company, even though not by a company with such a restricted membership as was desired by the London protagonists of a Spanish Company. English merchants in Spain were almost continually subjected to petty interference and occasionally to outrageous maltreatment by Spanish officials, and, in the absence of a permanent English consular service, some protection might have been afforded by membership of a powerful company with established depots in Spain. But despite the continued protests of London merchants, and even of a handful of provincials, their request was never granted. Even the sensible compromise suggested by Attorney-General Yelverton in 1616, whereby the London merchants were to be incorporated and merchants of the outports left free to trade independently was rejected by a government which feared the support which west-country interests were capable of mobilizing in parliament, and a similar fate befell renewed pleas from the Londoners in 1619–20.[15]

In the case of the French trade the Londoners, though thwarted in 1606, were ultimately to be more successful. The arguments of the so-called free traders of the western outports were here seen at their weakest, for the act of 1606 specifically exempted from its provisions a regulated company which had been formed at Exeter in 1560 for trade with France. In 1605 the citizens of Exeter had argued against the formation of a national company on the familiar grounds that it would result in the domination of the French trade by Londoners, and would 'hazard the estates of a great number of our western merchants, who (being made subject to their commands) shall adventure but what and how much and when they [the Londoners] list, and shall be disabled to do anything without directions from so distant and remote a place'. The success of the Exeter merchants in retaining their own organization and yet defeating the proposal to create a national company was short-lived, and the continued demands of the Londoners for the establishment of a French Company bore fruit in 1609, though only in the face of vigorous opposition, not only from Exeter, whose company maintained its separate existence after 1609, but also from a number of the other ports of the south-west, including Bristol. None of the merchants of Bristol, declared the mayor of that city, was in the least interested in joining the new company. Indeed, they desired only to avoid the 'many inconveniences and greate detryment which may otherwise happen

---

[15] B.L., Lansdowne MSS., 152, fos. 233–234(b); ibid. 487, fos. 187–194(b); P.R.O., S.P. James I, xii/64, xvi/118, xix/96, xxi/2; *H. of C. J.*, i, 275, 373, 380, 381; H.M.C., *Salisbury MSS.*, xviii, 3, 143, 171, 260, 263–5, xix, 9–10, 71, 72, 271–2, 304, 493; D. H. Willson (ed.), *The Parliamentary Diary of Robert Bowyer 1606–1607* (Minneapolis, Minn., 1931), pp. 30, 78, 116–17, 124, 138–9 & n, 144, 334–8; Gardiner, *History*, i, 348–54; Friis, *Cockayne's Project*, pp. 169–72; Ashton, *P. & P.*, no. 38 (1967), 42–3.

vnto them by the pollitique devises of the Merchantes of
London, who, for their own singuler gaine, doe alwaies seeke
to suppresse our chartres and priviledges for trade of Merchan-
dize, and have drawne 700 li. at a tyme from the Marchantes of
this Cytie for tradinge into Turkey and Venice, where this
Cytie . . . ought by their said Chartres to haue free Trafficke'.
The merchants of the south-western ports had every reason to
be apprehensive, for the apparently liberal conditions of entry
into the new company were largely illusory and, given the
relatively rudimentary division of economic function obtaining
in most provincial ports, the limitation of membership to
'mere merchants' was a factor which was bound to tip the
scales heavily in favour of the Londoners.[16]

II

On the whole, the events of the first parliament of James's
reign may be said to have underlined the broad community of
interest between the crown and the concessionary interest of
London. It is true that from time to time concessionaires might
feel certain misgivings about this alliance. The farmers of the
various branches of the royal customs, for example, had to put
up with successive enhancement of rent contrary to the terms
of their leases. The crown had, in fact, been quick to take
advantage of the fact that a prominent feature of the history of
customs farming during the decade which succeeded the
establishment of the great farm in 1604 had been the feuds
between the members of the successful Garway–Salter–Jones
syndicate and the disgruntled Sir John Swinnerton who had
also lost his lease of the French and Rhenish wines farm via a
reversionary lease to the earl of Devon, which was ultimately
worked by the hated Garway and Salter. His obtaining of the
lease of the sweet-wine farm, which he retained till his death in
1616 and which his wife farmed until 1623, was quite inadequate
compensation for these disappointments, and Swinnerton
spared no effort to oust the rival syndicate from its two more

[16] P.R.O., S.P. James I, xiii/49, xxi/1, xlv/88, 106; H.M.C., *Salisbury MSS.*, xvii,
453; Friis, *Cockayne's Project*, pp. 163–6; Lipson, *Economic History of England*, ii,
363–4; Ashton, *P. & P.*, no. 38 (1967), 45–6.

substantial concessions. In July 1607 he entertained James I and his queen at a sumptuous banquet, and earlier in the same year he succeeded in obtaining the backing of one of the most powerful personages of the day, the earl of Northampton, in an attempt to bring the great farmers to their knees, offering, so it was said, £4,000 more rent than they paid for the great farm in addition to an enormous entry fine of £100,000. Although Swinnerton failed on this occasion, the crown was the gainer by the resultant rise in the rent paid by the Garway–Jones–Salter syndicate from £112,400 to £120,000 as a result of his bid. However, five years later he made a further effort which brought him even nearer to success. In this he was joined not only by the earl of Northampton, the courtly ally of his 1607 bid, but, for a time at least, by the reigning royal favourite, Robert Carr, Viscount Rochester, later earl of Somerset, who was shortly to make his fateful marriage into the Howard clan. With the aid of Lionel Cranfield, an impressive case against the farmers was drawn up. As in 1607, however, it was successful only in the sense that it produced a substantial increase of the rent paid by the syndicate from £120,000 to £136,226. Northampton and Cranfield were rewarded for their pains, but Swinnerton had again failed to get his own way.

Concurrently with their attack upon the conduct of the great farm Swinnerton and Northampton had been questioning the conduct of the farmers in their lease of the French and Rhenish wine farm. On this issue too Rochester was an even more powerful potential ally than Northampton, and, at the beginning of 1613, we find Swinnerton offering him a pension of £1,000 per annum if he succeeded in obtaining the farm for him. However, the offer of the existing farmers was made through 'swete Rochester', to whose influence Northampton ascribed their success. What Rochester himself got out of the transaction is not known, but in view both of the suspicions which had been cast on the farmers' conduct of their lease and of Swinnerton's highly competitive offer, it must have been substantially more than the £1,000 per annum offered him by the latter. He must also have received some substantial reward from Swinnerton for helping him, in the autumn of 1613, out of an awkward situation which had arisen in connection with scandals about shady arrangements connected with his sweet-wine farm.[17]

Although Swinnerton's rivals, Garway, Jones and Salter, must certainly have resented bitterly the way in which the government was prepared to use his ambitions as a means of extorting higher rents from them, they would certainly be under no illusion about the far worse fate that would befall them if they had been left to the mercies of parliament. It is also true that the parliamentary offensive on the impositions might awaken a sympathetic response from those chartered companies such as the Levant Company which had not been subjected to notable attacks in parliament, and, indeed, that the government had failed in some respects to meet to the full the demands of the professional merchants of London. Nevertheless the latter were not unaware of the fact that its failure to do so was due in no small measure to the pressure to which it had been subjected by the House of Commons, and on the whole there is little to suggest that during these years the Elizabethan *mariage de convenance* between the government and metropolitan big business was very seriously threatened. During the next decade parliament met only once and then only for a few weeks in 1614. When it did meet, the newly created and London-dominated French Company presented an obvious target for attack. In the Addled Parliament of 1614 the members for Plymouth and Bristol launched a fierce attack on the practices of the new company, and more particularly on its domination by Londoners, and stressed the contribution which it was making to the ruin of the ports of the west country. In vain did the company's defenders cite the charter of the Exeter merchants as an equal violation of free-trade principles, as well as pointing out that the new company combined the advantages of relatively liberal terms of entry with much-needed regulation of traffic

---

17 On the customs farms, B.L., Harleian MSS., 1878, fo. 146; Lansdowne MSS., 169, fos. 87–90; P.R.O., Patent Roll 11 Jac. I, pt 22; Close Roll 11 Jac. I, pt 42; S.P. James I, LXX/49, 55, 62, 63, LXXI/3, 5, 16, 18, LXXII/1, 1 (i), 2, 4, 5, LXXIV/7, 8, 36, 37; S.P. 15/35/35; MS. Cal. of Sackville MSS., M202–4, 221; *Cal. S.P.D. 1611–18*, pp. 163, 199; H.M.C., *Sackville MSS.*, I, 282–96, 299–309; J. Spedding (ed.), *The Life and Letters of Francis Bacon*, 7 vols. (1861–74), IV, 337–9; N. E. McClure (ed.), *The Letters of John Chamberlain*, 2 vols. (Philadelphia, 1939), I, 243, 466, 474; Dietz, *English Public Finance 1558–1641*, pp. 332–3, 346–7; Ashton, *The Crown and the Money Market*, pp. 90, 106–7.

which saved the trade with France from some of the scandals which characterized the Spanish trade. It was nevertheless fortunate for the French Company that the issue of the organization of Anglo-French trade disappeared into obscurity as the attention of the House of Commons became riveted on the matter of the impositions, an issue which itself helped to cut short the life of the Addled Parliament. None the less the attack on the French Company underlined once more the distaste of prevailing opinion in the Commons for national chartered companies dominated by Londoners, and however much members of most of these companies disliked the impositions, they were well aware that, on balance, they had a great deal more to fear from parliament than they had from the crown.[18]

This seems to have been particularly true of the Levant Company. During this decade two events helped to strengthen the ties of economic interest between the company and the crown which had been weakened in the early years of the reign by the company's opposition to the impositions and to the personnel of the farmers of the duties on currants. The first of these events, the leasing in 1613 of the currant farm to members of the syndicate of great farmers who were dominated by the two Levant merchants Garway and Salter has already been mentioned. The second was the royal proclamation which was issued in 1615, following prolonged high-level pressure from the company. This reaffirmed in decisive terms the restriction to members of the company of the importation into England of 'currants, cotton wool, wines of Candy (muscadel), galles, [and] any other commodity whatsoever, brought from anie the forraine parts or regions wherein the said Company have vsed to trade'. On the face of it the proclamation appeared to concede no more to the company than its charter of 1605 had done, but the crucial issue turned on the precise interpretation of the phrase quoted above. Was it intended simply to confirm the area of monopoly of the company or to extend the company's hold from a monopoly of English trade with the eastern Mediterranean to a monopoly of trade in the *commodities* of the

[18] *H. of C. J.*, I, 461, 469–70; Friis, *Cockayne's Project*, pp. 167–8; T. L. Moir, *The Addled Parliament of 1614* (Oxford, 1958), pp. 90–1, 95.

eastern Mediterranean? If the latter were the case, a serious blow would be struck at those members of the Merchant Adventurers' Company who imported from their privileges in the Low Countries commodities which had been brought from the eastern Mediterranean by the Dutch. It was a matter of crucial importance to the fortunes of both interests and to the attitude of both to the crown that in 1617 the issue was decided in favour of the latter interpretation. In that year the Levant Company attempted to prevent a member of the Merchant Adventurers' Company from importing currants from the Low Countries. The decision that such practices should be forbidden in future was nominally the result of a settlement reached via private negotiations between the two companies concerned, but that the Merchant Adventurers made this concession under considerable pressure from the government is clear from their statement that they had yielded on this point 'because your Honours [viz. the privy council] . . . seem to judge that the present estate of the Levant Company standeth in need of some special favour'. It was a case of collision of interest between conflicting privileges, and the Merchant Adventurers had to yield. All in all, the second decade of the seventeenth century was not a good time for the Merchant Adventurers' Company, and, as will be shown later, they were given even more serious reasons for disquiet and doubts about the continuing good will of the crown.[19]

Such doubts were by no means confined to the Merchant Adventurers. During the first decade of its existence the East India Company had basked in the approval of both the crown and the House of Commons, and had shown its consciousness of the desirability of making the best of both worlds by unhesitatingly admitting both courtiers and officials and prominent members of the parliamentary opposition like Sir Edwin Sandys to the ranks of its investors. The need for the new charter which it had obtained in 1609 had, however, been emphasized by the royal inclination to violate its privileges by the issue of licences to adventurers like Michelborne and

[19] *Cal. S.P.D. 1611–18*, p. 283; Steele (ed.), *Bibliotheca Lindesiana*, I, no. 1160; Friis, *Cockayne's Project*, pp. 181–3, 385–6; Hinton, *Eastland Trade*, p. 25.

Penkewell. And even the new charter afforded less than complete protection to the company. For James was king of Scotland as well as of England, and the events of 1618 gave particular point to the company's need for powerful backing at court, not simply as a reassurance against a change in the attitude of members of the House of Commons to the company, but also as a means of defence against the schemes of the crown itself. In that year the company's privileges were infringed by a grant made under the great seal of Scotland to Sir James Cunningham and a group of court adventurers. The East India Company was sufficiently influential to get the grant revoked, but only at the price of incurring partial responsibility for indemnifying Cunningham. No less eloquent of the crown's willingness ruthlessly to exploit its position vis-à-vis the company was its demand in the same year for a loan of £20,000, prompted perhaps by a memorandum drawn up in the previous year which brutally asserted that 'Without his Majesty's vsinge his prerogative power, the said Companie and theire stock are at his Majesty's grace and pleasure to require of them what his highnes thinketh meete for his honner and proffit, which, as their case standeth, they nether may nor will deny.'[20]

The Cunningham incident had far more disastrous consequences for the Muscovy Company, since the adventurers' licence had also granted them what were in effect powers of poaching on the whaling preserves of that company off Greenland. The Muscovy Company had, therefore, to share with the East India Company the cost of buying Cunningham off, and its resulting financial difficulties forced it to seek help from the larger body. This was obtained only on the condition that the Greenland and Russian trades be separated in the future, and the former conducted as a new joint stock operated jointly with the East India Company. For all these difficulties the Muscovy Company had only the crown to thank, and it is uncertain how far its members regarded the support which they obtained

[20] P.R.O., S.P. James I, xc/54; *Cal. S.P. East Indies 1617–21*, pp. 78, 137, 147, 174, 175, 218; McClure (ed.), *Chamberlain's Letters*, II, 134–5, 150; Scott, *Joint-Stock Companies*, I, 147–8, II, 55, 104; Chaudhuri, *East India Company*, pp. 31, 35–7. As late as July 1619 the company seems still to have been concerned about the possible revival of Cunningham's patent (*Cal. S.P. East Indies 1617–21*, p. 286).

fairly consistently during this decade from the privy council against the claims of the fishing interests of east-coast ports, and notably of Hull and King's Lynn, as adequate compensation.[21] In sharp contrast to this was the privy council's attitude to disputes between Londoners and outport merchants in the Baltic trade. The fact that these were disputes within the ranks of the Eastland Company, rather than between a metropolitan-dominated privileged company and free-trade interests in the outports, does not make them any less relevant to our theme of the commercial interests of substantial London merchants. Since the London members of the company handled less than a third of the cloths exported to the Baltic and yet dominated its affairs, the constitutional arrangements of the company were particularly open to criticism, and in 1616 the privy council made concessions to provincial members of the company which, amongst other things, allowed the outports to send representatives to the meetings of its general court in London. Although this concession unquestionably irritated the London members of the company, in practice it did not amount to a great deal. The representatives of the outports were to have no voice in the determination of general policy, their only function being that of observers with a right of complaint to the privy council against any ordinances of which they disapproved. The crucial issue therefore remained the susceptibility of the government to the different demands of metropolitan and provincial interests. In one matter, however, both interests within the company were united against the government. This was the royal proclamation of 1615 relating to the enforcement of the Navigation Acts which insisted on the importation of goods in English ships, and which particularly menaced the interests of the Eastland merchants, since Flemish and Dutch ships were far more economical for use in this trade in commodities whose density was high in relation to their value. The company feared that its interests were being sacrificed on the altar of the growth of the native English shipping industry, and the concessions which were made by the privy

[21] P.R.O., S.P. James I, xciv/70, 71; *Cal. S.P.D. 1611–18*, p. 252; *Cal. S.P. East Indies 1617–21*, pp. 175, 336–7; Scott, *Joint-Stock Companies*, I, 147–8, II, 53; Friis, *Cockayne's Project*, pp. 174–7.

council in response to its complaints were far below what its members desired. More than the import trade was at stake, for, if the Eastland merchants are to be believed, the strictly bilateral nature of trade with the Baltic made it necessary for them to bring back imports if they were to find a market for their exports, and here the proclamation of 1615 put them at a distinct disadvantage.[22]

But of all the great chartered companies it was the Merchant Adventurers who had the greatest cause for discontent in the second decade of the century. The government's discrimination against the company and in favour of the Levant Company in 1617 has already been noted, but, serious though this was, it was a minor irritant when compared with the treatment which it had received at the hands of the crown over the previous three years. Subjected to frequent pillorying in the House of Commons during the first parliament of the reign and to more than one attempt to prevent its exportation of unfinished cloth, the company had its main prop of support, the backing of the crown, suddenly and spectacularly removed in 1614. Whether the notorious project of Alderman William Cockayne was inspired (as George Unwin thought) by the cloth-finishing interests of London who wished to prevent the export of unfinished cloth, or (in the interpretation of Astrid Friis) by members of other companies, and notably the Eastland Company, who wished to strangle the Dutch cloth-finishing trade and their re-export to the Baltic of cloths which had previously been exported unfinished to the Low Countries by the Merchant Adventurers, or (as Supple has suggested) by a group of racketeers whose ambitions extended no further than making a take-over bid for the privileges of the Merchant Adventurers using the project of exporting only finished cloth as a bait to catch royal support and to play on the susceptibilities of the free traders in the Commons (and the last interpretation probably comes nearest to the truth), there can be no doubt that it dealt a stunning blow to the Merchant Adventurers. When, in the Addled Parliament of 1614, Robert Middleton, himself a Merchant Adventurer, launched a violent attack on

[22] Friis, *Cockayne's Project*, pp. 172–4, 184–5; Hinton, *Eastland Trade*, p. 56.

the Cockayne projectors, there was perhaps for the moment a faint possibility that the company, which over the previous decade had come in for more consistent parliamentary abuse than any other – with the possible exception of the Muscovy Company – might find support in the Commons against the latest group of royal concessionaires. If the Addled Parliament had endured for another couple of years, such support might indeed have been forthcoming. As it was, although a few M.P.s spoke against the project, the House as a whole failed to rise to the bait. The real character of the Cockayne project had not yet revealed itself, and the specious free-trade arguments of the projectors, which so completely took in Sir Edward Coke, were equally persuasive to the House as a whole. Thus, in 1614, the Merchant Adventurers found themselves in a parlous position, since they had both forfeited the support of the crown and were faced by an implacably hostile House of Commons. Attempts to persuade individual Merchant Adventurers to throw in their lot with Cockayne were almost entirely unsuccessful and in 1615 a new company was formed with precisely the same privileges as the old except for an obligation to export a progressively increased amount of finished cloth, which was never properly fulfilled. After the disastrous failure of the project, it was left to the old company to make its peace with the crown and with the Netherlands government, and to obtain – at a price – the restoration in 1617 of most, if not quite all, of its old privileges. This, together with the more diligent activity of the privy council against interlopers, helped to patch up the old alliance between members of privileged export–import cartels and the crown at the point where it had been most seriously threatened.[23]

III

The events of the parliament of 1621 fully consolidated this alliance. The hostility of the Commons to privileged concessionaires was enormously sharpened by the economic depression,

---

[23] *H. of C. J.*, I, 291, 491–2; Unwin, *Industrial Organization*, pp. 181–93; Friis, *Cockayne's Project*, pp. 224–304, 367–76; B. E. Supple, *Commercial Crisis and Change in England 1600–1642* (Cambridge, 1959), pp. 33–51.

and no concessionary interest, monopolist, customs farmers, licensee or member of a privileged trading company was safe from attack.[24] Nothing better illustrates the renewed dependence of the companies on the crown than an event which took place on 3 May, when the Merchant Adventurers succeeded in diverting the Commons from an examination of their patents and rule books only by invoking the personal intervention of the king, who informed the House peremptorily that 'there have been diverse things between them [the Merchant Adventurers] and me not so fitt for yow to see and deale in. Medle not with those things that belong to me and the state.'[25] The Eastland Company, having failed to get the crown to grant it concessions similar to those afforded to the Levant Company in 1615, went cap in hand to parliament with a navigation bill which was designed to prohibit imports of Baltic commodities from the Dutch entrepôt and to promote legislation which would have facilitated a re-export trade in Baltic corn. They met with a very dusty response from those stern opponents of company privileges, the members for the western outports, though they obtained much of what they desired by royal proclamation in the following year.[26] A bill was introduced for general free trade,[27] another for free trade into France,[28] and the restrictive practices associated with the joint stocks of the Muscovy Company came in for the same sort of criticism that they had received in the parliament of 1604.[29] Even the East India Company, which had met with favour in the Commons debates on free trade in 1604, did not get off entirely scot-free. It was more or less inevitable, given the prevailing concern about the shortage of money in the depression, that the export

[24] The references to these matters in *C.D. 1621* are far too numerous to be cited in full, but can easily be located via the admirable index to this superb edition of the parliamentary diaries for 1621. On the parliament and the companies, see also Friis, *Cockayne's Project*, pp. 395–426; Supple, *Commercial Crisis*, pp. 52–70; Hinton, *Eastland Trade*, pp. 12–32; Stonehewer, 'Economic Policy and Opinion in the House of Commons, 1621', pp. 24–7, 38–9, 49–82.

[25] *H. of C. J.*, I, 598–9, 620; *C.D. 1621*, II, 365, III, 157, 247, IV, 298–9, 339, V, 138, 163, 365, VI, 155. The actual quotation is from Barrington's diary.

[26] *C.D. 1621*, III, 46–8, IV, 229; Hinton, *Eastland Trade*, pp. 24–6.

[27] *H. of C. J.*, I, 595; *C.D. 1621*, II, 330, III, 105–7, IV, 271–3, V, 109–10, 267, 353–4, VI, 107–8.

[28] *H. of C. J.*, I, 605; *C.D. 1621*, III, 147, V, 364, VI, 130.

[29] *C.D. 1621*, III, 48, 73–4, IV, 210–11, 230–1, 254, VI, 107–8.

of bullion to the orient should come in for parliamentary criticism. Although the company was ultimately exonerated, its image as the one privileged exporting agency which found favour with parliament was somewhat tarnished.[30] Faced with such attacks, the companies were in a state of disarray, and at times something approaching an atmosphere of *sauve qui peut* resulted. For instance, the poor relations which had existed between the Merchant Adventurers and the Levant Company since the government had, in 1617, persuaded the former not to import Levantine commodities from its privileges found expression in a speech made by Towerson, the deputy governor of the Merchant Adventurers, who argued that, although the export of money by the East India Company was a matter of small consequence in the crisis of monetary shortage, the unfavourable balance of trade between England and the eastern Mediterranean countries was of very real significance in this context.[31]

The parliament of 1621 represents the high point of the hostility of the Commons to the national chartered companies, and the alliance of the latter with the crown. In the face of fierce parliamentary attacks the grievances of the second decade of the century were forgotten. The parliamentary agitation for freedom of foreign trade, which had begun at the turn of the century, had developed out of the attack on internal monopolies in the last two parliaments of Elizabeth's reign. In the 1621 parliament, monopolists, customs farmers and members of export–import cartels were all indiscriminately lumped together for abuse. The blood of the English provincials was again up. The economic decline of the outports, argued Mr Alport, was a direct consequence of the restrictive practices of the national chartered companies, and especially the Merchant Adventurers' Company. The practices of these companies were in turn linked with the activities of holders of government financial concessions as part of a great metropolitan plot against the provinces.

---

[30] *Cal. S.P. East Indies 1617–21*, pp. 431–2; *H. of C. J.*, I, 510, 527–8, 552, 579, 645; *C.D. 1621*, II, 30, 138, 212–13, IV, 19, 97, 113, 149, 229–30, 436–7, V, 4, 36, 261, 262, 263, 440, 491, 514–18, 524, 527, VI, 10–12, 15, 16, 59, 296, 298.

[31] Ibid. v, 262, VI, 299. For similar views expressed by other speakers see ibid. v, 527, VI, 17, 61, 300. Howard's diary (ibid. VI, 299) gives the best account of Towerson's speech.

'*London* the Farmers of all Customs through *England*, and will, by their Restraints by Companies, overthrow all other Places'. It was no accident that the parliament of 1621 saw a proposal for financial decentralization added to the usual outport demands for commercial decentralization. This was Sir Dudley Digges's scheme whereby the outports should farm their own customs, which, he declared, 'will make them more industrious when they shall growe ritch by their industrye. The present Course drawes all the Trade to London, which is the place for men to growe wealthy in and then returne into the Countrye.'[32]

Attacks on the practices of chartered companies were also a notable feature of the parliament of 1624. It was largely as a result of such attacks that the government, yielding to parliamentary pressure, forced the Merchant Adventurers to broaden the basis of their company, to accept a measure of free trade to their privileges in a number of commodities, such as kerseys, coloured cloths and new draperies, and to lower the impositions which the company levied on its members. As Supple puts it, the most notable result of the parliamentary onslaught in the early 1620s was that 'a ten-year experiment in relative freedom was under way'.[33] Nevertheless, the temper of the Commons in 1624 was quieter than it had been in 1621, although both the tone and the content of the criticisms of the Merchant Adventurers, and especially those voiced by their most implacable enemy, Neale, were pretty abrasive. Moreover, the committee of trade remained critical of the company. The committee is reported in Pym's diary as desirous 'that the House would deliver a finall sentence against the Merchant Adventurers Pattent and that it might be presented to his Majestie as a Greivance'. It also recommended that the purchase of white cloths which had still been unsold six weeks after being brought to Blackwell Hall should be thrown open to all. The company

---

[32] *H. of C. J.*, I, 595, 611, 636, 638–9; *C.D. 1621*, II, 422–3, III, 394, IV, 228, 395, 408, V, 393; Stonehewer, 'Economic Policy and Opinion in the House of Commons', pp. 39, 60–1, 74–8. The passages quoted are taken from *H. of C. J.*, I, 595, and Pym's diary (*C.D. 1621*, IV, 408).

[33] B.L., Harleian MSS., 159, fos. 40–1, 115(b)–116; ibid. 6383, fo. 116(b); Add. MSS., 18,597, fos. 111(b)–112, 114–114(b); *H. of C. J.*, I, 695, 759, 780–1; Supple, *Commercial Crisis*, p. 71.

was ordered to submit for examination its court book, register book, ledger books and books of accounts showing all disbursements since it had first laid its private impositions on cloth exports, which were declared to be 'unlawful, unjust and a Grievance to the People'. Significantly on this occasion, and in complete contrast to what had happened in 1621, the parliamentary request to inspect these records was specifically conceded by the king. The domination of James by the prince and Buckingham, which is a central feature of the history of this parliament, clearly extended from political to economic matters. It was indeed via a message from the duke that the Commons learned that the king, notwithstanding the fact that he had forbidden parliamentary inspection of the Merchant Adventurers' records in 1621, 'so much trusts to the Judgment of this House, that he is very willing we should have them'.[34] The significance of this royal concession could hardly be lost on the Merchant Adventurers and may well have influenced their decision to pay the price demanded by parliament as a means of coming to an understanding with it. For all the hard knocks administered in debate and in committee the prevailing mood seems to have been one of sober criticism rather than violent hostility. One M.P. compared the company to 'a great old Tree, which hath borne good Fruit, yet now is grown mossy and too full of Branches'. The metaphor with its suggested cure of a paring and pruning exercise was, however, not altogether appropriate, since, as we have seen, the main remedy, apart from freeing the trade to the Merchant Adventurers' privileges in virtually everything but unfinished cloth, was to multiply the number of branches by widening the actual membership of the company. Although there were some parliamentary echoes of the sort of complaint which had been heard so frequently before Cockayne's project about the failure to set cloth-finishers on work due to undue concentration on the export of unfinished cloth, the twin remedies of the Commons' committee of trade of freeing trade in finished and many other cloths and

[34] B.L., Harleian MSS., 159, fo. 123; ibid. 6383, fos. 95, 97–8; Add. MSS., 18,597, fos. 66(b), 123(b), 139–139(b), 156(b)–158; Add. MSS., 26,639, fo. 43; Bodleian Library, Tanner MSS., 392, fo. 80(b); Northamptonshire Record Office, Finch-Hatton MSS., 50, fo. 85; *H. of C. J.*, 1, 672, 681, 689, 706, 717, 754, 758, 780–1.

enlarging membership of the company seem to have satisfied the House, which sought not a dissolution of the company 'butt rather that it bee reformed and reduced to that estate (or at least wise neare vnto it) wherein that trade did greatlie flourish'. Although the company's current patent was declared to be 'a Grievance both in the Creation and Execution', the way was paved for a new state of affairs in which the company, with its privileges suitably modified and its membership enlarged, might hope to remain unmolested in the future. With the crown's apparently complete withdrawal of protection from it, it had, in fact, little else to hope for.[35] Indeed, it is significant that some of the complaints which the Merchant Adventurers had made to the committee of trade ultimately appeared among the grievances of which parliamentary complaint was made to, and redress requested from, the king. Such were the royal levying of the so-called pretermitted customs on cloth and the Dutch exactions of 'licence money' and abatements for 'tare', viz. deductions for allegedly faulty cloth. Two complaints, in particular, anticipated what were to become crucial issues in the next reign and important factors in the change in the alignment of concessionary interests which is dealt with in the chapter which follows. The first of these relates to the relations between business and courtly concession-aires. This was the company's complaint against the operation by the earl of Cumberland of his licence to export unfinished cloth, and, more particularly, the reversionary grant of this concession to the recently deceased duke of Richmond and Lenox. In the hands of the duke's successor this licence was to become an outstanding grievance of the company during the next reign. The other matter complained of relates to the conflict of interests between the company and the concessionaires who farmed the royal customs, whose exactions, it was deemed, had grown to such a height 'that the ffees which they vniustly exact doe in manie cases farr exceede all the dutyes paid to

[35] B.L., Harleian MSS., 159, fos. 38–42(b), 46(b), 87(b), 117(b)–118, 119–119(b), 123; Add. MSS., 18,597, fos. 92, 97–8, 112, 120, 150, 156(b)–158, 170(b); Add. MSS. 26,639, fos. 15–19, 30–1, 35(b)–37(b), 43; *H. of C. J.*, I, 672, 681, 689, 695, 698–9, 702, 706, 710, 711, 717, 754, 758, 759, 771, 773–4, 780–1, 783–4, 787, 793, 795.

your Majestie'. Before the end of the decade this significant concessionary split would widen into open conflict.[36]

In 1624 as in 1621 some of the representatives of the outports and the proponents of free trade, who included in their number the Merchant Adventurers' old enemy William Neale, the M.P. for Dartmouth, and the future Attorney-General William Noy, were as critical as ever of the company. But there is, nevertheless, more than a suggestion that some M.P.s were abandoning simplist notions that the economic depression was explicable largely in terms of restricted export outlets. Echoing the Merchant Adventurers' statement of 8 April that the members of the company were perfectly capable of disposing of all the cloth produced, and that it was therefore futile to open the trade to more merchants who, 'by their Ignorance and vnskillnes would but give occasion to the makers of cloth to falsephye', one speaker concluded on 12 May that 'there needes noe enlargement of trade, for it is to [sic] greate alreadie'. An inevitable product of further expansion would be, in his view, a further flood of imports, whose proliferation, along with the constriction of the German market due to the ravages of war, he saw as a major contributory cause of the current difficulties. It is true that the parliamentary committee of trade dismissed the Merchant Adventurers' arguments as 'very light', and that the company had to make substantial concessions both as to membership and as to allowing non-members to trade in coloured cloths, kerseys and other fabrics far beyond what they thought proper and desirable. But even in the last matter they found some parliamentary support in surprising quarters, perhaps most surprising of all, that champion of the cause of free trade Sir Dudley Digges. To Digges, the proposal to allow free trade in coloured cloths to the Merchant Adventurers' privileges was questionable in the extreme, not least because those taking advantage of this concession would make no contribution towards the charges of the company. Sir John Savile, who in the course of debate had been highly critical of the inactivity of the M.P.s for the City of London, 'who in all

[36] B.L., Harleian MSS., 159, fos. 41–2, 111(b)–112; ibid. 6383, fos. 139–139(b); Add. MSS. 26,639, fos. 18(b)–19; *H. of C. J.* 1, 780–1.

this debate of trade . . . satt by and sayd not one word', also defended the Merchant Adventurers in this matter, arguing that 'if we take away the dyed and coloured cloths from them, they will give us the white and not medle with them'. It may be that it was considerations such as these which prevented the onslaught on the Merchant Adventurers from going further than it did, substantial though the concessions wrung from the company undoubtedly were. Indeed Digges's unaccustomed tenderness to the Merchant Adventurers in the matter of the coloured cloths may well reflect his consciousness of the magnitude of the concessions already made, though he certainly did not share Savile's fears about the danger of going further. Nicholas's notebook reports him as being of the opinion that 'the merchant adventurers are by what we have alreddy done dissolved alreddy in a manner and he would have trade opened . . . for all men to transport whyte and other clothes'.[37] Consistency was not Digges's strong suit!

It will be remembered that among the critics of the Merchant Adventurers during the free-trade agitation in parliament in 1604 had been interloping merchants not only from the outports but also from the capital itself,[38] for it would be a mistake to construe the issue of the organization of commerce simply as a dispute between London and the outports. None the less, there was a tendency for the latter, and more especially their representatives in parliament, to treat it as if it were, and to turn a deaf ear to the complaints of the London interloping interest. Many years ago Friis drew attention to the insensitivity of the parliamentary free traders in 1621 to the complaints of the metropolitan, as distinct from the provincial, interlopers, and their total lack of concern with cases where no provincial interest was involved. The identity of the London interlopers who received such miserably short shrift, the size of their enterprises and the extent to which they conformed to John Wheeler's classic picture of the interloping interest as pedlars, retailers and craftsmen not bred to commerce, and how far their ranks contained more substantial merchants, is something of a mystery

[37] P.R.O., S.P. James I, clxvi/211; B.L., Harleian MSS., 159, fos. 115(b), 117(b)-118; Add. MSS. 26,639, fos. 30-1, 36-37(b); *H. of C. J.*, i, 698-9, 783-4.
[38] See above, p. 86.

which, in the absence of any surviving records of the Merchant Adventurers' Company, will probably never be unravelled. But they were again among the most prominent critics of the company in 1624 complaining to parliament of 'restraint of trade' and 'vexation by suites'.[39]

The Eastland and Levant companies fared better than the Merchant Adventurers. Although there were complaints, especially from west-country interests, against the restraints imposed by the former body in the importation of naval stores, and although the parliamentary committee of trade called in the company's patent and other records for scrutiny, both the committee and the Commons in general seem to have been more impressed by the considerable numbers of finished cloths exported by members of the company and the amount of domestic employment which was created both by this and by the working up of imported naval stores. For these and other reasons the committee's verdict on the company was that it 'conceived it not, for the present, a Monopoly'.[40] As to the Levant Company, its traditional hostility to the impositions on currants may well have been a factor which helps to account for the fact that the House of Commons seemed to have looked with mild favour on its activities. At least there are no recorded complaints against its restrictive practices, and while the parliamentary committee of trade pronounced that nothing could be done about the company's complaint against an increased subsidy on imports of raw silk since this, being a subsidy, was 'the King's true Right', impositions were quite another matter. The committee therefore recommended that the king be petitioned to remove the offending levy and the matter was included among the nine grievances on trade complained of by the House.[41]

The criticism of the East India Company which produced a motion in the House of Commons for the arrest of its ships

---

[39] Northamptonshire Record Office, Finch-Hatton MSS., 50, fo. 48; Friis, *Cockayne's Project*, pp. 404, 410. For Wheeler, see above, p. 14.

[40] B.L., Harleian MSS., 6383, fo. 95; Add. MSS., 18,597, fos. 66(b), 195; *H. of C. J.*, I, 672, 681, 710, 712, 717, 793, 796; Hinton, *Eastland Trade*, pp. 64–5.

[41] B.L., Add. MSS., 18,597, fos. 191(b)–192; Add. MSS., 26,639, fo. 43; *H. of C. J.*, I, 710, 712, 794, 796.

which were then preparing for their annual voyage to the east is, to some extent at least, explicable in terms of rather special circumstances. These relate to the personal rivalry between Sir Edwin Sandys, the leading figure in the opposition to the crown since James's first parliament, and the champion of free trade and the cause of the outports, on the one hand, and that pillar of commercial orthodoxy and respectability Sir Thomas Smythe on the other. Since 1618 the struggle between these two formidable figures had raged within three companies, the East India Company, the Virginia Company and the Somers Islands Company. The struggle was not without political overtones, since Sandys's political career had earned him the hostility of the king. Sandys's party had won effective control of the Virginia Company in 1619, and a year later had circumvented an attempt by James I to prevent Sandys's re-election as treasurer – 'Choose the Devil, if you will, but not Sir Edwin Sandys' – by substituting for him one of his supporters, the earl of Southampton. In 1621 the Sandys faction had achieved a further notable success when they ousted Smythe and his supporters from the key offices in the Somers Islands Company. In contrast to his free-trade activities in this and other parliaments, Sandys had then sought in the parliament of 1621 to obtain a ban on the importation of all tobacco except from Virginia and the Somers Islands, and, moreover, to get the patent for the sole importation of tobacco vested in the hands of his supporters in both companies – strange conduct for a supporter of free trade. Even before the parliament of 1624 met, however, the conduct of the affairs of both companies by the Sandys faction had given rise to considerable misgivings, especially among those wealthier London mercantile interests who were members of both companies, and this had facilitated the launching of a powerful counterattack by Smythe and the earl of Warwick, Sandys's former ally but now his implacable foe. The result was the institution of a commission of inquiry in 1623, the placing of Sandys under house arrest, the election of Smythe as governor of the Somers Islands Company in December 1624, and the dissolution of the Virginia Company in the following year. These events form the background to the savage attack on the management of the East India Company, of

E

which Smythe was also governor, which was mounted in the parliament of 1624 by Sandys's supporters.[42]

With regard to domestic concessions, as in the previous parliament there were complaints against the extortions of the customs farmers which emanated both from the merchants of the western outports and the Merchant Adventurers. The parliamentary committee of trade pronounced it to be 'strange, and of ill Consequence, that the Farmers should alter the Book of Rates at their own Pleasure, and so fine the Kings Subjects to their own Profit'. Such practices were declared to be among the grievances which were to be submitted to the king for remedy.[43] But the most significant achievement of the parliament of 1624 in its dealings with the concessionary interest was undoubtedly the celebrated Statute of Monopolies.[44] There is every reason to believe that decisive parliamentary action against monopolies was welcomed both by the municipal government and the major livery companies. In the case of those monopolistic schemes which had developed out of the formation of incorporations of handicraft masters, as in the case of the Pinmakers, the attitude of both the municipality and the major companies requires no further emphasis,[45] though it is true that such corporate bodies were exempt from the provisions of the Statute of Monopolies. But aldermanic and company disapproval extended beyond such bodies as these. For instance, among the most powerful opponents of the notorious gold- and silver-thread monopoly associated with the names of Sir Giles Mompesson and Sir Edward Villiers was the Goldsmiths' Company, staunchly backed by the lord mayor and

---

[42] B.L., Harleian MSS., 159, fos. 71, 115; Add. MSS., 18,597, fo. 56; *H. of C. J.*, I, 676, 695, 710, 712, 780, 785, 795, 796; *C.D. 1621*, II, 139, 341, 371–2, 389, III, 7–12, 50–1, 147–8, 232–4, V, 73–4, 136, 524–5, VI, 168; *Cal. S.P. Colonial 1574–1660*, pp. 37, 44, 45–8, 50, 52–6, 59, 60–3, 65–8, 72–3; H.M.C., *Eighth Report*, app. II, pp. 4–8, 31–48; Lefroy (ed.), *Bermudas*, I, 289–91, 324–6, 336–7; S. M. Kingsbury (ed.), *The Records of the Virginia Company of London*, 4 vols. (Washington, D.C., 1906–35), I–II, *passim*; Scott, *Joint-Stock Companies*, I, 183–4, II, 106–7, 266–89; Craven, *Dissolution of the Virginia Company*, *passim*; Chaudhuri, *East India Company*, p. 131.

[43] B.L., Harleian MSS., 159, fos. 45(b)–46; ibid. 6383, fos. 139–139(b); *H. of C. J.*, I, 711, 712, 791, 794–5.

[44] 21 and 22 Jac. I, c. 3.

[45] See above, pp. 71–82.

aldermen. Mompesson's numerous monopolistic activities were, of course, effectively brought to an end by the 1621 parliament, but Villiers was irrepressible and, it would seem, too powerfully connected to be deterred by this. He is found at the back of another incorporation of gold- and silver-wire-drawers which was founded only two years later and which was in its turn to come to grief in the parliament of 1624. And even though this company was dissolved, Villiers, who farmed the duties on imported gold and silver thread and (more important) more than half of the duties payable to the crown by the short-lived wire-drawing company, had to be compensated for his loss by an annuity of £1,000. It was too much to expect the interests of such a powerfully connected courtier to share the fate of those of his unfortunate manufacturing associates.[46]

Insofar as any companies, other than incorporations of craftsmen, were in favour of existing patents, these were not major companies. For instance, the Plumbers' Company supported the income-raising project of Captain Henry Bell, a soldier who had done good service abroad, and had returned to England in 1618 with golden reports from the duke of Venice, several German princes, the king's own daughter, and, most useful of all, the marquis of Buckingham. James I had promised to Bell the grant of any reasonable suit, and after spending much time and money in search of one, he eventually hit on the idea of a patent to survey all English lead, to stamp all properly made lead and to prevent the sale or exportation of unstamped lead under penalty, half of which was to go to the king and half to the patentee, who would also impose a fixed charge on lead-producers for his services. But although the project found favour with the Plumbers' Company, it was not approved by the lord mayor and aldermen, to whom the privy council

[46] B.L., Harleian MSS., 159, fos. 102(b)–103, 113(b); C.L.R.O., Rep. xxxii, fos. 131(b), 259(b); *Cal. S.P.D. 1619–23*, pp. 444–5; *Cal. S.P.D. 1623–5*, p. 300; *A.P.C. 1619–21*, p. 252; *A.P.C. 1621–3*, pp. 284–5, 289, 453, 480–1, 495; *A.P.C. 1623–5*, pp. 91–2, 256; *H. of C. J.*, I, 726–7, 753; *C.D. 1621*, IV, 288–9, V, 274–7, VII, 364–72; *Remembrancia Index*, pp. 218–19, 220, 223–4; H. Stewart, *History of the Worshipful Company of Gold and Silver Wire-Drawers* . . . (1891), pp. 24–43; M. A. Abrams, 'The English Gold and Silver Thread Monopolies', *J. Ec. B. H.*, III (1931), 382–406. The Goldsmiths' Company was only one, though the most prominent, company opposing these schemes.

referred it for an opinion.[47] Another case of a patent which met
with the approval of an established gild was the monopoly of
using coal to manufacture glass which is especially associated
with the name of Sir Robert Mansell, a client of the Howards
and treasurer of the navy. This was in fact a virtual monopoly
of all glass production, since the use of wood fuel in the manufacture was forbidden by proclamation. In its early years the
project seems to have been welcomed by the London Glaziers
who went so far as to condemn the bill which was brought
against Mansell as a monopolist in the 1621 parliament.[48] But
on the whole City-company approval of patents of monopoly
seems to have been the exception rather than the rule. Probably
the most significant thing about the Statute of Monopolies of
1624 relates to its implications for the great chartered companies in foreign trade. In 1621 the Commons had shown
themselves to be hardly less hostile to the great chartered
companies than they had been to individual holders of patents
of monopoly. It is therefore not without significance that the
only exemptions from the operation of this statute, apart from
monopolies which were designed to introduce new industries or
to foster technical innovation, were those made in favour of
corporate bodies. It is a well-known fact that this provided an
important loophole in the field of domestic monopolies, and
accounts for the rash of corporate monopolies which were such
a marked feature of the next reign. But there can be no doubt
also that it was welcomed by the privileged chartered companies for overseas trade, whose members had every reason to
view anti-monopoly legislation as the thin end of a wedge
which, when rammed tightly home, might prove to be their
own ruin. This is emphatically not to argue that the proviso
exempting corporate bodies from the operation of the statute
was designed specifically and exclusively with the overseas

---

[47] *Cal. S.P.D. 1619–23*, pp. 68, 78, 102, 178–9; *Remembrancia Index*, pp. 220–3. The
patent having been disallowed, Bell is last heard of in September 1620, when he
petitioned from prison, to which he had been consigned for debt, to be allowed
the nomination of two Irish barons.

[48] *Cal. S.P.D. 1619–23*, pp. 243, 247; *A.P.C. 1616–17*, pp. 232–3; Ashdown,
Glaziers, pp. 29–31, 35–6. The Glaziers seem to have changed their tune during
the 1630s. In 1638 they complained to the privy council about the glass produced under Mansell's patent (*Cal. S.P.D. 1637–8*, pp. 153–4).

trading companies in mind. Such a saving clause was obviously necessary if municipal corporations, gilds and livery companies were not to be in danger of losing their privileges under the terms of the statute.[49] On the other hand, however, it would be equally misleading to see the exception of the overseas trading companies from the operations of the statute simply as an accidental by-product of a saving clause which was designed to benefit other corporate organizations. It would, after all, have been a perfectly simple matter to except the companies from the exemptions which the statute conferred upon other corporate bodies. The fact that no such exception was made is on any count highly significant and it is difficult to resist the conclusion that it betokened a more lively and realistic appreciation by a significant number of M.P.s of the importance of the companies in the economic life of the realm.

It is, however, easier to state such conclusions than to explain how and why they came about. It may well have been that the participation of some M.P.s not only in parliamentary but in royal committees on trade – thirteen of the M.P.s elected to parliament in 1624 had been members of the standing commission on trade set up by the government in 1622 – was an important medium giving them – and through them many of their fellow M.P.s – a better appreciation of the realities of economic life, and therefore of the rôle which company organization, shorn of its more objectionable restrictive practices, had to play in that life.[50] It is true that prominent members of the chartered companies were less well represented on the standing commission than they had been on the earlier committee for the decay of trade of November 1621. Two notable omissions were Sir Thomas Lowe and William Towerson, respectively governor and deputy governor of the Merchant Adventurers, while Dudley Digges, on the other hand, was a member of both bodies. But at least the standing commission, which had a much stronger complement of government office-

[49] See J. P. Cooper, 'Economic Regulation and the Cloth Industry in Seventeenth-Century England,' *Roy. Hist. Soc. Trans.*, 5th ser., xx (1970), 82.
[50] On the membership and work of such committees and commissions see ibid. pp. 78–84; Friis, *Cockayne's Project*, esp. pp. 412–13, 416–31; Supple, *Commercial Crisis*, pp. 66–8, 70–1.

holders, including the attorney-general and solicitor-general, contained none of the outport merchants who were among the strongest critics of the Merchant Adventurers. Moreover, Merchant Adventurers apart, there was a fairly substantial, if less generous, representation of the commercial concessionary interest, including the East India and Levant Company magnates Sir Paul Pindar, Henry Garway and Anthony Abdy and the economic pamphleteer and East India merchant Thomas Mun, whose participation helps to account for the commission's emphatic repudiation of the charges against the East India Company in connection with its export of specie. Indeed, while the commission was sharply critical of the Merchant Adventurers for their restrictive practices as to membership and the prevalence of price rings among their members, it was also at great pains to stress the value of government and order in overseas commerce, and the continued existence of the companies was never in doubt. Certainly they had to make some very substantial concessions. But unwelcome though these concessions were to most and perhaps all of their members, there is no denying the fact that they made possible the abandonment of that indiscriminate condemnation of *all* business concessionary interests which had been so prominent a feature of the economic debates in the parliament of 1621. Seen in the perspective of the developments of the next reign, it is arguable that the Statute of Monopolies marks the beginnings, however faint, of a more realistic differentiation on the part of members of the House of Commons between different sectors of the London concessionary interest. Aided by the prodigality with which Charles I was to dissipate some of his main sources of support in the business world, this was to be an important factor in ranging the vast majority of this interest against him.

4

Big business and politics under Charles I

I

Just as the Statute of Monopolies may be said to mark an important stage in the differentiation between the type of individual monopolist who had hitherto loomed so large upon the domestic concessionary scene and the privileged corporate bodies in overseas trade, so did the events of the early parliaments of the reign of Charles I succeed in bringing to the boil the hardly latent antagonism which prevailed between privileged export–import groups and the syndicates of business concessionaires who farmed the royal customs. It was largely the almost indiscriminate hostility of the Commons to every sort of concessionaire before 1624 which had helped to create the illusion that there was some common ground between the chartered companies and domestic concessionaires like the monopolists and customs farmers, if only on the grounds that they all had incurred the hostility of the Commons, and had indeed on occasions been lumped together as part of a metropolitan plot to undermine the outports. In the early parliaments of Charles I's reign this illusory identity of mutually incompatible interests disappeared for ever. By the opening of the period of non-parliamentary rule in 1629 not only had the traditional hostility of the Commons to the chartered companies burnt itself out, but the course of the events of the first four years of the reign had produced an hitherto unprecedented identity of interest between the opposition in the Commons and the chartered companies. This process was aided by the fact that, during these years, many of these companies had increasing cause to distrust the value of their traditional alliance with the crown. But, unlike the situation which had prevailed at the time of Cockayne's project, the disillusionment of the companies with the crown was no longer accompanied by the profound distrust of the companies on the part of the House of Commons.

On 4 July 1625, the solicitor-general exhibited in the House of Commons a royal answer to the grievances complained of by the last parliament of the previous reign, prominent among which had been complaints against the chartered companies, and especially the Merchant Adventurers. The solicitor stressed the benefits arising from the improvement in the cloth export trade since the previous year and the substantial concessions made by the Merchant Adventurers in the matter of participation in the trade in new draperies and coloureds and the abatement of the company's impositions. Similar concessions had been made by the Eastland Company in respect of the import trade in timber and naval stores. As to the Levant Company, the king's refusal to yield to its demands in the matter of the impositions on currants would, if anything, have had the effect of ranging that body more closely alongside the parliamentary critics of the impositions. It would have been surprising if the solicitor's pronouncement had produced the unanimous assent of the parliamentary critics of royal and company policies and, in fact, 'divers exceptions were made at manie of these answears & little satisfaction vpon all'. However, the parliamentary diarist goes on to say that 'the occasion & complaint being of former time, this was accepted for the present'.[1]

In the event it was accepted well beyond the present, at least as far as the chartered companies were concerned. It is, of course, arguable that the Commons had a multitude of other – primarily non-economic – matters pressing upon their attention in the early years of Charles I's reign: the growth of Arminianism, the appalling mismanagement of the war, the way in which the government had allowed English ships to be used against the French Huguenots, the impeachment of Buckingham and the unparliamentary levying of tonnage and poundage. But while it is true that other than economic matters command-

---

[1] A. B. Grosart (ed.), *An Apology for Socrates and Negotium Posterorum by Sir John Eliot*, 2 vols. (1881), I, 80–4. See also B.L., Add. MSS., 26,639, fos. 41(b)–44; Add. MSS. 48,091, fos. 7–11(b); S. R. Gardiner (ed.), *Debates in the House of Commons in 1625*, Camden Soc., n.s., VI (1873), 38–41.

ed the bulk of the attention of the Commons in these years, it does not follow that we can dissociate these issues completely from the commercial interests of the City. To cite but one example, among the articles of Buckingham's impeachment was the money which he had extorted from the East India Company in 1624 as the price which it must pay for royal disregard of Spanish complaints against the capture of Ormuz from the Portuguese. Another of the articles of impeachment was Buckingham's part in the detention of a French ship. This had given rise to retaliatory measures against English merchants in France which had threatened many members of the French Company with ruin.[2]

During these years a study of the proceedings of the House of Commons suggests a growing sensitivity to the needs of the chartered companies and a correspondingly diminished sensitivity to the demands of their opponents. If the Greenland Company still had any illusions about the reliability of royal support for its policies, these had received a sharp jolt in 1626, when the king, using a device which his father had favoured on more than one occasion, had granted a licence under the great seal of Scotland to one Nathaniel Edwards and his partners to pursue whaling operations within the privileges of the company. The licence was revoked only when the company agreed to compensate Edwards. In 1628, however, the balance was somewhat restored when the privy council renewed its prohibition of the importation of whale fins and whale oil except by persons free of the company, and the patent of the Greenland Company was denounced as a monopoly and declared a grievance. The attack on the Greenland Company was associated in the debates in the House of Commons with the general demand of the western outports for 'free fishing' off the American coast,[3] as well as with the grievances of the fishermen of Hull against the

[2] B.L., Egerton MSS., 2544, fos. 18–23(b); Gardiner (ed.), *The Constitutional Documents of the Puritan Revolution 1625–1660* (3rd edn, Oxford, 1962), pp. 11–14. On the French ships, see Gardiner, *History*, VI, 39–48, 65–7, 88–9, 100, 145–8. On the Ormuz incident, see *Cal. S.P. East Indies 1625–9*, pp. 174–5; Chaudhuri, *East India Company*, pp. 31, 64.

[3] *A.P.C. 1628–9*, pp. 384–5; *A.P.C. 1629–30*, pp. 181, 188–9, 311, 356; *H. of C. J.*, I, 919; *C.D. 1628*, III, 122, 343–4, 610–12, 614, 616, 618, 619–20; Scott, *Joint-Stock Companies*, II, 70–1; Ashton, 'Charles I and the City', pp. 151–2.

company. But in general attacks on the chartered companies were not a prominent feature of the proceedings of the House of Commons during these years, even though the voice of criticism was not entirely stilled. For example, the only echo of the once prominent hostility of the Commons to privileged trading companies in the parliament of 1629 is a complaint against the Guinea Company. One is tempted to assume that this complaint was directed against the court-backed association of Sir Nicholas Crispe, one of the court concessionaires *par excellence* of the 1630s, but although Crispe did trade to Guinea in the late 1620s, his company did not receive its charter till 1630. The complaint, however, almost certainly refers to the existing and now almost completely moribund Guinea Company which, having forsaken active trade itself, was using its privileged position to license other traders.[4]

That the attitude of the Commons in these years was a great deal more favourable to the chartered companies than it had been during the previous reign is also apparent from the Commons' reception of the petitions which the companies preferred to it. Moreover, since the House of Commons in June 1628 was collecting evidence to show that failure adequately to guard the seas in wartime had led to the disruption of trade and shipping, the House encouraged complaints from the chartered companies about their losses. The virtual cessation of the operation of the standing commission on trade which the government had set up in 1622 may have been another factor encouraging the companies to look to parliament for assistance. One such appeal came from the Somers Islands Company. It will be recalled that it was in alliance with James I that Smythe, Warwick and their following of opulent City merchants had finally succeeded in ousting Sandys and his party from control of the Somers Islands Company. But however grateful the new ruling clique might be for royal assistance, it soon had reason for dissatisfaction with royal policies, and, specifically, with the royal tobacco monopoly and the consequently ruinous price which tobacco fetched, as well as with the royal imposition

---

[4] *H. of C. J.*, I, 931; *C.D. 1629*, p. 225. The company had also been condemned in the parliament of 1624 (*H. of C. J.*, I, 710, 712, 771, 793–4).

of 9d. per pound on imported tobacco. The volte-face produced by this was startling. In the early 1620s Sandys had not hesitated to use his influence with the Commons as a counterpoise to the royal backing of his rivals. Once the latter were again entrenched in power, they emulated Sandys's tactics and appealed to parliament in 1628. They found the House of Commons sympathetic, and on the failure of a petition from the House to the king in June 1628, a bill was introduced in favour of the company in the following February.[5]

In March 1626 the Commons also considered two petitions from traditionally antagonistic elements whose interests were temporarily united by opposition to royal policies. These were the merchants of the western outports trading to France and the Londoners in the French Company, two groups whose battles had been a conspicuous feature of the debates on commercial organization during the first two decades of the century. Both groups were equally alarmed at the course of events which had been set in train by the seizure of French ships on the grounds that they were carrying contraband of war, and more particularly by the retaliatory action taken by French authorities against the property of English merchants in France, which was to culminate in November with the seizure of the cargoes of the English wine fleet at Bordeaux, an action which brought ruin to a number of importers. Since the prevalent popular rumour – however unfounded it may have been in fact – had it that Buckingham, as lord high admiral, had done well out of the proceeds of the French prizes, this incident provides yet another instance of the disastrous effects of the duke's rule on some of the main sources of royal support in the country.[6]

So, in some measure at least, do the rapidly swelling grievances of the East India Company. In July 1625 the disillusioned directors of that company were sharply rebuked by the privy council for defeatism in their apparent determination to abandon the trade altogether. The appeal which was made by the company to the House of Commons in 1628 also reflects

---

[5] B.L., Harleian MSS., 4771, fos. 160–160(b); Add. MSS., 36,825, fos. 329–31; Lefroy (ed.), *Bermudas*, I, 439–40, 480; Scott, *Joint-Stock Companies*, II, 291–2.
[6] *H. of C. J.*, I, 837.

the bitter disillusionment of its members, and not least its directors, who entreated the House

that . . . if vpon the due examination of the same [petition], the said trade be found vnprofitable to the Common-wealth, it may be SVPPRESSED. And if otherwise, that it may be SVPPORTED AND COUNTENANCED BY SOME PUBLIQUE DECLARATION for the satisfaction of all his Maiesties Subiects and better encouragement of the present Adventurers.

It would obviously be wrong to insist that at this juncture an appeal to parliament is by itself firm evidence that the East India Company was moving out of the royal protective orbit Indeed the governor of the company had taken the precaution of seeking the advice of Secretary Coke on the matter, though Coke's suggestion that they should wait until Michaelmas before submitting the petition was not adopted and it was presented to the Commons and referred by them to the committee of trade on 7 May. Probably more significant than Coke's opinion was that of the experienced parliamentarian Sir Dudley Digges, who had been approached by the deputy governor and had given his blessing to the petition, with the heartening observation that the gentry of the kingdom were now far more favourably disposed towards the company than had been the case only two years previously.[7]

There are a number of other indications that the tide may at last have been turning in the relations of the East India Company with crown and parliament. We have already seen how the company's bitterness at Buckingham's greed over the Ormuz incident in 1624 was reflected in the articles of impeachment which were drawn up against the duke. In the two years which followed the failure of the impeachment, the company accumulated numerous additional grievances, if not specifically against the duke, at least with the government in which he was the dominant force. Notable among these were the failure of the government to secure reparation for the Amboyna massacre and its shilly-shallying about securing satisfaction by taking

---

[7] *A.P.C. 1625–6*, pp. 122, 125–6; *Cal. S.P. East Indies 1625–9*, pp. 489, 490, 491, 492–3, 496; *H. of C. J.*, I, 893; *C.D. 1628*, III, 301, 308, 309–10, 319–31; *The Petition and Remonstrance of the Governor and Company . . . Trading to the East Indies Exhibited to the Honourable House of Commons . . . Anno 1628* (1628).

reprisals against Dutch ships in English waters.[8] Despite the buffeting which the East India Company had received in the Commons in 1624, the price of its alignment with the crown was already proving too high. In considering some of the company's domestic grievances, we at once come up against the turbulent figure of Thomas Smethwicke. Smethwicke first bursts into prominence in 1628, in which year he was responsible for delivering a violent attack on the policies of the directors of the company at a meeting of its general court, as well as seeking to set stringent limitations to their power to allocate stock. The incident is of particular interest, since it does not fit in very comfortably with the view that the directorate of the East India Company and the crown and court were natural allies.[9] On the contrary, Smethwicke's attacks upon the directors in 1628 seem to have been made with the full support of Charles I and were intimately associated with a proposal that the king should be admitted as an adventurer and credited with £10,000 worth of stock, a move which would, so Smethwicke and his associates argued, ensure the company of royal protection in the future. The company's response to this outrageous proposal was much the same as that with which it had greeted a similar suggestion in the opening year of the reign, when it had argued that if the king could protect the company in his capacity as adventurer, he 'may be pleased to do as much without'.[10]

The tussles between the East India directorate and its critics in the company's general court do not lend themselves so easily as is sometimes supposed to the notion of democratically inspired attacks on an entrenched and hidebound oligarchy which was closely allied by firm ties of economic interest with

[8] *Cal. S.P.D. 1627–8*, pp. 351–2, 355, 360, 368, 371, 374, 377, 389; *Cal. S.P.D. 1628–9*, pp. 136, 252; *A.P.C. 1628–9*, pp. 33–4, 95–6; *Cal. S.P. East Indies 1625–9*, pp. 77–8, 103–6, 109–11, 117, 413–14, 422, 424–5, 425–6, 462–4, 472, 478, 491, 492, 508, 519–20, 526, 527–9, 533, 539, 540–3; Chaudhuri, *East India Company*, pp. 65–6, 69; Ashton, 'Charles I and the City', pp. 154–5.
[9] See Pearl, p. 92 & n. For a more extreme statement of this view, see Brenner, *P. & P.*, no. 58 (1973), 73–6.
[10] *A.P.C. 1628–9*, pp. 308, 322; *Cal. S.P. East Indies 1625–9*, pp. 110, 499–503, 504, 505, 520, 522–4, 525, 528–9, 534–5, 538, 558–9, 591, 610, 611, 612–13, 614–17, 622–4, 631, 649, 651; Ashton, 'Charles I and the City', p. 157. Smethwicke went too far and was eventually censured by the privy council.

the crown and court. As William Foster long ago and Chaudhuri more recently have pointed out, the chief reason for these disputes is to be found in a significant divergence of interest between the directors, on the one hand, whose interest in the affairs of the company was deep and permanent, and on the other, a number of dissatisfied members of the general court, whose interest was more marginal, and who therefore consistently advocated policies which would bring speedy and spectacular returns but might, at the same time, be adopted only at the expense of the long-term interests of the company. Now there can be no question that among those marginal investors who desired quick and spectacular returns on their share capital the courtier-investor occupied a prominent position. In these circumstances it is hardly surprising that Smethwicke's criticisms of the directors were popular at court and backed by Charles I.[11] Far from driving the company still more firmly into the arms of the crown, they were more likely to have precisely the opposite effect. Nor does one need to seek for economic explanations of the company's refusal to lend £10,000 to Charles I in 1628. Even a loan for a few weeks was impossible, protested the directors, 'for they were now on a new subscription for prosecution of the trade, and, if this request should be known, it would utterly overthrow the work intended'. They might with reason have added that since current investment prospects had been seriously affected by the antics of Smethwicke, it was unreasonable for Charles to expect the company to provide money for him when his own irresponsible encouragement of this agitator was largely responsible for the current difficulties of the company. Smethwicke remained a thorn in the company's flesh throughout the next decade, when he continued to persevere with his attempts to associate the king and members of the privy council with a variety of complaints about the mismanagement of the directors. But he seems to have lost credibility long before 25 October 1639, on which date he was forcibly ejected from a court of committees for using 'opprobrious words' against the directors, though the

---

[11] W. Foster, introduction to *C.M.E.I.C. 1635–9*, pp. vii–x; Chaudhuri, *East India Company*, pp. 32–3, 58–9.

previous decade is crammed with examples of similar and
hardly less offensive attacks on them.[12]

II

These circumstances offer an adequate explanation of the
appeal which went out from a desperate East India Company
to the House of Commons in 1628 and 1629. We may finally
cite the petitions which were submitted to the Commons by
members of the Levant Company between March 1626 and
January 1629, since these lead us straight into that course of
events in the parliamentary history of these years which is most
significant in the context of the subject of this chapter.[13] From
the beginning of the reign of James I the company had been a
bitter opponent of the impositions, and in the early years of
Charles I, when the issue of the non-parliamentary levying of
tonnage and poundage was added to that of impositions, the
whole question of the unparliamentary exaction of customs
duties became a rallying cry which linked for the first time the
interests of many of the chartered companies – and notably the
Levant Company and the Merchant Adventurers – with those
of the leaders of the parliamentary opposition.

The king was infuriated at the refusal of members of the
Levant Company to pay duty, more especially when this
refusal was extended from impositions to customs duties in
general as a consequence of the failure of parliament to pass a
tonnage and poundage bill. He was prodded on for a time by
the earl of Arundel, the holder of the farm of the duties on currants, and once more the gap between export–import merchants
and business syndicates of customs farmers was significantly
widened. The tactics of Sir John Eliot and his associates in the
House were to widen it still further. The Venetian ambassador
in London saw the issue clearly, as is shown by his statement

---

[12] *Cal. S.P. East Indies 1625–9*, p. 521; *Cal. S.P. East Indies 1630–4*, pp. 235–6,
266–7, 286–7, 316, 335, 381–2, 383, 394–5, 398, 400–1, 594–6, 601, 608–10,
612–13, 632; *C.M.E.I.C. 1635–9*, pp. 6, 13, 17, 45, 54–5, 70, 118–19, 136–7,
139–40, 142, 153–4, 157–8, 165, 171, 201, 216–17, 218, 229, 258, 259, 300, 331,
335, 346–7, 352–3, 355, 356.
[13] B.L., Harleian MSS., 4771, fos. 161–161(b); Add. MSS., 36,825, fos. 331–
332(b); *H. of C. J.*, I, 839, 840, 923; *C.D. 1629*, p. 115.

that 'the King cannot levy duties which are not granted by the people, on which one of the chief discussions of the present parliament turns'. With even greater perspicacity he went on to argue that 'even if parliament grant to the King the customs, they cannot bear the burdens to which they have hitherto been subjected'.[14] Here lies the kernel of the situation. Constitutional issues left aside, taxes were never popular with the business community. But the fact that the House of Commons in 1628–9 devoted a great deal of its time and attention to the constitutional issue of the unparliamentary exaction of tonnage and poundage helped to harmonize its attitude with that of the business community of the City to a degree hitherto unknown. In these circumstances, the issue of the unconstitutionality of royal customs duties awoke an unprecedented echo in the hearts of business men. And the Commons in turn responded generously to the pleas of the latter. This is reflected in the deep concern of the House in May 1628 at the delays of royal officials both in releasing members of the Levant Company who had been imprisoned for refusing to pay what they regarded as illegal duties and in implementing the assurance given to the House on 19 May by Sir Humphrey May, chancellor of the Duchy of Lancaster, that their confiscated currants – which, it was emphasized, were 'bona peritura' – should be restored to them on their giving bonds that they would pay 'whatsoever shall be found due'. Unlike the debates on impositions in the parliaments of James I, commercial concessionaires were no longer confronted by a House of Commons which, though it might be in broad agreement with them on the issue of taxation, was violently hostile to them on everything else. Similarly, the events of 1629, when chartered companies like the Levant Company and the Merchant Adventurers again resisted the payment of unconstitutional duties and, after the dissolution of parliament, cited the Protestation of the Commons as the text for their behaviour, are eloquent testimony of a new alignment of forces.[15]

---

14 *Cal. S.P.D. 1627–8*, p. 594; *Cal. S.P.D. 1628–9*, pp. 10–11; *Cal. S.P. Ven. 1628–9*, pp. 552–3.
15 This account of the resistance to the payment of customs duties is based on P.R.O., S.P. Charles I, cxl/24; *Cal. S.P.D. 1628–9*, pp. 507, 524; *A.P.C. 1628–9*,

No doubt the motives of the bulk of the resisters were very
mixed. In September 1628 Richard Chambers, one of an early
group of recalcitrant merchants who were summoned before
the privy council for refusal to pay customs duties, had declared
that 'merchants are in no part of the world so screwed and wrung
as in England. In Turkey they have more encouragement.' In
these words he was giving expression to the nature of general
mercantile discontent with the level of taxation, a discontent
which parliamentary agitation on the constitutional issue
brought to boiling point in the following year. Few members of
the chartered companies were prepared to go as far as Chambers,
who suffered long imprisonment and a heavy fine as a result of
his devotion to the cause of constitutional propriety.[16] Some
indeed were prepared to take selfish advantage of the situation,
for example, those Merchant Adventurers who exploited the
constitutional scruples of their brethren by publicly urging
them to desist from active trade while themselves taking
advantage of this by purchasing cloth at absurdly cheap
prices.[17] The attitude of the majority lay somewhere between
this instance of unscrupulous self-seeking and the idealism of a
Chambers who was prepared to risk ruin for his beliefs. The
evidence suggests, however, that it was nearer to the latter
than to the former case, and it was the growing identification
of the mercantile interest with that of Eliot and his associates in
the House of Commons and the fear of reprisals if they voluntarily paid duties again which combined to produce this result.
The general strike against the payment of customs duties, which
persisted long after the dissolution of parliament, makes it
reasonable to suggest that during these years for the first time
constitutional notions were becoming a significant force in the
growth of big-business opposition to the crown. On 6 April the
Venetian ambassador wrote that the receipts of customs

---

pp. 123, 154–5, 292–3, 294, 295, 356–7; *Cal. S.P. Ven. 1628–9*, pp. 552–3; *Cal.
S.P. Ven. 1629–32*, pp. 7, 8, 19, 29, 44–5, 56, 75, 178, 290; *C.D. 1628*, II, 329,
330, 331, III, 447, 449–51, 452–3, 456, 457–8, 463, 593, 594, 595, 598–9, 600–1;
Gardiner, *History*, VII, 1–7, 31–7, 57–9, 82–7.
[16] On Chambers's resistance and punishment, see Gardiner, *History*, VII, 4–5, 37,
84–7, 114–15, 168.
[17] P.R.O., S.P. Charles I, CXL/24.

revenue, which were normally about £500 a day, had not been more than £30 over the past three weeks.[18] No doubt he exaggerated, but the evidence does suggest that the events in parliament in 1629 both captured the imagination and steeled the determination of the business community of London. And the new alignment between the Commons and the London export–import interests had other consequences which exacerbated the relations of the latter with the crown still further. In a mixture of despair and fury at the recalcitrance of the merchants, Charles was in March seriously considering withdrawing the charter of the Merchant Adventurers and substituting a company more amenable to the court.[19] But the situation had altered out of all recognition since the Merchant Adventurers had found themselves in an isolated position at the time of Cockayne's project. Then their pleas had been rejected by both crown and parliament. Now the cause of their breach with the crown was their fidelity to the constitutional position taken up by the recently dissolved parliament.

Resistance, of course, could not last for ever. The business community did not consist entirely of Chamberses. 'I have ever said', wrote Bishop Williams early in May, 'that the merchants would be weary of this new habit of statesmen they had put on, and turn merchants again by that time they heard from their factors that their storehouses began to grow empty. God send those men more wit who, living in a monarchy, rely upon the democracy.'[20] At the time of the dissolution of the parliament of 1629, no one could have realized that it would be eleven years before parliament was to be summoned again. Resistance in these circumstances was bound to break down sooner or later and not even the most extreme members of the Short and Long parliaments would be inclined to take literally that clause of the Protestation of 1629 which laid down that 'if any merchant . . . shall voluntarily . . . pay the said subsidies of Tonnage and Poundage, not being granted by Parliament, he shall . . .

[18] *Cal. S.P. Ven. 1629–30*, p. 8.
[19] Gardiner, *History*, VII, 83.
[20] Cited in ibid. VII, 84. The first decision to abandon resistance on the part of the Merchant Adventurers' Company was made by the narrow margin of two votes (*Cal. S.P.D. 1628–9*, p. 550).

be reputed a betrayer of the liberties of England, and an enemy to the same'.[21]

Their attitude to those who exacted duties was altogether different. In its attack upon the farmers of the customs in 1629 in connection with the collection of unparliamentary customs duties, the House of Commons was setting a precedent which was to be followed by its successor twelve years later.[22] In concentrating their attack on a small but very wealthy and influential section of the London concessionary interests – the monopolists in 1624 and the customs farmers in 1629 – the Commons were now able to draw freely upon the support of that vast mass of privileged export–import merchants who had until 1624 met with almost equal hostility from them. To some extent perhaps this development was a constitutional accident. The need to fall back on attacking the king's servants rather than the king himself was a commonplace of seventeenth-century constitutional practice and a necessary corollary of the doctrine that the king may do no wrong. Hence Eliot's determination to make the farmers the scapegoats for the unparliamentary exaction of tonnage and poundage and the confiscation of the property of merchants who refused to pay up. On 12 February he made it clear that the House should fix responsibility firmly on the customers, even though they claimed that 'they stay those goods for duties to the King and noe other interest: wheras it appeareth they had an interest by the Kings grant: having farmed it'. Eliot found a great deal of support in the House. 'The sole of the Common wealth', stated one member, '[is] Religion: the body is the Entercource betwixt man and man: ther is obstruction in the Liver: which suffers [viz. hinders] the blood from free passage. The Customers have abused the King in his Custome and Revenue, and are the cause of the Stop of trade.' The argument was clearly to rest on the fact that since the king had alienated his interest in the customs revenue to the farmers they were solely responsible for the illegal exactions. But the case, which had a number of obvious flaws, was not easy to prove. When the customers

---

[21] Gardiner (ed.), *Constitutional Documents*, p. 83.
[22] This account is based on *H. of C. J.*, I, *passim*; and *C.D. 1629*, *passim*. See also Gardiner, *History*, VII, 59–65.

were called before the bar of the House, they made a clear
distinction between their rôle as royal officials – many of them
were royal collectors of customs as well as farmers – and as
customs farmers, and insisted that only those farmers who were
also customs officials had taken action to distrain the goods of
merchants refusing to pay duty and, moreover, that they had
done this in obedience to royal command. This comes out most
clearly in the evidence given by Sir John Wolstenholme to the
House on 20 February. Wolstenholme insisted that 'he went
downe to seize the said goods as an officer of the Kings, not as
a farmer, for if he had not bene an officer he would not have
gone noe more then the rest of the farmers, but did this be
especiall comand from the King to assist the rest of the officers
of the Customes, and if he had not bene an officer . . . he would
not have gone with them to seize the said goods noe more then
Sir P. Pindar and the rest of the Farmers did'.[23]

Eliot, Selden and their associates were not convinced. The
farmers were sheltering behind royal authority and acting 'on
pretence of the Kings comand'. The situation could be resolved
only by either leaving the farmers to their fate or by the direct
intervention of the king. On 23 February, Secretary Coke
made the position unequivocally clear.

The ground to punish these men is because we have divided ther
case from the King. I must lett you know that the King hath taken
knoledge of the late debate . . . concerning the farmers of his Customs,
and of the care they [viz. the Commons] had in laboring to sever
ther case from that of his Majestie. But the King finding this concerned him in a high degree of Justice and honor thought it nott fitt
the truth should be unknowne and that what these men did they
did it by his expresse command: or by the Counsell board, he being
by in person or directing; that this can not be divided from his own
act and that there be noe proceeding agaynst them: as highly
concerning his honor.

---

[23] *H. of C. J.*, I, 929, 930, 931, 932; *C.D. 1629*, pp. 60–3, 73–4, 81, 83–93, 140–4,
155–61, 162–6, 195–201, 217–18, 221–4, 225–34. It would be quite impossible
to reconstruct the course of these debates from the official journal alone, and
the clerk of the House of Commons may have refrained from detailed reporting
on account of the highly contentious nature of the debates. The accounts given
by different diarists printed in *C.D. 1629* vary in detail but not in essentials. The
quotations from Eliot's speech and the speech made by an unnamed M.P.
(actually Waller) are both taken from Grosvenor's diary (*C.D. 1629*, pp. 160–1).

The ground was cut from beneath Eliot's feet and although he moved the adjournment of the House still insisting that 'the Customers are the occasion of this, the goodnes of the King wronged', in a later speech he transferred his attack to the king's advisers.

It is the practise of ministers about him who feare some reflection upon themselves . . . these clouds are blowne by such as seke ther owne security not the Kings honor.

With these words Eliot makes the transition from his all-out attack on the customs farmers to that wild onslaught on Lord Treasurer Weston, whom many saw as the tool of the farmers, which was to become such a dominant feature of his argument in the dying stages of this parliament. Charles's message to the House informing it that the customers had acted in accordance with his express command put the opposition in an impossible position, to which Eliot responded with the attack on Weston and other ministers, and Selden with the argument that the farmers had deceived the king into commanding them to collect illegal duties and had thereby compounded their offence. In truth, of course, it was becoming increasingly difficult to attack government policy without extending the attack from the king's servants to the king himself.[24]

III

In the parliament of 1621 it had only been the intervention of James I which had rescued the Merchant Adventurers from the fury of the House of Commons. In that of 1629 it was the intervention of Charles I which saved the customs farmers from a concerted attack by Eliot, Selden and their supporters in parliament backed by the Merchant Adventurers and other privileged chartered companies outside it. The tonnage and poundage disputes helped to produce a new alignment of forces and widened irreparably that split between different parts of

---

The fullest account of Wolstenholme's statement and that cited here is drawn from Nicholas's notes (ibid. pp. 197, 198).

[24] *H. of C. J.*, I, 932; *C.D. 1629*, pp. 93–5, 102–3, 167–71, 234–8, 241–2, 259–61. The quotations from both Coke's and Eliot's speeches are from Grosvenor's diary (*C.D. 1629*, pp. 237, 238).

the London concessionary interest which survived more or less unaltered to the early years of the Long Parliament. For while attacks upon privileged export–import interests were no more a feature of parliamentary debates between 1640 and 1643 than they had been in 1628–9, the Long Parliament was as merciless in its treatment of other concessionary interests – and notably of the monopolists and the customs farmers – as its predecessor would have been in 1629 if Charles I had given it the opportunity.[25]

This suggests that the events of the 1630s did not produce any profound alteration in the new equilibrium which had been achieved by 1629, despite the fact that during this decade some of the companies regained many of the privileges which they had lost as a result of parliamentary pressures upon the government in the early 1620s.[26] For instance, despite Charles I's rritation with them at their disobedience in 1629, the Merchant Adventurers succeeded in getting some support from the crown, whose aid they needed if they were to obtain the desired transfer of their Netherlands mart town to Rotterdam. With royal connivance they also succeeded both in raising their entry fines and in tightening their hold on the export trade in cloth to Germany though they seem to have had a great deal of trouble from the interlopers in the Netherlands trade.[27] But the concordat with the crown was at best only partial, and the company still had a number of grievances. Some of these were of a non-economic nature. Such was the royal attempt to force the unwilling company to accept Edward Misselden, a person who is today best known for his contributions as an economic pamphleteer, as its deputy governor at Delft and Rotterdam. Misselden's candidacy was in turn connected with the Laudian policy of attempting to reduce the company's overseas factories to religious conformity, which was persisted in long after the attempt to secure Misselden's appointment had been abandoned, and occasioned a great deal of resentment and opposi-

[25] See below, pp. 149–56.

[26] Similar arguments about the 1630s can be found in my essay 'Charles I and the City', pp. 149–59.

[27] P.R.O., S.P. Charles I, cclxxiv/51, cclxxvii/124(i); P.C.R., P.C. 2, xliv, fos. 89–90, 224; ibid. l, fos. 170–1; *Cal. S.P.D. 1634–5*, pp. 257, 346; Supple, *Commercial Crisis*, pp. 121–2, 124–5, 241.

tion in the company.[28] Another cause of resentment was the
government's concessions to provincial towns, and notably the
granting by the privy council of permission to the baymakers of
Colchester to export their new draperies to the Merchant
Adventurers' privileges, and the council's refusal to prohibit
the trade in so-called 'Spanish medley cloth' from west-country
ports.[29] In addition, there were bitter complaints at the government's failure to press the company's case against the Dutch on
the matter of 'tare', that is, the compulsorily exacted abatements in the price of allegedly faulty cloth.[30] It might, of
course, be argued that a better way of dealing with this problem
would be via the effective enforcement of domestic English
regulations against the manufacture of faulty cloths, which
would at least have tackled the problem at its source. But this
hardly disposed of the company's objection that its members
would still be at the mercy of the Dutch in the matter of 'tare',
which would continue to be exacted irrespective of any improvement in the quality of the cloth achieved via the agency
of improved methods of internal regulation and control. Moreover, from the Merchant Adventurers' standpoint, the forms
taken by such regulations left a good deal to be desired. While
the company seems initially to have welcomed the government's conferring of wide powers of inspection of cloth manufacture on one Anthony Withers in the early 1630s, it was not
long before it became involved in bitter disputes with Withers
over his remuneration and other matters. Similarly while it may
well have approved of the creation in September 1638 of a
royal commission on the clothing industry which numbered at
least four Merchant Adventurers among its thirty members,
the addition of four new members in the following January was
probably greeted less than enthusiastically. It is true that one

[28] P.R.O., P.C.R., P.C. 2, xlii, fo. 114; ibid. xliii, fos. 185–6, 188, 261–2, 279–81;
ibid. xlviii, fo. 213; ibid. l, fo. 309; *Cal. S.P.D. 1631–3*, pp. 445, 575; *Cal.
S.P.D. 1633–4*, pp. 74–5, 225, 364, 449; *Cal. S.P.D. 1634–5*, p. 87; *Cal. S.P.D.
1635*, pp. 77, 151; *Cal. S.P.D. 1635–6*, pp. 36, 37; *Cal. S.P.D. 1637*, p. 420;
Cal. S.P.D. 1637–8, p. 102; *Cal. S.P.D. 1638–9*, pp. 250–1; *Cal. S.P.D. 1639–40*,
p. 213; *Cal. S.P.D. Addenda 1625–49*, p. 500.
[29] P.R.O., P.C.R., P.C. 2, xlv, fo. 15; ibid. xlviii, fos. 476, 516, 535–6; *Cal. S.P.D.
1635*, pp. 91, 103–4; *Cal. S.P.D. 1637–8*, pp. 164, 176, 185, 218.
[30] *A.P.C. 1630–1*, pp. 62–3, 395–7; Lipson, *Economic History of England*, ii, 235–6;
Supple, *Commercial Crisis*, pp. 115, 121.

of these newcomers, Laurence Halstead, was a member of the company, but Halstead's economic interests lay more in domestic monopolies than in the export of cloth. None of the other three newcomers to the commission, and least of all the objectionable Anthony Withers, could be regarded as particularly sympathetic to the interest of the Merchant Adventurers. The other two were Sir John Brooke and the notorious George Mynne, the Clerk of the Hanaper, who had been suspended from the exercise of his functions for the exaction of excessive fees.[31]

Probably the main reason for the Merchant Adventurers' disquiet in the 1630s was their disputes over one of the most valued of their economic privileges, the licences to export unfinished cloth. By this time, the most important of these licences which the Merchant Adventurers had formerly subleased from the earl of Cumberland had come into the hands of the duchess of Richmond and Lenox from whom it was to descend to her son. The duchess succeeded in obtaining a greatly augmented rent from the company, but in 1636, when they had held the concession for three and a half years, the Merchant Adventurers announced that they had had enough, and the relations between the crown and the company during the closing years of Charles's personal rule were further embittered by these disputes in which the king took the side of the duke against the company. He supported the duke when the latter in 1640 seized a consignment of cloth that was about to be shipped and threatened to license interlopers to trade unless the company acceded to his immoderate terms. At a difficult time the Merchant Adventurers were thus faced with the unpleasant alternatives of either a sharp increase in their operating costs or the royal countenancing of the activities of at least some of those interlopers who were such a thorn in their side over these years. The incident widened the split between the court and the company which had first been opened by Cockayne's

---

[31] P.R.O., S.P. Charles I, cccxcviii/118, ccccviii/15, ccccix/210; *Cal. S.P.D. 1638–9*, p. 240; G. D. Ramsay (ed.), 'The Report of the Royal Commission on the Clothing Industry, 1640', *Eng. Hist. Rev.*, lvii (1942), 485–93; G. E. Aylmer, *The King's Servants: The Civil Service of Charles I 1625–1642* (1961), pp. 117–21.

project, partially healed by the parliamentary onslaught on the company in 1621, and reopened by the events of 1629.[32]

The other most prominent participant in the refusal to pay customs duties in 1629 had been the Levant Company. From the beginning of the reign, the company had also engaged in another dispute with the crown, over its refusal to accept a nominee of Buckingham as ambassador at Constantinople. The dispute was prolonged long after the death of both Buckingham and his client and the company had to accept a succession of court nominees. One of these, the monopolist and concessionaire, Sir Sackville Crow, who was appointed to the embassy in 1633 but was unable to take up his position till 1638, further exacerbated matters by laying claim to the consulage which was levied by the company from alien merchants who shipped their goods in English vessels. The bitter dispute over this matter lasted well into the period of the Civil War and naturally enough merged into the wider political struggle, since Crow was a royalist and the bulk of the company, which had now got rid of its royalist minority among the directors, supported parliament.[33]

But of all the chartered companies it was the East India Company which took the hardest knocks in the 1630s. Not only did the government fail to take decisive action against the Dutch to secure a just settlement of the Amboyna dispute, but subsequent aggressions by the Dutch in the East Indies also went unpunished.[34] Moreover, in the mid 1630s two connected enterprises, each backed by powerful court interests, the leading figure among whom was Endymion Porter, brought the members of the company to despair, not least because they were supported by many of those marginal investors who had in the previous decade been the main critics of the policies of the directorate. The first of these incidents was the privateering

[32] P.R.O., P.C.R., P.C. 2, XLVI, fos. 334–5, 339, L, fos. 520, 540–1, LI, fos. 192–3, 223, LII, fo. 497; Bodleian Library, Bankes MSS., 5/57; *Cal. S.P.D. 1635*, p. 96; *Cal. S.P.D. 1636–7*, p. 106; *Cal. S.P.D. 1639*, pp. 539–40; *Cal. S.P.D. 1639–40*, pp. 234–5, 298, 333–4, 417–18, 599; *Cal. S.P.D. 1640*, pp. 21, 163, 176.

[33] Wood, *Levant Company*, pp. 87–91.

[34] P.R.O., P.C.R., P.C. 2, LI, fos. 165–6; *Cal. S.P.D. 1633–4*, pp. 259–60, 300; *Cal. S.P. East Indies 1630–4*, p. 579; *C.M.E.I.C. 1635–9*, pp. 168, 274, 284, 289, 303, 333, 336–41, 351–2; *C.M.E.I.C. 1640–3*, p. 24.

expedition of Kynaston and Bonnell in the Red Sea, which produced among other things the arrest of the entirely blameless East India Company's factors at Surat as a consequence. The protection which one of the privateers received from the king effectively prevented the company securing redress for the damage which it suffered.[35] Secondly, there was the foundation of the East India Association by Sir William Courteen, who was backed by powerful interests at court and secured some financial support in the City, notably from Sir Paul Pindar, the leader of the customs-farming syndicates of the 1630s. The king himself, who had been unceremoniously refused a free adventure by the East India Company in 1628, was credited with an investment of £10,000 gratis by the new association, whose existence the East India Company naturally regarded as a dangerous threat to its continued prosperity. The fact that by the time of the Civil War the pitiful remnants of Courteen's association had fallen under the control of radical merchants with extensive interests in colonial trade ought not to be allowed to obscure the significance of the original Courteen project as a royally licensed and court-backed association, which stood in much the same relationship to the East India Company in the fourth decade of the century as Cockayne's project had done to the Merchant Adventurers in the second. It was only in December 1639, after the disastrous failure of successive expeditions, that Charles repudiated the survivors of the Courteen adventurers and the way was again open for an uneasy rapprochement with the East India Company.[36] But in the very next year Charles's forced seizure of a consignment of pepper belonging to the company in return for worthless tallies on the customs was hardly an act which was likely to restore

[35] *Cal. S.P.D. 1635*, p. 96; *Cal. S.P.D. 1636–7*, pp. 342, 426, 528–9; *Cal. S.P.D. 1638–9*, p. 46; *C.M.E.I.C. 1635–9*, pp. xiv–xv, xxi–xxii, xxiv, xxvii, 211–13, 215–20, 226, 232, 240–1, 283–4, 289, 299, 337.

[36] B.L., Sloane MSS., 3515, *passim*; P.R.O., P.C.R., P.C. 2, LI, fos. 165–8; *C.M.E.I.C. 1635–9, passim*; *C.M.E.I.C. 1640–3*, pp. 23–7; G. Carew, *A Vindication of the Several Actions at Law Brought against the Heirs of Sir Peter Courten and Peter Boudaen* (Middelburgh, 1675); T. Carew, *Hinc Illae Lacrimae: or An Epitome of the Life and Death of Sir William Courteen and Sir Paul Pindar* (1681); *A Brief Narrative of the Cases of Sir William Courteen and Sir Paul Pindar* (n.d.); Chaudhuri, *East India Company*, pp. 73, 167. My interpretation of this incident differs crucially from that of Brenner, *P. & P.*, no. 58 (1973), p. 71.

confidence after the shocks which had been administered in the middle of the decade.[37]

IV

Finally, the conflict of interest between different types of concessionaire to which the tonnage and poundage dispute had given such scope was also a prominent feature of the 1630s. The marked divergence of interest between different elements of the concessionary interest, such as customs farmers and domestic monopolists on the one hand and privileged members of chartered companies on the other, does not betoken complete harmony among the latter. For example, since 1615 there had been plenty of scope for disputes between the Levant and Merchant Adventurers' companies, and the proclamation of 1630, which did for the Eastland Company what that of 1615 had effectively done for the Levant Company by giving to it the sole right to import eastland commodities as opposed to simply the sole right to trade with the Baltic, was bound to excite the hostility of Merchant Adventurers who had imported eastland goods from the Netherlands.[38] There is also evidence in the 1630s both of continued hostility to the customs farmers as collectors of duties which were not only burdensome but also illegal, and of resentment at the way in which the proliferation of internal monopolies militated against the interests of some of the chartered companies, since even when a grant of a monopoly was not coupled with a prohibition of the importation of the commodity in question, it involved the restriction of demand for it. The way in which the successive monopolies of the Westminster and London soapboiling companies conflicted with interests of the Eastland and Greenland companies as importers

---

[37] P.R.O., Audit Office, A.O.1/1948/1; S.P. Charles I, ccccLXV/64, ccccLXXIII/83; *Cal. S.P.D. 1640–1*, p. 271; *Cal. S.P.D. 1641–3*, pp. 67–8, 266–7, 275, 305, 365; *Cal. S.P. Ven. 1640–2*, p. 74; *C.M.E.I.C. 1640–3*, pp. 80–4, 242–3, 247, 256, 269, 325, 333, 343, 370; Ashton, *The Crown and the Money Market*, pp. 44, 45, 178–80, where the emphasis laid on this transaction differs markedly from that of W. Foster, 'Charles I and the East India Company', *Eng. Hist. Rev.*, XIX (1904), 456–63.

[38] On the Levant Company, see above, pp. 87, 101–2, 108. On the Eastland Company, *A.P.C. 1629–30*, pp. 276–7, 284–5, 393, 415; P.R.O., P.C.R., P.C. 2, XLI, fos. 272–4, XLII, fos. 324–5; Hinton, *Eastland Trade*, pp. 76–7, 175–8, 183–5.

of potash and whale oil is a case in point.[39] And the Westminster Company in particular aroused the antagonism of a large number of other interests: of the Grocers and Salters who sold soap; of the consumers of soap, who had to pay higher prices for an inferior product, or, insofar as the Westminster Company exercised its right to license independent producers, higher prices for the same product; and of the independent soap-boilers who were either totally excluded from production or had to pay heavily to continue to do what they had formerly done as of right. Some of the former were imprisoned for offering spirited resistance to attempts to force them to close down. One of them, a chandler of East Smithfield, 'armed with sword, pistols and a great mastiff dog', threatened to kill anyone attempting to enter his premises to prevent him from boiling soap. The most powerful friend at court of the Westminster Company with its numerous genuinely Catholic as well as crypto-Catholic investors was Lord Treasurer Portland, whose own Catholic sympathies were no very well-guarded secret in both court and country. Its most implacable court opponent was no less a person than Archbishop William Laud who, after Portland's death in 1635, still had to contend with the support which the chancellor of the exchequer, Sir Francis Cottington, continued to give to the monopolists. It was not until Cottington's ambition to succeed Portland had been finally scotched and the interim treasury commission had been succeeded by Laud's protégé, Bishop William Juxon, who took the white staff in 1637, that the hated Westminster soapers were finally ousted. They were, of course, replaced not by a return to free trade in soap, but by a more broadly based corporation of the formerly excluded producers, which, moreover, had to buy out its predecessors for £43,000, as well as to meet an increase in the king's tax per ton of soap produced from £4 to £8. Although the interests of the new company, as a restricted buying agency for raw materials, still conflicted with those of some substantial London importing interests, it did, unlike its

---

[39] The Eastland Company stressed the essentially bilateral nature of the Baltic trade and the consequent likelihood of a fall in English cloth sales if the company was unable to take potash as a return cargo.

predecessor, have firm roots in the City, and its leading figure, Sir Edward Bromfield, was in fact lord mayor in 1636–7. Here, indeed, at last is an aldermanic monopolist; but the political significance of this fact is minimal, since the Long Parliament excepted the new company from its denunciation of monopolies.[40]

The lord mayor and aldermen and the members of the Grocers' Company were also consistent opponents of the successive monopolistic schemes for the manufacture of starch in the early Stuart period. In the 1630s, however, the most numerous complaints came from humbler people, the excluded starch producers, whose arguments were treated with contempt by the monopolists, who dwelt in detail on the mean status and dubious moral character of the complainants, one of whom was described as a man 'altogether illiterate [and] of a meane capacitie'; another 'a seditious person'; and yet another as 'a druncken deboyst [debauched?] dangerous person'; and so on. The new company's friend at court was the earl of Ancram, a Scot who was Gentleman of the Bedchamber to Charles I and a notable virtuoso at the Caroline court; but court culture and the energetic pursuit of court rackets are by no means mutually incompatible and Ancram had invested substantial amounts in the starchmaking project. He also farmed at a rent of £200 to the crown both the four-shillings duty paid by the monopolists on every ton of starch they produced and the duty of ten shillings on every hundredweight of starch imported, on which transactions it was reckoned that he was the clear gainer to the tune of about £600 yearly. Naturally enough, Ancram was greatly disturbed in 1638 when the monopolists came under particular heavy attack from the excluded starchmakers, who

---

[40] P.R.O., P.C.R., P.C. 2, xlviii, fos. 28, 30–1, 140, 151, 299–300, 337–8, 544, 546, xlix, fos. 14, 36; *Cal. S.P.D. 1634–5*, pp. 393–4; *Cal. S.P.D. 1635*, pp. 298, 305, 311–12, 525, 566–7; *Cal. S.P.D. 1635–6*, pp. 45, 200; *Cal. S.P.D. 1636–7*, pp. 67, 157, 235–6, 249, 303; *Cal. S.P.D. 1637*, pp. 53–4, 68–9, 100, 127, 174, 219, 313, 480, 513; *Cal. S.P.D. 1637–8*, pp. 196, 260, 370; *Cal. S.P.D. 1638–9*, p. 374; *Cal. S.P.D. 1639*, pp. 45, 135–6, 215–16, 363–4, 539; *Cal. S.P.D. 1640*, p. 157; H.M.C., *Fifth Report*, pt I (H. of Lords MSS.), p. 88, *H. of L. J.*, vi, 66; *H. of C. J.*, ii, 259–60; *Remembrancia Index*, pp. 224–5; Gardiner, *History*, viii, 71–6, 284; W. H. Price, *The English Patents of Monopoly* (Boston, Mass., 1906), pp. 119–28; Scott, *Joint-Stock Companies*, i, 210–18, ii, 71–2; Hinton, *Eastland Trade*, pp. 45, 81, 185–7. See below, p. 153.

now seem to have been benefiting from the organizing abilities of two men, Robert Smyth and Leonard Stockdale, the former, so it was alleged, a bricklayer, and the latter a pasteboard-maker. An attempt by the company to buy off its chief antagonists by admitting them as members was unsuccessful, and, attracted by a spectacular offer from Smyth, Stockdale and their associates, the king authorized the creation of a new company to replace the old. The new company engaged to keep the price of starch down and to appoint Thomas Meautys, the clerk of the privy council, as their treasurer, which would ensure that priority would be given to the payment of the king's rent of £1,500 in the first year, £2,000 in the second and £3,500 thereafter before any dividends were distributed among members of the new company. Against such terms not even Ancram's influence could prevail, but Smyth and Stockdale had in fact badly overreached themselves. It is significant that among those complaining most bitterly about the new company's practices were artisan starchmakers of the new company who complained in November 1639 that most of its governors were men inexperienced in starchmaking, that they laid excessive and unnecessary charges on their members, and – most damning of all – that there was no possibility of the new company's being able to meet its obligations to the king.[41]

There is one significant difference between the examples of the corporate monopolies of the 1630s which have already been cited and the less familiar case of the London and Westminster Company of Brickmakers and Tilers, which was founded in 1636 and had as its official *raison d'être* the need to enforce government regulations about the price and quality of building materials. Although at least one projector saw in these regulations attractive openings for courtly capital seeking investment, there is no evidence to suggest that the new company was connected with influential court interests, other than of the

[41] P.R.O., S.P. Charles I, ccLxxix/77, 77(i); P.C.R., P.C. 2, xLvii, fos. 288–9, 327, xLviii, fos. 59, 303, 427, 542, xLix, fos. 349, 391–2, L, fos. 157–8, 262, 373, 378–9, 461–3, Li, fos. 50–1, 56, 61, 87–9, 168, 198–200; *Cal. S.P.D. 1628–9*, pp. 593, 596; *Cal. S.P.D. 1633–4*, p. 226; *Cal. S.P.D. 1634–5*, pp. 394–5, 454; *Cal. S.P.D. 1636–7*, pp. 302–3; *Cal. S.P.D. 1637*, p. 240; *Cal. S.P.D. 1637–8*, pp. 105–6, 109, 552; *Cal. S.P.D. 1638–9*, pp. 9, 24, 165, 242–3; *Cal. S.P.D. 1639*, pp. 211, 216; *Cal. S.P.D. 1639–40*, pp. 92, 93–4, 230, 238–9; *A.P.C. 1630–1*, p. 187.

crown itself. However, its malpractices were certainly bound up with those fiscal considerations which loomed so large in royal industrial policy. The crown was to receive sixpence on every thousand bricks and tiles made. But this imposition appears to have been no more an occasion of worry to the members of the new company than the similar tax per unit sale was to the Westminster Soapmakers, since, as one brick-maker boasted, they would be able to pass on three times its incidence to the hapless consumer. In the event, moreover, the aims of the government in terms of quality seem to have been as little regarded as those relating to price, though interlopers seem to have abounded, including persons who, under colour of making bricks for their own use, sold them for profit. The company's privileges were ultimately revoked as part of that great holocaust of patents in the summer of 1639 which heralded the end of Charles I's personal rule.[42]

A central feature of all the case-histories of Caroline mono-polies which have been dealt with so far was the opposition both of the City fathers and the major companies to such schemes. To this rule the last and perhaps the nastiest of these monopolies provides a very partial exception, at least in the case of one alderman and perhaps of one major company. As to the latter, it is by no means easy to determine how far the Vintners' Company in general, as opposed to a small minority of its members, was willingly involved in the celebrated scheme for the sale of wines associated with the names of Alderman William Abell, the master of the company, and Richard Kilvert, an ecclesiastical lawyer with a sharp eye for the possi-bilities of this sort of profitable enterprise. In the orgy of self-exculpation which characterized the response of all concerned to the Long Parliament's determined assault on this monopoly, Kilvert insisted that the scheme had originated long before his association with Abell. He maintained, moreover, that the members of the court of assistants of the company had been enthusiastic participants in the scheme from the beginning. The

[42] *Cal. S.P.D. 1635–6*, p. 292; *Cal. S.P.D. 1637*, pp. 253, 569; *Cal. S.P.D. 1637–8*, pp. 327, 347, 388; *Cal. S.P.D. 1638–9*, p. 36; *Cal. S.P.D. 1639*, pp. 66, 116, 374, 470; *Cal. S.P.D. 1639–40*, pp. 8–9, 410; *Cal. S.P.D. 1640–1*, pp. 31–2, 548.

latter maintained, on the other hand, that they had been drawn into the business only with the greatest reluctance as part of the train of events which had succeeded the star-chamber prosecution of the Vintners for illegally dressing meat, and the crown's subsequent failure to honour its undertaking to leave them unmolested in return for a loan of £6,000. But however great the uncertainty on this matter, the nature of the courtly interest is clear enough. The grantee of the fines for illegally dressing meat was the king's Scottish favourite, the marquis of Hamilton. Hamilton's action in persuading the Vintners to submit to the king's demand that they pay 40s. on each tun of wine sold, in return for the right to dress meat and other concessions, was not quite the exercise of noble altruism which it perhaps appears at first sight. For the tax in question was farmed to a syndicate of which Abell was the principal figure, and Hamilton was amply compensated for his sacrifice of the fines for dressing meat illegally by a cut of £4,000 per annum out of the syndicate's rent of £30,000 as well as an additional £1,500 per annum to other members of his family. The attempts of the main body of the company to pin the blame for the monopoly on a few persons, and notably on Abell and Kilvert, harmonized well with the mood of the House of Commons, with its desire not to spread responsibility for such acts of economic delinquency over too wide an area of the business world.[43] Among the main opponents of the scheme had been the consumers of wine, for the Vintners were author-ized to raise their prices as a *quid pro quo* for the virtual excise duty which they paid; wine importers who, although offered a guaranteed sale, were rightly suspicious of the opportunities which the scheme afforded to the Vintners as a sole purchasing agency, as well as being disgruntled that not all of the promised quotas were taken off their hands; and both metropolitan and provincial retailing vintners and taverners who were forced to accept a quota of what many of them claimed to be either excessive amounts of, or inferior quality, wine on pain of the closing of their establishments. Nevertheless, some refused to submit, and there is one example of a Whitsuntide orgy in

[43] See below, p. 153.

1639 outside the shop of a Bedlam vintner who refused to accept a cask of monopoly wine, which nevertheless proved acceptable enough to a horde of passers-by who broke open the cask and helped themselves liberally to its contents. Whatever the rôle of the Vintners' Company in general, Abell himself is clearly a case of a London alderman whose monopolistic interest brought down on him the wrath of an avenging Long Parliament.[44]

V

From the Caroline monopolists we turn to the customs farmers. Despite the fact that the constitutional struggle over tonnage and poundage in the later 1620s had further emphasized the mutual dependence of the customs farmers and the crown, the farming syndicates of the reign of Charles I were not by any means sure that they could continue to rely upon the royal support which had been so strikingly manifested in the face of the parliamentary onslaught of 1629. Over the later 1620s and the 1630s schemes for the resumption of direct royal administration of the customs revenue, emanating, oddly enough, from the petty farmer John Harrison, attracted some support at court. They were frustrated, so Harrison claimed, only as a result of the support which Sir Paul Pindar and the farming syndicate received from the duke of Buckingham and, after Buckingham's death in 1628, from the lord treasurer, the earl of Portland, during whose term of office 'there was no meanes to divert this revenue . . . out of the ould way of farming, as being against the interest of that great man and of some of the farmers his creatures'.[45]

During the same period the farmers' security of tenure also appeared to be threatened by the adoption of a policy of

[44] P.R.O., S.P. Charles I, cccxxxviii/70, 71; cccxliii/79; cccxliv/75; C.L.R.O., Rep. xlvii, fos. 83–83(b); *Cal. S.P.D. 1634–5*, pp. 396–7, 513, 520–1, 556; *Cal. S.P.D. 1638–9*, pp. 244, 364, 379–80; *Cal. S.P.D. 1639*, pp. 183, 184–5, 196, 240, 256, 300–1, 356, 530; *Cal. S.P.D. 1639–40*, pp. 96–7, 161, 240; *Cal. S.P.D. 1640*, pp. 226–7; *Cal. S.P.D. 1640–1*, pp. 289–90, 325, 410; *Cal. S.P.D. 1641–3*, pp. 32–3, 56–7; *A True Discovery of the Proiectors of the Wine Proiect* (1641); *The Vintners' Answer to Some Scandalous Pamphlets* (1642); Gardiner, *History*, VIII, 286–7; Unwin, *Gilds and Companies*, pp. 323–6; Pearl, pp. 289–91.
[45] B.L., Stowe MSS., 326, fos. 89–89(b).

F

letting the great farm on very short leases, annually between 1628 and 1632 and triennially thereafter. But they rose to this challenge magnificently, as perhaps they were intended to, by making large-scale anticipatory payments of rent due beyond the dates at which their leases were due to expire. Nevertheless the potential menace of the policy of short leases became a firm reality in 1635 when the death of Lord Treasurer Portland robbed the syndicates of great and petty farmers of their most powerful protector. Laud and his allies at court had been bitterly opposed to Portland and his allegedly corrupt practices, and their most spectacular triumph came in March of the following year with the appointment of Laud's protégé, William Juxon, bishop of London, as lord treasurer in preference to Portland's chancellor of the exchequer, Sir Francis Cottington. But although Juxon's appointment boded no good for the Pindar syndicate, he does not seem to have been particularly sympathetic to Harrison's schemes to nationalize the customs either. His enemies claimed that he had his own personal axe to grind, and that he was being manipulated by the courtly multi-concessionaire Lord Goring.[46] The detailed story of the attempt to force Goring and his City associates, Sir Nicholas Crispe, Sir Job Harby and Sir John Nulls, on Pindar's syndicates and the consequent withdrawal of Pindar and all but two of his colleagues has been told elsewhere.[47] But Goring's career as a customs farmer was short-lived, and in the summer of 1640, Pindar was persuaded to join Goring's former associates in a new syndicate which lent enormous sums to Charles I in the crisis in his affairs in 1640 and in the next year was hammered unmercifully by the Long Parliament. It is ironical to find John Harrison, that most determined and intelligent opponent of customs farming, as a member of it.

The prodigality with which Charles I dissipated his traditional sources of business support is one of the least familiar but certainly not the least significant factor which contributed to his isolation in 1640. The customs farmers whose treatment

[46] Ibid. fos. 62–3.
[47] See Ashton, *The Crown and the Money Market*, pp. 98–105, 108–12, and 'Revenue Farming under the Early Stuarts', *Econ. Hist. Rev.*, 2nd ser., VIII (1956), 313, 316–19, 320–1.

represents a spectacular example of this tendency were, of course, especially vulnerable, since, as farmers of customs revenue which had not been granted in a parliamentary way, they could expect no mercy from parliament. The events of the later 1620s had, however, demonstrated that the same was not true of commercial concessionaires, and this was to be confirmed by the history of the Long Parliament before the Civil War.

VI

The view that the new balance of forces in the City, achieved as a result of the events of the early years of Charles I's reign, survived into the 1640s is attested by the contrast between the Long Parliament's severe handling of internal monopolies and the customs farmers, on the one hand, and, on the other, its failure to mount an attack on the privileges of the chartered companies in foreign trade. It is true, of course, that some members of the latter had other concessionary interests which made them persons who were bound to be picked out for destruction by Pym and his associates – Sir Henry Garway is an obvious example. But such persons represent a very small minority of the London business élite in 1640. The Long Parliament could easily wreak its vengeance upon them without alienating that élite as a whole.

And the Long Parliament began precisely where its predecessor had left off in 1629. At the end of 1640 and in the opening weeks of 1641 some of the familiar names which had created such a stir in the constitutional crisis of 1629 were once again heard in the House. On 2 December the petition which the pertinacious Richard Chambers had filed against the customs farmers in 1628 for their non-parliamentary exaction of tonnage and poundage was read, together with another of his petitions, 'by which hee shewed the wrongs offered him since the peticion in 1628'. These included his censure in the star chamber in May 1639, his subsequent imprisonment in the Fleet, and the forced sale of his goods to the value of nearly £7,000 to pay the fine imposed upon him in the star chamber. 'And that first and last hee suffered 6 yeares imprisonment, his losse hath been

10,000 £, and himselfe, wife and 10 children weere neare utter-
lie undone.' Another opposition stalwart of 1628–9 was Samuel
Vassall, a member of the Levant Company, who had refused
to pay duties on currants, and who, like Chambers, had got into
trouble during the 1630s for refusal to pay ship money. 'In
seven yeares he was 16 times committed, with divers other
losses, wrongs and oppressions to the losse of above 10,000 £.'
But a name which probably evoked even more poignant
parliamentary memories was that of John Rolle, the seizure of
whose goods for non-payment of duty had, more than any other
factor, sparked off the crisis of 1629, and, since he was an M.P.
at that time, had coupled the issue of the constitutionality of
the royal exaction of tonnage and poundage with that of parliamentary privilege. After eleven years of freedom from parliamentary attacks, the heat was again turned on to the customs
farmers. The relentlessness of the attack is reflected in John
Hampden's possibly apocryphal threat to Pindar that 'the
people should know or be informed that the farmers had bene
the cause of all the evells of the Kingdome, which uniust
language he vttered with much vehemence'. And on this occasion
the king was as powerless to protect the farmers as he was to
save the life of the earl of Strafford, though for a short time,
during January 1641, it looked as if they might extricate
themselves from the worst of their difficulties by their willingness to lend £60,000 to the hard-pressed parliament. The
debate on this matter on 14 January raised important issues of
principle, and is reported in these terms by the parliamentary
diarist Sir Simonds D'Ewes.

SIR JOHN HOTHAM moved that it might bee resolved by the Howse
whether wee should accept of the 60,000 £ offered from the customers or not . . . Some moved that wee should accept of it, others that
wee should refuse it, because the customers weere men guiltie of
great crimes. I moved that wee weere now in a great strait: necessi-
tie and danger pressing us to borrow; and dishonour dehorting us to
borrow of criminall men. But rather then the kingdome and the
safetie therof should runn anie hazard, I conceived wee might
borrow of these men though not *eo nomine* as of Customers. For they
had a double capacite, first as men, secondlie as officers. The Jewes
whilest they lived heere in England weere of all men most execrated
and hated for ther usurie, and yet the Kings of England did often

upon urgent occasions borrow of them. Nor did I see why this act of ther lending should putt anie obligation upon us either not to question or to pardon ther crimes. I wished all other wayes and meanes to borrow might bee assaied; but if none could bee found, then to accept ther offer, in which, as long as wee gave them securitie and damages, I saw nothing for which wee weere beholding to them, seeing wee had but an Oliver for a Rowland.

D'Ewes's argument was logical enough, but, desperate as the Commons were for ready money, their scruples proved too strong for them. Moreover, the preservation of their virtue was by no means entirely incompatible with the satisfaction of their financial needs. As Denzil Holles was later to argue, 'one good meanes to raise monies might bee the questioning of the customers'. It proved to be a very good means. On 24 February the House appointed a committee to examine the abuses of the customs farmers, and it was as a result of the recommendations of this committee that the farmers were forced to compound for their delinquency by the payment of a fine of £150,000, as well as to make satisfaction to merchants whose goods had been illegally distrained for failure to pay duty in 1628–9 and afterwards. Pindar and his colleagues were already owed enormous sums by Charles I for the loan which they had made to him in 1640, and the crushing fine which was imposed upon them in the next year was the final blow which shattered this sector of the London concessionary interest which had always been most intimately connected with the crown and the court.[48]

In their attack upon the customs farmers the Commons were completing the unfinished business which had been interrupted by the dissolution of parliament in 1629. The similarity in this matter between the arguments of 1629 and those of 1640–1 is most striking testimony to the continuity between the two parliaments, and can be illustrated by reference to a speech made on 6 July 1641 by no less a person than Edward Hyde,

[48] B.L., Stowe MSS., 326, fos. 72–72(b), 85–6, 91–93(b); Harleian MSS., 1769, fo. 205(b); *Cal. S.P.D. 1641–3*, p. 278; *H. of C.J.*, II, 43, 66, 67, 77, 106,109, 116, 122, 154, 155, 157, 161, 163–4, 167–8, 169, 179, 216, 217, 221, 238, 251, 315–16, 348, 387, 420, 514, 525–6; Notestein (ed.), *D'Ewes's Journal*, pp. 93–4, 246, 248–9, 252–3, 255 & n, 311, 398 & n; J. Bruce (ed.), *The Verney Papers: Notes of Proceedings in the Long Parliament . . . by Sir Ralph Verney, Knight, Member for the Borough of Aylesbury* (Camden Soc., o.s., XXXI) (1845), pp. 78–80, 81; Ashton, *The Crown and the Money Market*, pp. 110–12.

who was, of course, later to become the main spirit in the organization of support for the king in the Long Parliament during the winter of 1641-2. Here, however, Hyde adopts an argument and tone which are strikingly reminiscent of those characterizing the contributions of Selden, Eliot and Pym in the closing stages of the parliament of 1629. Indeed, in his view,

to call a seizure by the Farmours (of whose interest the Court will not deny the notice, and if his Majesty had any right, they well knew he had transferred it to these men) or the Ware-houses of the Customers, the Kings possession to defeat the Subject of his proper remedy, was the boldest piece of *Sophistry* we have met with in a Court of Law.[49]

It will be remembered that the earlier attack on the farmers had followed the victory which had been won by the parliaments of 1621 and 1624 over another sector of the concessionary interests, the holders of patents of monopoly. But that victory had turned out to be a great deal less than complete, and the Statute of Monopolies of 1624 was in actual fact no more decisive than the celebrated Elizabethan decision of 1601. The loopholes in the statute had provided ample opportunities for new monopolistic projects, and, after a decade of Charles's personal government, the Augean stables again needed cleaning. To some extent parliament's work was made easier by the government's panic measures of 1639, which had swept away a large number of the existing monopolies. The House of Commons hardly required the encouragement of numerous anti-monopolistic petitions, including one from the London Grocers' Company, to proceed mercilessly against most of the remaining patentees. On 9 November 1640 it ordered that 'all proiectors, Monopolizers, Promoters or Advisers of them should bee made uncapable of sitting in this House', and by January 1641 measures were already being taken to unseat the offending members. Among these were Sir Nicholas Crispe, the former customs farmer and patentee for copperas, dyewoods and vending beads; William Sands, who held a patent for sea coal; Sir John Jacob, the customs farmer, 'being a Monopolizer for tabaccoe in which

---

[49] 'Mr. Edward Hydes Speech . . .' (1641), *Lord Somers' Tracts*, 2nd coll., II (1750), 276-7; J. Rushworth (ed.), *Historical Collections*, IV (1691), 342. Cf. above, pp. 133-5.

the Lord Goring had a share'; and Thomas Webb, 'a Monopolizer for bone-lace'. And, needless to say, the anger of the Commons was not confined to those monopolists who were also M.P.s. Few of the monopolistic privileges which had mushroomed during the 1630s escaped, and the vast bulk of existing patentees were declared delinquents. Among them were the notorious Alderman William Abell and the no less notorious members of the now dissolved Westminster Society of Soapboilers, though parliament was content to leave intact the monopolistic privileges which had been so dearly bought from that body and the crown by the formerly excluded soapboilers of London and Bristol.[50]

This last incident mirrors what had, since the mid 1620s, become the parliamentary attitude towards the London concessionary interest. No longer, as in the period before 1624, were almost all concessionaires lumped together for indiscriminate condemnation. A distinction had come to be made between those privileges from which a relatively large number of people benefited, even though an even larger number of less influential persons were excluded from these benefits, and the sorts of privileges, like monopolies and customs-farming concessions, where a very few men held the rest of the community, including the first and now favoured type of concessionaires, to ransom. It was a distinction which was to be of incalculable importance in securing a very wide basis of influential support for the parliamentary cause from the business interests of the City of London. Needless to say, it was of profound significance to the most numerous of these concessionaires, the members of the privileged charter companies engaged in foreign trade. In December and January 1640–1

---

[50] *Cal. S.P.D. 1639*, pp. 30, 116, 374, 470; *Cal. S.P.D. 1640–1*, pp. 31–2, 289–90; *H. of C. J.*, II, 24, 27, 30, 31–2, 34, 35, 37, 51, 55, 58–9, 70–1, 75, 77, 83, 156–7, 161, 184, 207, 218, 259–60, 298, 299, 432, 516, 519, 527, 533–4, 581, 727; Notestein (ed.), *D'Ewes's Journal*, pp. 5, 14 & n, 19–20, 34n, 42 & n, 54, 68, 159, 174, 190, 224, 267–8, 299–300, 312, 351, 444, 456, 503–4, 529, 531, 533, 537, 539, 543–4, 546–7; W. H. Coates (ed.), *The Journal of Sir Simonds D'Ewes from the First Recess of the Long Parliament to the Withdrawal of King Charles from London* (New Haven, Conn., 1942), pp. 52, 55–8; Bruce (ed.), *Verney Papers*, pp. 80–1; *A True Discovery of the Proiectors of the Wine Proiect; The Vintners' Answer to Some Scandalous Pamphlets*; Gardiner, *History*, IX, 6, 238–9; Price, *The English Patents of Monopoly*, pp. 45–6; Unwin, *Gilds and Companies*, pp. 323–8.

representatives of the principal chartered companies were ordered to attend the House of Commons 'to the end that they may give Information . . . what is the cause of decay of Trade, what their principall greevances are; and what Remedy they conceive is fitt etc.' It was at this point just conceivable that the companies would again become the object of a parliamentary attack as a contributory factor to the prevailing economic depression, as had been the case in the parliament of 1621. But far too much water had passed beneath the bridge during the intervening period. Far from preparing themselves for a parliamentary onslaught on their restrictive practices, the Eastland Company preferred a complaint to parliament in January 1641 against a certain Valentine Beale 'for being an Interloper into their Trade, being noe Merchant nor Free of their Company'. Although there is no evidence that the House acted upon this complaint, the fact that it was made at all is significant. It is true that the Merchant Adventurers had to release one William Sikes, whom they had detained in Rotterdam 'for not conforminge himselfe to the orders of their Company beyond Seas'. Sikes was to be allowed to return to England where he would be free to make his complaints against the company. The Merchant Adventurers were also called upon to answer certain complaints which had been made against their restrictive practices by the clothiers of Worcester, but nothing seems to have come of this. The members of the company may have experienced some uneasiness in the early months of the Long Parliament when they were made to hand in their patent for parliamentary examination during 1640–1, but what is far more significant is the fact that, before the Civil War had begun, a new bill for a fresh incorporation of the company had already received two readings. The Merchant Adventurers, in short, although they may have had some anxious moments, were never subjected to the sort of pressure which they had experienced in 1621. One factor which may have further predisposed parliament in their favour was the loans, amounting to £70,000, which they made in 1641–2. On 27 December 1641 the governor and deputies of the company were called into the House of Commons and were thanked and warmly congratulated by the Speaker for the patriotic way in which they had risen to the occasion and helped parliament out of its financial difficulties. The contrast with the parliamentary attitude to the proposed loan from the customs farmers is too obvious to require stressing. Finally, in October 1643 a parliamentary ordinance upheld the existing government of the company as beneficial to both the trade in and manufacture of woollen cloth. This ordinance sets the seal on the change in the relations between the company and parliament which had taken place since the days of the free-trade bill of 1604 or even the parliament of 1621. Membership of the company was to continue to be restricted to mere merchants,

And . . . no person shall trade into those parts limited by their incorporacion but such as are free of that Corporacion . . . Provided that the said fellowship shall not exclude any Person from . . . admission . . . which shall desire it by Way of Redemption, if such person by their Custome be capable thereof & hath bin bred a Merchant, and shall pay one Hundred pounds for the same if he be free and an in habitant of the Citty of London & trade from that Porte, or ffifty poundes if he be not free and no inhabitant of the said Citty & trade not from thence.

This ordinance must indeed have gladdened the hearts of the old guard of the company.[51]

None of the companies seem to have been under the same pressure that they had experienced in the early 1620s. The continued split in the concessionary interest is again emphasized by the Levant Company's complaints in 1640 against the manifold malpractices of the customs farmers who were soon to be ruined as a result of parliamentary action. Not so the Levant Company. In February 1642 representatives of the company were ordered to attend a parliamentary committee which had been appointed 'to consider how the *Suffolk* Cloths may be vented in *Turkey*, as formerly they had been; and to consider of the Obstructions in that Trade, and what Remedies may be applied vnto it'. There is at no time even a hint of a suggestion that the company itself was considered by parliament to be one

[51] *Cal. S.P.D. 1641–3*, p. 492; *H. of C. J.*, II, 56, 179, 214, 296, 357, 358, 363, 380, 569, 578, 587, 592, 595, 629, 689, 702; *H. of L. J.*, VI, 255; Notestein (ed.), *D'Ewes's Journal*, pp. 523, 524–5, 526, 527; Coates (ed.), *D'Ewes's Journal*, pp. 42, 348, 352.

of these obstacles. In April 1642 the Commons gave a sympathetic hearing to the Levant Company's complaints against the royalist ambassador at Constantinople, Sir Sackville Crow, and his predecessor, Sir Peter Wyche, in the interminable dispute about the rights to strangers' consulage, although it was another two years before parliament finally recognized the company's right to this money. In the meantime, the royalist minority among the directorate, including the arch-concessionaire Sir Henry Garway, had been deposed, and Garway had been replaced as governor of the company by the radical lord mayor, Isaac Penington. With these events the way was completely open for the mutually sympathetic attitudes, which had increasingly characterized the relations between the company and parliament since the accession of Charles I, to bear their full fruit. In March 1644 a parliamentary ordinance confirmed all the company's privileges, including the right to exact enormously greater entry fines than those which had been laid down by the government as a direct result of the parliamentary agitation of the early 1620s. The security of the company reflects the successful establishment of a *mariage de convenance* between big business and parliament, as secure and as mutually advantageous as had been that between the companies and the Elizabethan government. The breaking down of the barriers of mutual distrust, tentatively begun in the parliament of 1624 and enormously accelerated in that of 1629, was now complete.[52]

[52] P.R.O., S.P. 105/143 (Register Book of Levant Company), no foliation; *Cal. S.P.D. 1641–3*, p. 467; *Cal. S.P.D. 1644*, pp. 37, 59; *H. of C. J.*, II, 297, 429, 465, 471, 532–3, III, 131; *H. of L. J.*, VI, 455, 474; Wood, *Levant Company*, pp. 52, 89–90.

5

The crown and the municipality:
local issues

The principal object of the next two chapters of this book will
be to inquire how far the disillusionment and dissatisfaction
which affected, to a greater or lesser degree, so many members
of the London concessionary interest were reinforced by the
experiences of some of them as City fathers. The present
chapter deals with the significance in this context of what may
loosely be described as local issues peculiar to the relations
between crown and municipality but none the less significant
for that. The succeeding chapter looks at some of the issues
which divided crown and court from what came to be the great
majority of the political nation with the aim of seeing how far
and in what manner they were reflected within the City. In the
final chapter the story will be taken up to and beyond the outbreak of civil war so as to parallel the treatment of the fortunes
of the concessionary interest in chapter 4 and to attempt to
throw some new light on the problem of London's allegiance in
the struggle.

I

Insufficient attention has hitherto been paid to the multiplying
occasions of friction between the municipal governors of London
and the government of Charles I during the two decades or so
before the constitutional revolution of 1641–2 in the City. Seen
in conjunction with the experiences of many aldermen as
business concessionaires there is in fact an impressive body of
evidence relating to the issues in dispute which when brought
together has the effect of casting very serious doubt on the
notion that the City of London was the polite client of the

crown and was emphatically ranged alongside the court rather than the country over these years. Among these issues were a number of local disputes which, far from being relatively minor disagreements between natural allies, were bitterly contested and of major historical significance. These in turn lend themselves conveniently to subdivision between those issues which, while being potent causes of friction, were settled by the City's agreement in the summer of 1637 to pay a composition fee in settlement of its differences with the crown[1] and the other questions at issue which were not settled by these means.

II

Thanks to Moody's definitive study the most familiar of the issues settled in 1637 is the dispute over the City's and its Irish Society's conduct of the Londonderry Plantation.[2] Like most of these issues its history stretched back long before the 1630s, almost indeed to the time when the City had first yielded to royal persuasion to undertake the plantation in 1610. As early as March 1612 the City presented a catalogue of its own grievances relating to Londonderry, while in the following month Sir Arthur Chichester, the then lord deputy of Ireland, made complaint to the privy council about the manifold deficiences of the City's Irish Society; more particularly, tha the citizens were the most backward of all the Ulster planters in sending over tenants to people the land and, in consequence of this, the most willing to accept the native Irish as tenants, thus jeopardizing the success of the whole plantation policy. Further information unfavourable to the City was built up as a result of a series of royal surveys made in 1614, 1616 and 1618–19, the last by Sir Thomas Phillips, the governor of Coleraine, who was

---

[1] C.L.R.O., Jor xxxvii, fos. 345–345(b); Jor. xxxviii, fos. 103–104(b).

[2] My treatment of this dispute is based primarily on Moody, *Londonderry Plantation*, *passim*, and a collection of documents made available by Sir Thomas Phillips to Charles I in 1629, illustrating the history of the plantation from its foundation (*Londonderry and the London Companies 1609–1629, Being a Survey and Other Documents Submitted to King Charles I by Sir Thomas Phillips* (Belfast, 1928). For an invaluable critical examination of this – for all Phillips's exaggerations – extremely valuable source, see Moody, *Londonderry Plantation*, pp. 252–8. The plantation also receives extensive treatment in R. Bagwell, *Ireland under the Stuarts*, 3 vols. (1906–16; repr. 1962), i, *passim*.

to become the City's arch-enemy in Ireland and the person who, more than any other, was responsible for legal proceedings ultimately being brought against the citizens. It was primarily due to his efforts that the government singled out the City's Irish lands for its special attention, that its Ulster rents were twice sequestered during the 1620s, and that an action was brought in the star chamber in the same decade only to be withdrawn on technical grounds. By the end of the decade, however, the government had accumulated enough additional information to recommence the serious preparation of its case, and an attempt by the court of aldermen in April 1633 to fend it off by offering £20,000 – the sum was raised to £30,000 in the following year – as the price of being freed from this and other royal suits was unsuccessful.[3] The crown was hunting for far bigger game, and legal proceedings against the City were opened in the star chamber in 1635.

It was not difficult to prove that the City was by no means blameless in its conduct of affairs in Ulster. It had failed to encourage and attract adequate numbers of English settlers, had tolerated and even positively encouraged native Irish tenants and had made less than adequate arrangements for fortification and housebuilding. But that it had been guilty of the deliberate and wanton hazarding of the settlement and the brazen fraud of which it was accused in the star chamber was untrue. Its faults had been magnified by fantastically exaggerated estimates, mostly proceeding from the fertile but jaundiced imagination of Phillips, both of the number of native tenants and of the citizens' enormous profits, an estimated £98,233, which is palpably absurd. As in the case of so many of the royal expedients of the years of personal government, the government's motives were mainly fiscal, but the City had additional cause for resentment in the fact that, as well as the swingeing fine of £70,000, which like so many star-chamber fines was later reduced, it was deliberately and publicly humiliated in the process. Since final settlement involved other matters currently at issue between crown and City, it must for the moment suffice to say that the Irish lands were forfeited as a result of the dispute, the crown's naming of £125,000 as the price of their retention

[3] C.L.R.O., Rep. xlvii, fos. 203(b)–204.

being far higher than the Londoners were prepared to pay. The incident can hardly be passed off as a rather unpleasant tiff between natural allies, and the bitterness of City resentment was to find eloquent expression in the petition presented by the common council to the Long Parliament in 1641, which resulted in the complete reversal of the verdict of 1635. In the circumstances of 1641, however, lands in Ulster were not to be a greatly sought-after asset.[4]

In 1632 the City had to face a royal inquiry – which ultimately resulted in a case in the court of exchequer – into its management of the sale of the royal contract estates, which had been conveyed to its trustees in 1628 as a means of satisfying individual creditors of the crown for loans raised through the municipality between 1617 and 1628.[5] There can be no doubt that its proceedings had left much to be desired. Of the advances of 1628 the first instalment bore interest at only 6 per cent, but the subsequent instalments of the £120,000 were charged with the full statutory maximum rate of 8 per cent. Moreover, the loans of 1617 and 1625, which had originally borne interest at a statutory maximum rate of 10 per cent and 8 per cent respectively,[6] had now become the cheapest of all these debts to service as the result of a decidedly arbitrary order of common council of 20 December 1627 which reduced the subsequent rate applicable to these loans to a paltry 5 per cent. Expediency thus dictated that in the matter of repayment the first lenders should be last and the last should be first. But this was the least of the hardships which the unfortunate lenders of 1617 and 1625 or their heirs and assigns had to endure. In January 1630 the City committee in charge of the land sales had the bright idea of making the terms of sale more attractive by allowing individual creditors to use their City financial securities as part of the purchase price, and (far more important) by permitting individual purchasers who were not creditors to buy up such securities – in actual practice normally at a very heavy

---

4 H.M.C., *Fourth Report*, pt I, p. 99; *H. of C. J.*, II, 272; Moody, *Londonderry Plantation*, pp. 355–89, 406–15.

5 See Ashton, *The Crown and the Money Market*, pp. 132–41.

6 The statutory maximum rate of interest had been reduced to 8 per cent in 1624, and this rate applied to both loans. A very few lenders were repaid privately before 1627.

discount – and present them at their face value towards the purchase price of the land they desired. This practice unquestionably gave just occasion for scandal, and the king rightly took strong exception to it, even though, in so doing, he laid himself open to the retort that if he had discharged his obligations promptly in the first place rather than resorting to this tardy and cumbrous procedure of settlement in lands, none of these things would have happened. In addition, the crown lawyers made extensive reference to the so-called 'unexpressed trust', a gentlemen's agreement not contained in the contract between king and City whereby the latter had indicated its willingness to restore to the crown any profits from the land sales, but on which matter its representatives took their stand on the reasonable ground that it was still far too early to predict the ultimate financial outcome of the sales. Finally, and most damaging of all, came the royal charge that certain well-placed citizens had feathered their own nests by arranging land sales at undervalues and committed other malpractices. In face of such charges of gross dishonesty and breach of trust, it is not unreasonable to assume that the royal proceedings on this issue left at least as nasty a taste in the citizens' mouths as had those on the Londonderry Plantation. By the agreement of 1637 the crown, in return for £12,000 to cover this and other matters, agreed to overlook the City's misdeeds, and the City was freed from the unexpressed obligation to return any surplus from the land sales and was naturally to refrain from allowing purchasers to discount the debts of the creditors thereafter.[7]

On another of the matters currently in dispute which the City had hoped to include in the settlement of 1637 the king refused to yield. This was his claim, contested by the City, to the urban land constituting the manor of Blanche Appleton, and therefore the legitimacy of a royal grant of that manor to a private individual. On two other matters, however, Charles was ultimately more accommodating. The first of these was his dispute with the City as to who had the right to estreats under

---

[7] See Ashton, *The Crown and the Money Market*, pp. 142–53, for a detailed account of these developments.

the greenwax, casual revenues which the City had taken ever since its charter of 23 Henry VI, but which the crown was contesting vigorously in the 1630s. The second was the right to fines for encroaching on the wasteland or streets of the City which was claimed by the City by virtue of the same charter and by the crown by virtue of a subsequent royal act of resumption. As early as 1610 and 1614 the City had successfully stood its ground on this matter, and it seems to have been left free to prosecute offenders for the next two decades. The impression which is conveyed by an examination of the cases of encroachment coming before the court of aldermen is that the aldermen were genuinely interested in the suppression of abuses rather than in filling the City's coffers by compounding with offenders. Unfortunately the same cannot be said of the motives of the crown when it revived its old claims in 1636 and established a royal commission to compound with encroachers. The City's rights in this matter were finally confirmed as part of the package deal of 1637 and by the new charter which it received in the following year.[8]

The tale of the relentless wearing down of the City which is the central feature of the events just described invites the conclusion that this might be expected to result in a significant deterioration of its relations with the crown. The fact that the aldermen ultimately came to terms with the crown ought not to be taken to denote anything more than acceptance of the need to yield to *force majeure*. It would surely be unrealistic to blame the City, which was totally dependent on the crown for the maintenance of its privileges, for not offering a more determined resistance than it did at this juncture. It is however one thing to yield to the inevitable; quite another to adopt this course with enthusiasm. The serious misgivings which aldermen must have come to entertain about royal behaviour towards the municipality might well have prompted heart-searchings

[8] P.R.O., S.P. James I, LII/42, LXXVI/10–15; S.P. Charles I, CCCXLVIII/44; CCCLXXVII/107; C.L.R.O., Jor. XXXVII, fos. 202–202(b), 345–345(b); Jor. XXXVIII, fo. 103(b); Rep. XXIX, fos. 212(b), 219(b)–220, 222(b), 226(b)–227; Rep. XXXI, pt ii, fos. 290(b)–291, 322(b); Rep. XXXIV, fos. 195(b)–196; Rep. XLII, fos. 3, 10(b), 13–13(b), 58(b), 296(b)–297; Rep. XLIII, fos. 23–23(b), 47(b), 83, 95(b), 107; Rep. XLIV, fos. 89(b)–90, 115–115(b); Rep. XLVI, fo. 220(b); Rep. LIII, fos. 50(b), 130–130(b); Pearl, pp. 21–2, 84–5.

about royal policy similar to those which, as chapter 4 suggested, must have affected many of them in their capacity as
business men and concessionaires.[9]

III

Any such impression of rapidly accumulating aldermanic misgivings can only be heightened when one turns to disputes
other than those which were nominally settled by the agreement of 1637. Two of these matters, the royal encouragement
of pressure to obtain the translation of many members of
livery companies to companies appropriate to the crafts which
they pursued, and, more important, the favour which the crown
showed to splinter groups of craftsmen seeking incorporation
have already received attention elsewhere, and emphasis has
been laid upon the opposition which they evoked from those
prominent gildsmen the lord mayor and aldermen on account
of the palpable breach which they threatened to force in the
oligarchic citadel.[10]

Another threat to the power and prestige of the City fathers
came from alarming developments in royal policy with regard
to the vexed problem of suburban control. Throughout the
period complaints by gildsmen against the mushroom growth
of unregulated suburban industry, the ease with which suburban craftsmen poached on the preserves of similar but distinct
crafts, and the suburban employment of unapprenticed labour
and 'ye poorest and weakest workemen that will doe the worke
cheapest' were legion. It was especially to the suburbs, rather
than to the City, that unskilled immigrants from the provinces,
'porters, laborers, Tapsters, hostlers, Broomemen and such
like' thronged. Here too prostitutes, thieves and vagabonds
and young men brought up by waggoners or sent to be apprenticed to honest trades but subsequently falling into bad company
and living in alehouses and less reputable institutions abounded.[11] And some immigrants came from still further afield,

---

[9] For a different view, see Pearl, pp. 81–7, where she plays down the significance
of these issues.
[10] See above, pp. 58–70, 71–82.
[11] B.L., Lansdowne MSS., 169, fos. 130–131. See also ibid. 92, fos. 47–50(b);
ibid. 160, fos. 95–6; ibid. 165, fo. 261; P.R.O., S.P. Charles I, ccxlviii/40;

from abroad as well as from provincial England, and, like native immigrants, gravitated more often than not to the suburbs and the so-called 'liberties', those pockets of exception from the control of the municipal authorities of the City of London which yet lay within the square mile between Temple and Holborn bars and Aldgate. In both suburbs and liberties alike, the obstacles to the employment of untrained and immigrant labour were less formidable and the power of the City gilds and livery companies far weaker. One of the reasons why the great court painter Van Dyck chose to live in Blackfriars is that, the district being a liberty, he would escape from the unwelcome attentions of the Painter–Stainers' Company. For less exalted immigrants an additional factor favouring residence in liberties or suburbs was the abundance of cheap accommodation due to the laxer enforcement of the regulations against the subdivision of houses and the harbouring of 'inmates'. In great part the history of the expansion of London is the history of the outlying districts where the lord mayor's writ did not run, and where, so he and his colleagues continually alleged, crime, disorder and squalor were rife.

Suggested remedies for this state of affairs were at no time wanting. In 1610 a committee of aldermen and common councilmen advanced the standard City solution that the rights of search of the City gilds should be extended to within five miles of the City boundaries. Two other remedies canvassed in the same year were more radical and less likely to meet with the approval of the City fathers. One was the creation of a number of suburban gilds distinct from those of the City. The other was voiced in a petition from long-established and respectable suburban tradesmen and artificers who had 'neither Halle nor Governers', but were as appalled as the City gildsmen themselves at the swarms of newcomers who 'shrowde them selves neere the Citye . . . greatly hurtinge as well the auncient Inhabitants which dwell nere the Citie and have duely served their Apprenticeshippes, as the Inhabitantes and Companyes of the said Citye, and abvsinge your Highnes Subiectes generally

---

P.C.R., P.C. 2, XLII, fos. 305–6; C.L.R.O., Remembrancia, VII, 76, 78; *Cal. S.P.D. 1631–3*, p. 446.

by falce and insufficient Wares'. The proposed solution was an
incorporation of all suburban producers and tradesmen with
general jurisdiction in the suburbs within ten miles of London,
a significant anticipation of some of the main features of the
royal scheme of the 1630s. But none of these proposals, nor the
project advanced on more than one occasion of dividing the
suburbs into four parts with a body of commissioners attached
to each, was adopted at the time.[12]

Of course the need for more effective suburban controls
extended far beyond regulation of industry and labour, to
matters such as disease, sanitation and perhaps above all, the
efficient enforcement of the royal building regulations. During
the period of Charles I's personal government the crown again
took the offensive. The privy council responded to a complaint
of the lord mayor and citizens in November 1632 against the
growth of unregulated suburban production, which was causing
'the freedome of London . . . to be [of] little worth' with a
proposal 'to enlarge the government of the cittie on euerie side
as far as anie contiguous buildings extend, together with the
number of wardes & Aldermen to make the government vni-
forme'. The reasons for the City's refusal to entertain these
proposals are largely a matter for conjecture, but in general
there is no reason to doubt Pearl's suggestion that, except in the
unlikely contingency that the anomalous arrangements for
representation in the courts of aldermen and common council
which had prevailed when Bridge Without had become the
twenty-sixth City ward[13] could be repeated in the proposed
new wards, the aldermen probably feared that the extension of
the City would have undesirable, and perhaps ultimately
disastrous, effects on the social composition of these two staid
and respectable organs. Whatever their reasons, they soon had
cause to regret their hyper-cautious approach to the problem,
for the government, lacking co-operation from the City,
attempted a unilateral solution to the problem. By March 1636
an extremely jumpy court of aldermen was doing its best to
delay the implementation of the privy council's new proposal

---

[12] B.L., Lansdowne MSS., 92, fos. 47–8, 49–50; Lansdowne MSS., 169, fo. 130;
P.R.O., S.P. James I, clviii/79.
[13] See above, p. 6.

for 'the incorporating of the Suburbes and priuiledged places in & about London', but by May this incorporation of the suburbs, roughly along the lines of the body proposed in 1610 except for the fact that its jurisdiction extended to within only three and not ten miles of the City of London, had become an established fact. Although the control and maintenance of industrial standards, the exclusion of foreigners and the better government of the suburbs were all prominent among the reasons given for the creation of the new authority, its subsequent short history suggests that, like so many of the other government-inspired schemes of the 1630s, fiscal considerations loomed very large indeed. For as to the maintenance of standards, the regulation of the crafts and the prevention of the employment of unskilled workers, persons who had never served an apprenticeship were to be admitted to the freedom of the new corporation on payment of a fine of twenty shillings to the king's use (as opposed to four shillings paid by those who had served apprenticeship); as to the exclusion of foreigners, they too might be admitted on paying forty shillings; while as to the better government of the suburbs and the maintenance of public order, in December 1637 a reply given by the officers of the new incorporation to an inquiry made by Secretary Windebank stated that, as a body of simple tradesmen, they had neither the resources nor the inclination to appoint a provost marshal for the area under their control.[14]

As far as the City itself was concerned, the creation of the incorporation of the suburbs came as a very rude shock. But worse was to follow. On 15 March 1637 the privy council responded to the City's complaints that freemen of the City dwelling in the suburbs were being pressed to take out the freedom of the incorporation of the suburbs, by ordering the officers of that body to desist, and disclaiming any intention of trespassing on the rights of City freemen. But only four days later it reversed this decision, and although the City was asked

[14] P.R.O., S.P. Charles I, ccxxv/71, ccl/51; C.L.R.O., Rep. xlvi, fos. 330–330(b); Rep. l, fos. 151(b), 191(b), 205(b); Bodleian Library, Bankes MSS., xii/46; *Cal. S.P.D. 1635–6*, pp. 359–60; *Cal. S.P.D. 1636–7*, p. 10; *Cal. S.P.D. 1637–8*, p. 19; *Remembrancia Index*, pp. 227–9; Brett-James, *The Growth of Stuart London* (1935), pp. 223–45; Pearl, pp. 31–7.

to devise an oath whereby City freemen entering the new incorporation were obliged to bind their apprentices to their City companies, such persons were put in an unenviable position, faced by the expense of belonging to two bodies. Perhaps as a further reassurance to the City fathers, who must have been horrified at the rapid reversal of the decision of 15 March, they were told that, although the rights of the new incorporation extended not only to the suburbs, but also to the so-called liberties within the City boundaries – over which the City had been striving to acquire control since at least the time of the dissolution of the monasteries – those liberties over which it had obtained some measure of control as a result of its charter of 1608 were to be exempt from the new incorporation's jurisdiction. But this assurance suffered much the same fate as that of 15 March 1637. As a result of consistent pressure from the new incorporation the privy council resolved in June 1638 that it should be allowed to recruit members even from these liberties, and that if the City wished to challenge the new incorporation on this issue, it must proceed via the law courts. The City not only prosecuted a number of such suits, which were still undecided when the events of 1640 brought an abrupt change for the worse in the fortunes of both the crown and its suburban protégé; it also did all it could to assist those City freemen dwelling in liberties such as Blackfriars and the Duke's Place who had been imprisoned for their refusal to join the new incorporation. The creation of that body, which did not outlast the period of personal government, was not the least important of a number of causes which helped to embitter the relations between crown and City in the 1630s.[15]

IV

In all the issues which have so far been considered the fiscal advantage of the crown was a consideration which loomed very large. This is also emphatically true of another major City grievance against the crown, the activities of the royal com-

---

[15] P.R.O., P.C.R., P.C. 2, XLVII, fos. 242–3, 254–5, XLVIII, fo. 346, XLIX, fos. 137, 211, L, fo. 173; C.L.R.O., Rep. LIII, fos. 28–28(b); Rep. LIV, fos. 322–322(b); *Cal. S.P.D. 1637–8*, p. 417; *Cal. S.P.D. 1638–9*, p. 20; *Remembrancia Index*, pp. 228–9.

missioners for buildings, which rapidly degenerated into a blatantly revenue-raising device via the familiar process of licensing offenders. This is not to deny the sincerity of the first two Stuart kings' desire to make of London and Westminster, or at least the most prominent parts of them, a more civilized urban environment worthy of a great capital city. One of the most striking examples of this was the government's determination that the dilapidated Goldsmiths' Row in Cheapside should be repaired and its unpopular attempt to force the goldsmiths who had moved to the West End to take up residence in the Row.[16] Another was the pressure for the repair and re-edification of St Paul's cathedral.[17] No less eloquent of royal intentions is the concern for the use of comely and durable materials which is expressed in a number of proclamations. One of these, issued on 16 July 1615, while bestowing praise on the City's zeal for public works, went on to stress the king's ambition to emulate the achievement of Caesar Augustus. Just as Augustus was said to have found a Rome built of brick and left it built of marble, so it might be said of James 'that we had founde our Citty and Subvrbes of London of stickes and left them of bricke, being a Materiall farre more durable, safe from fire and magnificent'. A stream of such proclamations from 1605 onwards, which gradually formulated a code of building practices regulating such matters as materials and the heights and numbers of storeys, testifies to the royal concern, despite the facts that many of the regulations were applicable only to the main streets and were vitiated by abuses in the practice of licensing offenders.[18]

---

[16] P.R.O., S.P. Charles I, cccxv/76; C.L.R.O., Rep. xxxvii, fos. 176, 186; *Cal. S.P.D. 1629–31*, pp. 100, 278; *Cal. S.P.D. 1634–5*, pp. 288–9, 374–5; *Cal. S.P.D. 1635*, pp. 79, 119, 167, 237–8, 304; *Cal. S.P.D. 1637*, p. 145; *Cal. S.P.D. 1637–8*, pp. 151, 161, 330–1; *A.P.C. 1621–3*, p. 515; *A.P.C. 1623–5*, pp. 20, 233–4, 298–9; H.M.C., *House of Lords MSS.*, xi, *Addenda*, p. 375; *Remembrancia Index*, pp. 105–6, 108, 109, 110–11, 213; T. F. Reddaway, 'Goldsmiths' Row in Cheapside, 1558–1645,' *Guildhall Miscellany*, ii (1963), 181–206.

[17] See below, pp. 197–8.

[18] B.L., Cottonian MSS., Titus Bv, fo. 213; C.L.R.O., Jor. xxix, fos. 351–351(b); Jor. xxxi, fos. 208(b)–210 (old foliation); Rep. xxix, fos. 128, 128(b); *Cal. S.P.D. 1603–10*, p. 200; *Cal. S.P.D. 1619–23*, p. 165; J. F. Larkin and P. C. Hughes (eds.), *Stuart Royal Proclamations*, i (Oxford, 1973), pp. 111–12, 171–5, 193–5, 485–8, 597–8; Steele (ed.), *Bibliotheca Lindesiana*, i, nos. 1049, 1063, 1114, 1167, 1218, 1248, 1420, 1616.

The original object of the royal commission for buildings was to remedy the deficiences of the regulation which was exercised by local authorities such as the burgess court of Westminster and the corporation of the City of London.[19] The first such commission established in March 1608 had proved abortive, but another commission was established in the summer of 1615 with widely ranging membership, including the privy councillors and City and suburban magistrates, though the most active commissioners were a relatively small core of officials.[20] Despite the emphatic declaration that it was a matter of royal honour 'That the procedure of a publique Reformacion be not turned to any private benefitt', there is abundant evidence that almost from the first different ideas prevailed and that many people 'not regarding his Majesty's strict commaundement, but presuming upon the easines of a composicion, have and do continually erect tenements and other buildinges to the manifest contempt of his Majesty's proclamacions and the scandall of gouvernment'.[21] The royal regulations seem to have had little effect on the large-scale offender, and it is significant that the vast bulk of the delinquents who were sent before the privy council and ultimately to prison were 'the poorer and meaner sorte of offendors, and others of better quallitie and worth [are] omitted and leafte out'. Proclamation followed proclamation, one of which, issued on 12 March 1619, freely admitted that offenders were now so numerous that it was quite out of the question to demolish all illegal buildings. This, together with the statement of the commissioners for buildings on 8 July 1619 that a few judicious demolitions might facilitate the prompter

---

[19] The machinery of the City of London for the discovery and presentment of these and other abuses was the wardmote inquests, sworn juries which in each ward presented cases to the alderman or his deputy. There were many complaints about the defects of this machinery, though in 1644 it was significantly suggested that the chief blame lay not with the inquests as such but rather with the continued failure of the municipal authorities to act on their presentments (C.L.R.O., Jor. XL, fo. 83(b)).

[20] C.L.R.O., Jor. XXIX, fos. 351–351(b); *Cal. S.P.D. 1603–10*, p. 415; *Cal. S.P.D. 1611–18*, pp. 286, 295; *A.P.C. 1615–16*, pp. 121–2; Larkin and Hughes (eds.), *Stuart Proclamations*, pp. 111–12, 345–7; Steele (ed.), *Bibliotheca Lindesiana*, I, nos. 1167–8.

[21] *A.P.C. 1615–16*, pp. 434–5 (letter from privy council to Middlesex J.P.s, 12 March 1616). For similar letters in the following month to the J.P.s of both Middlesex and Surrey, see ibid. pp. 483–6.

payment of composition fines is eloquent testimony of the reality which lay behind royal policy.[22]

The years of Charles I's personal government saw some notable stiffening of royal building controls, the first of which was a proclamation on 16 July 1630 which established sanctions not only against workmen building on new foundations but also against magistrates who refused to suppress such activities. In October 1632 the privy council inaugurated an inquiry into abuses in building licences, many of which had been obtained under false pretences. The king was to be asked to grant no further licences, and those already granted but not yet acted on were to be revoked. There is some evidence to suggest that the operations of some fashionable builders such as the earl of Bedford and Scipio Squire in Covent Garden and Long Acre were seriously hampered by this new stringency, although it was during the same decade that William Newton, with the aid of the queen, succeeded in obtaining licences to build in Lincoln's Inn Fields, which it had formerly been hoped would be preserved as a public amenity.[23]

A welcome glimmer of sanity in the dark history of the royal building regulations is to be found in the privy council's order of 25 January 1637 that all who compounded should be compelled to take out letters of pardon with the condition that their patents would be cancelled if they subdivided the buildings or took inmates. Here at last was a clear recognition of the fact that the great evil was not new building *per se* but the creation of slums by subdivision, which the regulation against building on new foundations had tended to encourage. The order is, of course, also evidence that illegal building was still going on despite regulations such as an order of the previous month against both new building and compounding with offenders. In 1638 a list of 447 persons who had compounded was pro-

[22] P.R.O., S.P. James I, xcix/13, 14, cxxii/139; *Cal. S.P.D. 1611–18*, pp. 557, 558; *Cal. S.P.D. 1619–23*, pp. 23–4, 59; *Cal. S.P.D. 1629–31*, p. 7; *A.P.C. 1615–16*, pp. 483–6; *A.P.C. 1619–21*, pp. 21–2; Steele (ed.), *Bibliotheca Lindesiana*, i, nos. 1218, 1248; Larkin and Hughes (eds.), *Stuart Proclamations*, pp. 428–31; *Remembrancia Index*, pp. 47, 48–9.
[23] P.R.O., S.P. Charles I, clxxi/3, cccv/20, 73, 74, ccclxx/35, 40; *Cal. S.P.D. 1629–31*, pp. 308, 554; *Cal. S.P.D. 1631–3*, p. 428; *Cal. S.P.D. 1635*, pp. 532–3; Steele (ed.), *Bibliotheca Lindesiana*, i, no. 1616.

duced, including 68 living within the fashionable parish of St Martin-in-the-Fields.[24]

Many of these developments occurred outside the confines of the City of London, but the building commission had not been in existence for five years before it became common knowledge that the City fathers, although they were nominally commissioners, disapproved of its activities. In October 1619 the court of aldermen expressed alarm at the fact that many of those who disobeyed the orders of the royal proclamations were excusing themselves on the grounds 'that this Court did countenance or favour their inconformitie'. The aldermen could not afford to give the impression that they were encouraging disobedience, and some of them were deputed to consult with the commissioners in general so as to 'take away all iealovsyes in the rest of the Commissioners of our backwardnes to further the same'. This was no more than a papering over of very obvious cracks, and it was at the instance of the City fathers that royal building policies were presented as grievances before the parliaments of 1621 and 1624. These grievances did not abate during the period of stiffer enforcement in the 1630s, and the City petitioned for redress in November 1632; in vain, for the activities of the commission continued and were later to be roundly condemned by the Long Parliament and to receive specific mention in clause 30 of the Grand Remonstrance of December 1641 dealing with 'the sale of pretended nuisances, as building, in and about London'.[25]

V

It is arguable that the damage wrought to relations between the crown and the City by the issues recounted above might have been less serious if the monarchy had presented a more sympathetic personal image to the citizenry. Arthur Wilson, admittedly a by no means unprejudiced observer but one whose account is borne out by other contemporaries, points the

[24] P.R.O., S.P. Charles I, ccccviii/65; *Cal. S.P.D. 1636–7*, pp. 359, 384.
[25] C.L.R.O., Rep. xxxiv, fos. 202, 223, 238(b)–239(b); Rep. xxxv, fos. 155–155(b); Rep. xlvii, fo. 9; *C.D. 1621*, vi, 24, 292; Gardiner (ed.), *Constitutional Documents*, p. 212; Pearl, pp. 20–1.

contrast between James I and his predecessor early in the new reign.

> While he remain'd in the *Tower*, he took Pleasure in baiting Lions; but when he came aboard, he was so troubled with Swarms, that he fear'd to be baited by the People. And the Parliament now drawing on . . . the King, with the Queen and Prince, Four Days before, rode from the Tower to *Whitehall*; the City and Suburbs being one great Pageant, wherein he must give his Ears leave to suck in their gilded Oratory, tho' never so nauceous to the Stomach. He was not like his Predecessor, the late Queen, of famous Memory, that with a well-pleased Affection, met her People's Acclamations, thinking most highly of her self when she was born upon the Wings of their humble Supplications.

If Sir Simonds D'Ewes is to be believed, there was, however, a most noticeable improvement in the royal attitude and demeanour when James rode in procession through London to open his third parliament in 1621:

> he spake often and lovingly to the people standing thick and threefold on all sides to behold him, 'God bless ye! God bless ye!' contrary to his former hasty and passionate custom, which often, in his sudden distemper would bid a p[ox] or a plague on such as flocked to see him.

Whether the alleged improvement was permanent or temporary, it did not survive James, whose frigid and withdrawn successor was if anything even less capable of responding to manifestations of civic enthusiasm. The story of his abandonment of plans for royal entries into London in 1626 and 1633 has recently been told by D. M. Bergeron. On the former occasion the elaborate and costly arrangements for street shows and pageants which had been made by the citizens in response to the instructions of the earl marshal had to be dismantled, the Lord Chamberlain's peremptory letter to this effect coming near to reducing the traditional demonstration of civic loyalty to the level of a public nuisance obstructing the passage of courtiers in their coaches. In 1633 the City experienced a similar though less expensive disappointment when the king failed to make an expected official entry into London on his return from Scotland where he had honoured Edinburgh with the sort of occasion which he consistently denied to London until, returning from the same land eight years later, he at last deigned to make a ceremonial entry into the capital. This was a successful if unduly and perhaps disastrously belated exercise in royal charm and persuasion which is important in the context of the determined royal attempt to regain lost ground in the City.[26] But the disdain and lack of consideration which were far more characteristic of the courtly attitude in the 1630s are exemplified by an incident in November 1633, when the lord mayor and aldermen were censured by the privy council both for the slovenly and irreverent manner in which they had taken their oaths on an official occasion and for returning home in coaches rather than on horseback in formal procession. All this was part of that increasing emphasis on formality and propriety which characterized the reign, as well as reflecting the government's determination not to allow the citizens to forget their proper place.[27]

Although the lord mayor and aldermen were the recipients of similarly sharp rebukes about their handling of the affairs of the Honourable Artillery Company, a voluntary organization of citizens and gentlemen practising arms and undergoing military training in the Artillery Garden in London, royal interference on this front was by no means entirely unwelcome to the City fathers. No less important than the desirability of encouraging such practices and fostering the martial virtues was that of keeping organizations which were dedicated to these laudable ends in the right hands, an objective which the regulations of the company, whose membership had been doubled to 500 in 1614, had lamentably failed to achieve. As the author of a celebrated royalist tract of the 1640s put it,

For *first* you may well remember when the *Puritans* here did as much abominate the *Military Yard* or *Artillery-Garden*, as *Paris-Garden* it self; they would not mingle with the prophane: but at last when it

---

[26] See below, p. 209.
[27] P.R.O., P.C.R., P.C. 2, XLIII, fos. 322–3; Arthur Wilson, 'The History of England, Being the Life and Reign of James the First' (1653), in White Kennett, *The Complete History of England . . .* II (1719), 667; J. O. Halliwell (ed.), *The Autobiography and Correspondence of Sir Simonds D'Ewes, Bart. during the Reigns of James I and Charles I*, 2 vols. (1845), I, 170; R. Ashton (ed.), *James I by His Contemporaries* (1969), pp. 63–5; D. M. Bergeron, *English Civic Pageantry* (1971), pp. 66–89, 91–2, 94–6, 101–2, 105–9, 111–21, and 'Charles I's Royal Entries into London', *Guildhall Miscellany*, III (1970), 91–7.

was instill'd into them, that the blessed Reformation intended could not be effected but by the sword these Places were instantly filled with few or none but Men of that Faction: We were wont you know to make very merry at their Training, some of them in two Yeares Practice could not be brought to discharge a Musket without winking . . . but after a while they began to affect, yea and compasse the chief Officers of Command, so that when any Prime Commanders dyed, new Men were elected, wholy devoted to that Faction.

Mercurius Civicus may have been exaggerating, but there can be no doubt that by the end of the third decade of the century the infiltration into the company, both of notable Puritans and of other associates of Sir John Eliot and his colleagues in the early parliaments of Charles I, was giving serious cause for alarm. Accordingly on 18 April 1630 the king announced his intention of reverting to the mode of appointment of officers which had originally prevailed when the company had been reconstituted in 1610. Henceforth all the officers of the company, except the treasurer who was to be elected, were to be royal nominees. This state of affairs might well have given rise to the sort of dispute which had occurred during the second decade of the century, when the City had tried in vain to rid itself of an unpopular captain-general who had been appointed by the crown. But the arrangements of 18 April were not adhered to literally. The nomination of all officers except the captain-general was left in practice to the lord mayor and aldermen, and even in the case of the captaincy-general, the king did not insist on appointing to the first subsequent vacancy. This arose from the death of Captain Henry Waller, who had been M.P. for the City in the parliament of 1628–9 and a close associate of Eliot and the other members who had opposed royal policies so bitterly in that parliament. Indeed, the result of the procedure whereby members of the Artillery Company presented the names of a number of candidates from which the court of aldermen selected that of Captain Marmaduke Rawden in November 1631 was eminently satisfactory to the king, though not, it would seem, to the more radical members of the company. This much is made clear by the complaints of an aldermanic deputation to the privy council in March 1632 against 'divers disorderly and mutinous

cariages of sundry persons of the Artilery yard', who had refused
to accept Rawden and elected their own candidate in his place.
The lord mayor and aldermen were sharply rebuked by the
council, which ascribed this and subsequent disorders to the
fact that they had been 'so remisse in vsing that power where-
with his Majesty hath entrusted you'. They were required to
institute an inquiry into the incidents and to punish the offenders. Moreover, it was made clear that, while the pressure of
business might force the king to continue to delegate the
appointment of officers to the lord mayor and aldermen, he
would insist on the full exercise of his right to appoint future
captains-general himself. In these circumstances it is peculiarly
difficult to explain the appointments of a radical president and
deputy of the Artillery Company in 1639, and, more important,
the replacement of Rawden as captain-general by the seasoned
veteran of numerous continental campaigns Philip Skippon, a
man of strong Puritan sympathies who was to play an even
more notable part on the parliamentary side during the Civil
War than his predecessor was to do on that of the king.[28]

Another military question, the appointment of a muster
master, was a source of bitter dispute between crown and City.
As Boynton has demonstrated, the widespread opposition in
England to the government's determination to create a more
efficient militia trained by professional soldiers was due, in part
at least, to local opposition to the county lieutenancy and its
rôle in connection with the allegedly centralizing proclivities of
royal policy. Similarly, from September 1635, when the king
wrote to the lord mayor and aldermen stressing the need for the
City trained bands to be properly instructed under the command of a muster master and recommending his own candidate,
Captain John Fisher, for the post, until the end of the period of
personal government, the issue was to bulk large among the

---

[28] P.R.O., P.C.R., P.C. 2, XLI, fos. 438–9, 450–1, 462–3, 500, 520–1; C.L.R.O., Rep.
  XLVI, fos. 4(b)–5, 7(b)–8, 106(b), 122(b), 127–8, 132, 134–134(b); Rep XLVII,
  fos. 131(b)–132, 143–143(b), 153(b)–154(b); Rep. XLVIII, fos. 118–118(b),
  340; Rep. LII, fo. 104; Rep. LIII, fo. 328; *Remembrancia Index*, pp. 19–24; 'A
  Letter from Mercurius Civicus to Mercurius Rusticus . . .' (1643), *Lord Somers'
  Tracts*, 2nd coll., I (1750), 399; G. A. Raikes, *A History of the Honourable Artillery
  Company*, 2 vols. (1878–9), I, 47–8, 50–6, 70–80, 84–9, 95–6; G. Gould Walker,
  The Honourable Artillery Company (1926), pp. 28, 33–5; Pearl, pp. 170–3.

factors exacerbating royal relations with the City. *Mutatis
mutandis*, the City's objections paralleled those of numerous
local authorities all over England. It pleaded that the care and
ordering of arms and armour traditionally belonged to the lord
mayor and aldermen; that the functions of the muster master
had hitherto been performed with commendable efficiency by
the aldermen, their deputies and the common councilmen in
their various wards; and that the appointment of a professional
muster master would impose additional financial burdens on an
already hard-pressed citizenry, and was likely to prove a potent
disincentive to the practice of those military exercises which
they had hitherto performed so assiduously. These arguments
were successful only insofar as they caused a further delay of
two years before Fisher was finally appointed by the king in
December 1637. But opposition did not end here, and municipal feet continued to be dragged to the great annoyance of
Charles I, who was the recipient over the next two years of a
stream of complaints from Fisher about the City's refusal to
pay his allowance and arrears of salary. Royal rebukes grew
progressively sharper, culminating in a letter of 1 November
1639, informing the lord mayor that any further delays in co-
operating with Fisher would be treated as being in contempt of
royal authority, and would occasion severe disciplinary action
against the City.[29]

Here then is yet another case of what were at best extremely
edgy relations between crown and City, which has been treated
here in the context of military affairs and local grievances,
though it could equally have been considered in chapter 6 as
one of the numerous royal policies which were creating widespread resentment both in the City and in England in general.
It is to such considerations that we must now turn.

[29] C.L.R.O., Jor. xxxviii, fos. 212, 284; Jor. xxxix, fo. 12(b); Rep. l, fos. 1(b)–2
155, 157; *Cal. S.P.D. 1635–6*, p. 286; *Remembrancia Index*, pp. 536–9; Raikes,
Honourable Artillery Company, i, 92–3, 107–9; L. Boynton, *The Elizabethan Militia
1558–1638* (1967), pp. 244–97 and esp. 287–91.

6

The municipality and national issues

The last two chapters have described the large number of serious inconveniences, irritations and frustrations experienced by the business and municipal élites of the City of London. But it might nevertheless be argued that even in the cases where the rôles of business concessionaire and City father were combined in the same person, the evidence, impressive though it may be, does not add up to irrefutable proof of their total alienation from the court, though it certainly goes a long way in that direction. For the principle of hierarchy, subordination and obedience was, after all, indivisible, and was it not better to grit one's teeth and submit uncomplainingly rather than risk the danger that disobedience to the king might spark off similar behaviour in one's own subordinates? The concluding pages of this book will be at pains to emphasize how powerfully such considerations operated as factors drawing the lord mayor and his colleagues towards support for the king and resistance to the policies of Pym and his associates in the autumn and winter of 1641–2. But it would be dangerous to read back the very exceptional circumstances of 1641–2 into previous decades, and if earlier chapters have demonstrated that business concessionaires and City fathers had perforce to yield to royal dictation in the 1630s, this was no more than recognition of a necessity which was accepted reluctantly but not without complaint and serious misgivings. How far did these things contribute to, and how far were they reinforced by, the attitude of the municipal governors to the nation-wide opposition to royal policies which manifested itself with increasing prominence over a wide variety of issues during the 1620s and 1630s?

I

An obvious starting point for this inquiry is to ask whether
the municipality may be said to have developed a distinctive
attitude to any of those events of the 1620s which form so conspicuous a landmark in the development of constitutional
opposition to the crown and, not least, in that of the attitudes
and fortunes of the concessionary interest. It has for instance
been suggested that many contemporaries attached a distinctly
sinister significance to the municipality's willingness to raise
money for the crown on a number of occasions, since this
clearly militated against the success of the strategy of the leaders
of what was fast becoming a co-ordinated parliamentary
opposition.[1] But what stands out more clearly than anything
else from the record of the financial relations between crown
and City is the sorry tale of brutal pressure, unfulfilled obligations, and hard words and abuse. This story may be begun in
1617 when James I raised about £96,400 – he had originally
demanded £100,000 – from the citizens, the vast bulk of the
lenders being secured not by the crown but by the City itself.
To cite in this context the abundant details of the various forms
of coercion applied to the citizens would be to invite the inevitable retort that the unpopularity of the loan with individual
citizens is hardly evidence of the attitude of the governing élite.
On this latter point, official records are, not surprisingly, un-
illuminating, except insofar as it is feasible to draw any conclusions from the complaints of the privy council that delays in
the service of the loan were due 'either to backwardnes and ill
affeccion (which wee would be loath to find in you . . .) or to
the negligent and indescreete carriage of the same', and its
insistence that what it now required from the lord mayor and
his colleagues was 'no further excuses and pretences, but service
and performance'. This rough edge of the council's tongue
brings us far nearer to the realities of the situation than the
decorous platitudes about the City's rôle as the valued and
trusted royal Chamber with which negotiations had begun.
Moreover, the aldermen had been threatened that they might

---

[1] Pearl, pp. 74–6.

be called upon to supply any deficiency in the total sum provided irrespective of whether they had already contributed. This threat at least was not implemented.[2] Certainly no sinister political significance attaches to the loan of £60,000 which was made by the City to Charles I in April 1625, shortly after that king's accession. James I had failed to honour his obligations of 1617, and it was very much in the City's interest to accede to his son's request, since it now received mortgage security to cover both advances. In any case it would have been difficult for the City to refuse to help to tide the king over the expenses incident upon his accession, while the summoning of parliament in the following month made it very clear that the loan had been no part of a royal policy of dispensing with the need to call parliament.[3] However, there were not wanting observers who found political explanations for the City's refusal to lend £100,000 to the king in the summer of the following year. For instance, both the Venetian and the Tuscan envoys in London ascribed this to the widespread feeling in the capital that the money was intended to serve as a substitute for a parliamentary supply, and indeed parliament was dissolved in the same month to rescue Buckingham from the impeachment. The government claimed that the money was needed to meet the danger of foreign invasion, but when ultimately the aldermen themselves consented to raise £20,000 as a poor substitute for the hoped-for £100,000, what seems to have struck contemporaries was not so much the relation of the loan to royal political strategy as its total inadequacy in respect of royal needs – 'scarce enough to buy a dozen points', as one of them put it. To advance such a small sum may well have been an uneasy and ineffective compromise between courses which would have incurred either the censure of the parliamentary opponents of Buckingham or the anger of the privy council, which had already treated the City's refusal to comply with its request for £100,000 with a mixture of scorn and incredulity.[4]

[2] P.R.O., S.P. James I, xc/135; C.L.R.O., Remembrancia, iv, 75, 77, 82, 84; *Cal. S.P.D. 1611–18*, p. 481; *A.P.C. 1616–17*, pp. 219–20, 256–7, 285–6, 298–9; McClure (ed.), *Chamberlain's Letters*, ii, 85; Gardiner, *History*, iii, 197; Ashton, *The Crown and the Money Market*, pp. 122–7.
[3] On this loan see Ashton, *The Crown and the Money Market*, pp. 127–9.
[4] C.L.R.O., Rep. xl, fos. 266(b), 272–272(b); Remembrancia, vi, 89; *A.P.C.*

G

It has been suggested that the City's dissatisfaction with the royal securities offered was more important than political objections in explaining its refusal to lend the full sum demanded by Charles I in 1626 and that this verdict is confirmed by its willingness to make a large advance of £120,000 eighteen months later.[5] But there was nothing wrong with the security offered, and, moreover, very special circumstances attach to the later advance of 1627–8, which make a simple comparison between the two incidents inapposite. For this was no straightforward loan, but one made in return for final settlement of all the crown's outstanding obligations to the citizens, dating back to 1617, by the conveyance of royal lands – the so-called royal contract estates – to trustees for the City who were to sell them off and repay the lenders out of the proceeds. This is not to deny that the City's agreement to the contract and its willingness to advance the first instalment of the £120,000 in January 1628 and the remainder over the succeeding six months was a blow to those who hoped for a speedy recall of parliament following the previous autumn's disaster at the Isle of Rhé and the consequent mounting of agitation against Buckingham to a new crescendo. But there is no reason to assume that these advances in any way reflect municipal support for royal policies or indifference to parliamentary hostility to them, rather than simply a very understandable eagerness to seize any opportunities of escaping from the uncomfortable consequences of the fact that the lenders of 1617 and 1625 held securities from the City rather than from the crown.

It is impossible to discover how far the recorded cases of opposition to the loan from officers of a number of the livery companies, the Brewers, Founders, Plumbers, Saddlers and Girdlers, were due to political and how far to economic considerations. One case, however, did come to acquire a momentous political significance. Nicholas Clegate, a member of the Vintners' Company, was gaoled for refusing to pay his share of the money which that company had assessed upon him and

---

1626, pp. 20–1; Ashton, *The Crown and the Money Market*, pp. 129–31; Pearl, p. 72.

[5] By V. Pearl, pp. 73–4. For a different view of the loan, see Ashton, *The Crown and the Money Market*, pp. 132–41.

twenty-one other brethren. In May 1628 Clegate's case was taken up by an irate House of Commons, which pronounced that he had been imprisoned unlawfully and that the lord mayor and common council had no right to assess the livery companies other than for causes tending to the good of the City, into which category a loan to the crown was not deemed to fall. The Mercers' Company was to use this decision – so clearly derogatory to the lord mayor's authority – as a pretext for making difficulties about providing its contribution towards the last instalment of the £120,000 in the summer of 1628. In the meantime two of the aldermen had in February protested against being assessed towards the provision of a small intermediary instalment, and it comes as a surprise to find that one of them was William Acton, who, later in the same year, was to incur parliament's displeasure for his refusal to grant a replevin in the tonnage and poundage dispute. On this occasion, however, he is found playing a more parliamentary game.[6]

II

It would obviously be unwise to attempt to draw firm conclusions about municipal political sympathies from the evidence relating to royal borrowing. While it is possible that the City's behaviour in 1626 had been influenced by the need to avoid antagonizing influential members of the parliamentary opposition, it might also be argued that in its eagerness to obtain repayment of the contributors to the loans of 1617 and 1625 it had shown itself to be insensitive to the political consequences of its actions and the danger that they might be misconstrued by the parliamentary opponents of the court. The blow struck at mayoral authority by the House of Commons in Clegate's case may well have been in the nature of a parliamentary

---

[6] C.L.R.O., Rep. XLII, fos. 59(b)–60, 61(b), 99–99(b), 167; Remembrancia, VI, 144–6; Vintners' Hall, Transcripts of Court Minutes of Vintners' Company for 1626–9, pp. 29–35, 38–9, 42–3, 48–9; Mercers' Hall, Acts of Court of Mercers' Company 1595–1629, fos. 333–6, 337–9; *Cal. S.P.D. 1627–8*, p. 554; *A.P.C. 1627–8*, pp. 274, 287; *H. of C. J.*, I, 875, 891; *C.D. 1628*, II, 119, 120, 127, 128, 139, 181, 184–5, 380, 381–2, 387, III, 76–8, 81–2, 86, 90; J. R. Jones, 'The Clegate Case', *Eng. Hist. Rev.*, XC (1975), 262–86.

reprisal for this. Against this must be set the crown's successive default on its obligations since 1617, and its peremptory and almost contemptuous treatment of the citizens. Similar rebukes were administered to the municipal authorities when they met a request of 4 August 1626 to provide twenty fully equipped and manned ships for the royal service with a reply that this was quite impossible. The privy council informed the lord mayor and his colleagues that their refusal 'we cannot impute truly to anything but want of duty'. The tale of further threats, the ultimate yielding of the City authorities and their subsequent foot-dragging has been well told by M. C. Wren, who is also at pains to emphasize that it was the opposition of aldermen and common councilmen which first set the example of resistance to the king with which they themselves had ultimately to contend once they had belatedly agreed to the levy. It may well be true that they were moved less by any deeply held political convictions of their own than by their fear – justified in the event – that most of the money would ultimately have to come out of the City funds. Moreover, they were very conscious of the difficulties presented by the sort of conscientious scruples which were held by at least one recalcitrant citizen who went to prison for refusing to pay a levy which he insisted was the thin end of the wedge of arbitrary government. But whatever their motives it is difficult not to see the incident as contributing to the worsening of relations between central government and municipality. For instance, a City deputation which had attempted to compromise with the government by offering only half the number of ships which it demanded plus two pinnaces, to be supplied on impossibly stringent conditions, and had dared to raise the question of precedents for the royal demand, met with an icy reception from the lords of the council, one of whom commented waspishly

that whereas they mention precedents, they may know that the precedent of former times was obedience and not direction; and that there are also precedents of the punishment of those who disobey His Majesty's commandments signified by the Board in the case of the preservation of the State.

The notion of the City fathers acting as the willing henchmen of the government is no more applicable here than it is in the case of government borrowing.[7]

The ship levy was not the only extra-parliamentary exaction which the City had to face in 1626. The autumn of that year saw a nation-wide effort by the government to raise a forced loan whose title, the Loan of Five Subsidies, blatantly underlined its significance as a substitute for the money which Charles I had hoped to raise from parliament before the attempted impeachment of Buckingham had made dissolution inevitable. The growing national opposition to the loan is graphically described by a number of observers, among them the Tuscan envoy in London, who remarked that, if it succeeded, the very name of parliament might be forgotten in England. The five knights whose imprisonment for refusing to pay gave rise to one of the most celebrated cases in Stuart constitutional history had humbler metropolitan counterparts, among them seafaring men dwelling in the eastern suburbs of Wapping, Ratcliffe and Limehouse, who, while declaring their willingness to contribute to a parliamentary subsidy, refused to have any truck with a Forced Loan.[8]

Perhaps because it was loaded with other burdens in 1626, the City itself appears not to have been troubled at first, the government's attention being directed towards Westminster and the suburbs. However, in December 1626 Edward Bate suggested to the Duke of Buckingham that a rich and neglected source of potential contributions was to be found in those citizens who were living obscurely in the country where they were assessed at absurdly low sums. At any rate by the spring of 1627 the City was under severe pressure. As in the suburbs and the provinces, there is evidence not only of widespread resistance but also that the government's displeasure was not confined to obdurate individual citizens but extended to the lord mayor and aldermen themselves. On the failure of all but a few aldermen to appear when summoned before the privy council to be informed of the royal displeasure, the lord mayor was com-

---

[7] M. C. Wren, 'London and the Twenty Ships, 1626–7', *Amer. Hist. Rev.*, LV (1950), 321–35.

[8] P.R.O., S.P. Charles I, LII/72; *Cal. S.P.D. 1625–6*, p. 459; *Cal. S.P.D. Addenda 1625–49*, p. 166; H.M.C., *Eleventh Report*, pt I, pp. 78, 88–9, 92; Gardiner, *History*, VI, 143–4; Sharpe, *London and the Kingdom*, II, 100–1.

manded to recall all those who had taken themselves off to rural retreats, and to allow no one to leave the City until its contribution was paid in. The obdurate were severely dealt with here as elsewhere in England. Apart from the imprisonment of some who, like the celebrated Samuel Vassall, refused to contribute, others in Greater London were made to appear in the Military Gardens near St Martin-in-the-Fields to be enrolled as soldiers. Of the inhabitants of the City, Lord President Manchester reported that they had been roundly dealt with 'as your Majesty commanded and find them to come off this way better than by fair words'. His observation aptly characterizes the government's attitude to the City over matters of finance. It was hardly an attitude designed to foster a sense of mutual trust or harmony of interest. The so-called 'royal Chamber' was a sponge to be squeezed dry.[9]

In an earlier chapter great importance was attached to the issue of tonnage and poundage as one of chief occasions of the splitting of the concessionary interest.[10] Although some prominent City merchants such as Richard Chambers, Samuel Vassall and John Fowke played a prominent part in the dispute, and while at least one of the aldermanic bigwigs, Sir Morris Abbot, himself a prominent commercial concessionaire and former customs farmer, was conspicuous among those refusing to pay duties, the municipality as such was not directly involved. There had, however, been a possibility that it might have been drawn into the dispute, when one of the London sheriffs, William Acton, was called before the bar of the House of Commons in February 1629 to answer the complaint that he had treated a committee of the House with contempt when it was questioning him about his refusal to grant a writ of replevin to John Rolle, the M.P. who was trying to regain possession of his goods which had been confiscated for refusal to pay unparliamentary duties. But Eliot and his colleagues seem to have been conscious of the danger, and made it clear that it was the

[9] P.R.O., S.P. Charles I, LXXI/39, 59, LXXII/60, 62, 63–5; *Cal. S.P.D. 1627–8*, pp. 253, 262, 275; *Cal. S.P.D. Addenda 1625–49*, p. 178; *A.P.C. 1627*, pp. 208–9; *Remembrancia Index*, p. 195; Gardiner, *History*, VI, 144; Sharpe, *London and the Kingdom*, II, 102–3; Pearl, pp. 74–5; D. A. Kirby, 'The Radicals of St. Stephen's Coleman Street, London, 1624–1642', *Guildhall Miscellany*, III (1970), 105–6.

[10] See above, pp. 129–36.

'prevarications and contradictions' of the sheriff rather than the City magistracy itself which was the object of their wrath. In his speech of 9 February 1629, Eliot emphasized that Acton 'was not snared suddenly: but with great caution in regard to the dignity of this house and that Citty'. The point was sufficiently made by sending Acton, who was later rewarded by Charles I with a baronetcy, to spend a few days in the Tower.[11]

III

If ship money had figured prominently as a cause of contention between the City of London and the crown in 1626, it was, of course, to become the most celebrated constitutional issue of the next decade, in London as in the realm as a whole. The immediate reaction of the court of aldermen to the first ship-money writ in November 1634 was to appoint a select committee, not to consider the most expedient way of providing and equipping the required ships, but to ascertain whether the City ought not to be completely exempt from such demands. The committee's report was opposed by common council which, on 2 December, informed the government that its demand was contrary to 'their auntient liberties, Charters and actes of Parliament'.[12] It might be argued that, instead of resting its case on the narrow localist issue of its privileges and liberties, the Londoners should have appealed to more general constitutional principles in the hope of evoking thereby a more truly national response.[13] But if the work of regional historians in recent years has taught us anything it is surely that the defensive conservative localist responses to arbitrary royal policies is connected intimately with the evolution of the so-called country opposition to the Stuarts. Moreover, it is the verdict of a number of them that it was not the initial unconstitutionality, but the threatened permanence of the levy as the result of the issue of later writs, which was the prime cause of local opposition to

---

[11] *H. of C. J.*, I, 928, 929; *C.D. 1629*, pp. 52–3, 56–7, 133–4, 136–7, 181–2, 187–9, 195; Pearl, pp. 78, 190, 244, 291, 314, 316. Eliot's words are in the version given in Grosvenor's diary (*C.D. 1629*, p. 182).

[12] C.L.R.O., Jor. xxxvii, fos. 12–12(b), 19–20; Rep. xlix, fos. 18, 18(b), 45–6, 46(b), 97(b)–98(b); Sharpe, *London and the Kingdom*, II, 111–13.

[13] This would appear to be the view of Pearl (pp. 88–9).

ship money.[14] As to the first writ, as Gardiner long ago pointed out, the action of the lord mayor and his colleagues was unique in its appeal to precedent and principle, at a time when other local authorities were contenting themselves with complaints, not against the levy *per se*, but at the weight of the burdens which were being imposed upon them.[15] Of course, it is possible to contrast the behaviour of protesting and recalcitrant individual citizens, such as the indomitable Richard Chambers, the hero of the tonnage and poundage dispute of the previous decade,[16] with the official policy and the behaviour of the sheriffs of London who attended the privy council weekly to report on the collection.[17] But far too much can be read into these facts, which one suspects are indicative less of shrieval zeal than of the council's need to keep the sheriffs up to the mark. Moreover, in distraining the goods of defaulters and committing some of them to prison,[18] the London sheriffs were doing no more than was being done by their counterparts all over England, among whom were to be found many men who were ultimately to fight against the king in the Civil War. Above all, shrieval obedience to royal commands reflects the fact that the sheriffs were held personally responsible for their collections, and a sheriff who did not wish to court personal financial disaster had little choice but to comply. The details provided by

[14] E.g. T. G. Barnes, *Somerset 1625–1640: A County's Government under the Personal Rule* (1961), p. 206; A. M. Everitt, *The Community of Kent and the Great Rebellion 1640–60* (Leicester, 1966), p. 64; H. A. Lloyd, *The Gentry of South-West Wales 1540–1640* (Cardiff, 1968), pp. 122–3; J. S. Morrill, *Cheshire 1630–1660: County Government and Society during the 'English Revolution'* (1974), pp. 28–30. Cliffe argues that purely constitutional considerations were of greater importance in Yorkshire, but that there was little opposition to the early ship-money writs there (J. T. Cliffe, *The Yorkshire Gentry from the Reformation to the Civil War* (1969), pp. 142, 305). R. W. Ketton-Cremer's chapter on ship money in Norfolk (*Norfolk in the Civil War: A Portrait of a Society in Conflict* (1969), pp. 89–103) offers no opinion on the matter.

[15] Gardiner, *History*, VII, 375–6.

[16] See above, pp. 131, 184.

[17] Pearl (pp. 88–90) is at pains to emphasize the failure of the City government to countenance outright refusal to pay and its co-operation in punishing offenders. But what else could it do?

[18] C.L.R.O., Rep. L., fos. 219(b)–220; Rep LI, fos. 93–93(b); Rep LII, fo. 282(b); Rep. LV, fos. 32(b), 63–63(b), 70, 75, 100–100(b), 127(b), 135–135(b), 199–199(b), 389(b); H.M.C., *Twelfth Report*, pt IV, p. 521; *Remembrancia Index*, pp. 467–8.

Barnes's eloquent account of the wretched lot of the Somerset sheriffs in the ship-money era have parallels all over England.[19] There is, indeed, some evidence that, in the government's view, the behaviour of City officials left much to be desired. At the time of the earlier ship-money writs, when the City had to provide manned and equipped ships and not money, a committee of senior aldermen had been charged with the duty of provision by making arrangements with individual contractors. In January 1638 the members of this committee were called before the privy council in connection with charges contained in an information which had been laid by the attorney-general in the court of exchequer. They were accused of 'undue practices and deceipt' in the year 1636, when the ships provided through their agency had been 'furnished with lesser number of Men, Victualles and Municion, and staid lesse time at Sea then was required by his Majesty's Writt, for the private proffit and gaine to themselves of One thousand poundes and more.' Even though the crown ultimately abandoned the charges against the aldermanic members of the committee, contenting itself with the prosecution of William Bushell, the contractor, it is unlikely that this step was sufficient to bring about a restoration of mutual confidence between city and crown. Moreover, in the following month, the sheriffs of London were severely reprimanded by the privy council for their dilatoriness in the service of ship money.[20]

In January 1639 the court of aldermen sent a deputation to the lord high admiral informing him that the City, with the returns to a previous writ still heavily in arrears, was totally incapable of raising the money for a further ship which had been demanded the previous November. In the event the government refused to yield and the money was provided by assessing the twelve major livery companies, the arrears of £1,800 on the earlier writ being provided out of the City chamber, doubtless to the great relief of the sheriffs who would otherwise have been liable for this sum. As Pearl has emphasized, the last royal

---

[19] Barnes, *Somerset*, pp. 208–41.
[20] P.R.O., P.C.R., P.C. 2., XLVIII, fos. 517–18; C.L.R.O., Rep. L, fos. 75–75(b); Rep. LI, fos. 68(b)–69; Rep. LII, fos. 70–70(b); *Cal. S.P.D. 1637–8*, p. 165; H.M.C., *Twelfth Report*, pt II, p. 175.

attempt to raise ship money in the City in June 1640 was attended by a house-to-house search by the lord mayor, the royalist Sir Henry Garway, and the sheriffs. But their zeal, if zeal it was, did not save them from a sharp rebuke for their neglect. In the matter of ship money, as in so many other matters in the 1630s, the municipal governors appear to have been the unwilling executants of royal policy and the recipients of a great deal more blame than praise.[21]

IV

It remains to inquire what importance should be attached to religion as a divisive issue. Since the question of confessional and ideological differences is a complicated one, it is perhaps as well to begin by examining one source of dispute which, at least on the face of things, was of a more material nature. Tithes, as Christopher Hill has shown in his illuminating chapter on the controversy between the Laudian clergy and the citizens over this matter,[22] were levied, in accordance with the provisions of two Henrician statutes, at 2s. 9d. in the pound on the rental value of property. However, as in the case of so many other institutional revenues, the yield had tended to ossify at an absurdly unreal level. There was a variety of ingenious devices whereby the burden of tithes to the house-holder was kept down, among them the tendency to minimize the level of rents and maximize that of fines, since the latter did not count for tithing purposes. In addition, it was naturally difficult to get newly built or newly divided houses realistically accounted for. Recognizing these deficiences, the court of exchequer had in 1618 decreed that tithes should in future be assessed on the basis of the true annual value of property. Important as this decision undoubtedly was, it raised as many problems as it solved, and although in December 1620 Lord

[21] P.R.O., P.C.R., P.C. 2., LII, fos. 559, 620; C.L.R.O., Rep. LIII, fos. 81, 142(b), 232, 317(b); Bodleian Library, Bankes MSS., v/41; H.M.C., *Twelfth Report*, pt IV, p. 521; Sharpe, *London and the Kingdom*, II, 118, 125–6; Pearl, pp. 90–1. In a letter written on 2 July Edward Taylor states that the sheriffs refused to aid Garway (Bodleian Library, Tanner MSS., 65, fo. 93).

[22] C. Hill, *Economic Problems of the Church from Archbishop Whitgift to the Long Parliament* (Oxford, 1956), pp. 275–88.

Chancellor Verulam was appointed to arbitrate in a dispute which had arisen between the citizens and the London clergy, who were pressing for the implementation of the decision of 1618, nothing specific seems to have emerged by way of a solution. Indeed it was not until William Laud's appointment to the see of London in 1628 that the matter again achieved prominence, coming to a head in 1634, the year following Laud's elevation to Canterbury. In that year the London clergy petitioned the king, reminding him of their poverty and of his failure to implement the decree of 1618. As a result a royal commission was set up, which called before it individual Londoners of whom the parsons had made particular complaint. At the same time the municipal authorities were required to enter into negotiations with the London clergy, with a view to establishing a *modus vivendi* about assessment of tithes. There ensued a prolonged exercise in municipal delaying tactics, the City insisting on separate negotiations being conducted in every parish.[23]

At the end of December 1634 the business was referred to royal arbitration. But, as late as the spring of 1638, when the clergy again petitioned Charles I and at last succeeded in obtaining the important concession that tithe cases should be heard in the spiritual and not in the temporal courts, a royal decision in the matter of assessment was still not forthcoming. Perhaps, as Hill has suggested, the king was reluctant to add yet another issue to the already lengthy catalogue of matters in dispute between himself and the municipality. Rather than make the decision himself, he probably still hoped that the matter would be settled by negotiations pressed forward at his own insistence. But there can be no doubt that, as in so many other issues of the 1630s, the citizens were pressed on to the defensive and, when ordered either to accept or to refute with their own alternative figures the clergy's estimate of rental values – now calculated on the new basis of a so-called 'moderated rent', some 25 per cent below the true rent – they again

[23] C.L.R.O., Jor. xxx, fo. 320; Jor. xxxi, fos. 72, 121(b); Jor. xxxvii, fos. 11–12 12(b), 20–20(b); Rep. xlii, fo. 24(b); Rep. xlviii, fos. 362(b)–363, 367(b) 385(b); Rep. xlix, fo. 18(b); Remembrancia, v, 86, 93; *Remembrancia Index*, pp 137–8.

had recourse to delaying tactics. These seem to have been successful, although it is very likely that, if it had not been for the crisis resulting from the outbreak of the Scottish war, Laud would have succeeded in the aim, noted in his diary and later brought up against him at his impeachment, 'To see the Tythes of London setled betweene the Clergy & the Citty'.[24]

The case for improvement was a strong one. The position of the incumbent of the substantial parish of St Magnus London Bridge was by no means untypical. His tithes – not all of which he was able to collect – amounted to £81 2s. 8d., while the 'true tithe' calculated on the revised estimate of 'moderated rents' was reckoned at £287 12s., which is unlikely to be a wild overestimate, since it was subject to counter-check against the citizens' figures. The parson of St Faith under St Paul's complained of the practice of double-think in the sphere of property assessment, pointing out that 'I have no parsonage house and though when they pay tithes they reckon houses to me at £4 per ann. rent, yet when I come to hire them I cannot have them for £30 per ann.' It could well be that Thomas Westfield who, while well aware of the desirability of improvement, pronounced himself to be 'so well satisfied as that I find no cause to complain for relief', was fortunate in that no part at all of his annual parochial income in the parish of St Bartholomew-the-Great, amounting to about £100, consisted of tithes. But he was also exceptional, and for most incumbents tithes, as opposed to casual revenues such as the Easter collection, fees for weddings, funerals and (where applicable) lectures, made up by far the most important part of their income.[25] Parishes such as St Peter upon Cornhill, where the tithe revenue amounting to £100 was supplemented by substantial additional revenues amounting in all to £69 10s., all but £11 10s. of which came from the very extensive glebeland, were relatively unusual. And there were some parsons who were even unable to lay their hands on the parish tithes. Sometimes this arose

---

[24] C.L.R.O., Jor. xxxvii, fos. 34–34(b), 36–8; Jor. xxxviii, fos. 107, 108–9, 133–133(b), 168–168(b); H.M.C., *House of Lords MSS.* xi, *Addenda 1514–1714,* 379; *Remembrancia Index,* p. 138.

[25] The relationship between tithing and other forms of parochial revenue can easily be checked from the clerical returns of the value of livings reproduced in T. C. Dale (ed.), *The Inhabitants of London in 1638* (1931), *passim.*

from their difficulty in coping with recalcitrant property owners like the Mr Banks in Cheapside who 'refuseth to pay the old tithes' due to the parish of St Vedast Foster Lane. And sometimes tithes were in the hands of an impropriator. Not only the tithes but also all the casual revenues including even the Easter collection and amounting in all to £89 12s. went to the impropriator of the parish of All Hallows Staining who paid the working curate a beggarly stipend of £8. St Gregory near St Paul's was an impropriation of the warden and petty canons of that cathedral who farmed out the tithes to the parishioners at a rent of £40 6s. 4d. and refused to provide details of the actual tithe yield – one estimate put it at about £80 – out of which they paid their curate a mere £10 per annum. More generous were the dean and chapter of Windsor, impropriators of the rectory of St Benet Fink, who allowed £26 13s. 4d. to their curate out of a total net parochial income of about £64.[26]

The Londoners' determination not to play Laud's game may owe something to a belief, still common today, that it ill befitted clergymen, however hard pressed they might be economically, to seek improvement in their incomes. It may have been in response to such arguments that, as early as 1620, the London parsons had been at pains to emphasize that

the Ministers seeke not such an excessive increase as they are vniustlie charged withall, but desire in all peace that some course may bee taken that seinge the Raker of your streets hath had his wages in some wardes raysed thrice within xx^tie yeare and little more, you would not with contempt cast of those that are to give accompt of your soules in the great daie of the lord Jesus Christ, especiallie in this Case of soe great equitie and conscience.

On balance, however, dislike of Laudian ecclesiastical practices was probably a more potent factor than civic meanness, for the citizens were generous enough in contributing towards religious causes of which they approved. According to the Laudian rector of St Martin Orgar, among the chief influences persuading the citizens to keep down the level of tithes were the Puritan non-beneficed lecturers in whose interest it was to divert resources from the incumbents to themselves. Moreover,

[26] Ibid. pp. 38–9, 59–61, 65–8, 94–6, 176–8, 198.

as Hill points out, the reduction of fixed payments to a minimum allowed of their supplementation by voluntary augmentations which were not only in the control of the citizens, but could also be restricted to clerics of whose religious views and practices they approved. This was not the least important reason why the problem of lectureships was to become a crucial bone of contention.[27]

To understand this problem[28] it is necessary to appreciate certain basic facts about the nature of church patronage in London. As both Williams and Seaver have emphasized, the main reason why so few London parishes had Puritan incumbents in this period is that the right to present to more than two-thirds of the benefices in the City was in the hands either of the church or the crown.[29] Clearly if the word of Puritan truth were to be diligently preached, other means had to be adopted and the response of many godly parishioners to this situation was to introduce what a hostile observer described as 'that *Gibbus* or *Excresency* of the Clergy called *Lecturers* over their *Parochiall Ministers* Heads'.[30] To a churchman of high clerical temper such as William Laud, who became bishop of London in 1628, such arrangements were an abomination, since they necessarily involved a strong measure of secular control over spiritual activities. In cases where the incumbent met with the approval of those of his parishioners or the other lay authorities who controlled the finance for lectureships, he might be allowed to give the lectures and receive the appropriate augmentation to his stipend. For example, a number of the successive incumbents of the parish of St Bartholomew-by-the-Exchange also held parish lectureships. By a will dated 30 March 1625 this parish was to become the grateful recipient of a bequest of £500 from Richard Fishborne, the income from which,

---

[27] C.L.R.O., Remembrancia, v, 86; C. Hill, *Economic Problems of the Church*, pp 277–9.

[28] My research on the London lectureships was completed before the appearance. of the admirable and definitive study of Paul S. Seaver, *The Puritan Lectureships: The Politics of Religious Dissent 1560–1662* (Stanford, Calif., 1970), the second part of which is an exhaustive account of the situation in London.

[29] D. A. Williams, 'London Puritanism: The Parish of St. Stephen, Coleman Street', *Church Q. R.*, CLX (1959), 464–5; Seaver, *Puritan Lectureships*, pp. 171, 191–2.

[30] 'A Letter from Mercurius Civicus to Mercurius Rusticus' (1643), *Lord Somers' Tracts*, 2nd coll., i (1750), 400.

administered through the Mercers' Company, was to finance an additional weekly lecture. The incumbent's position in respect of this lecture is made abundantly clear by the terms of the bequest:

> ye parish from *time to time* [is] to make *Choyce* of ye Preacher, wherein ye *parson of ye parish* if he be a *fit* man to giue ye parish Content [is] then to be *preferred* before others. But if ye parish shall not *like* of him to this purpose, then they [are] to make Choice of *some other* as they in *their discretion* shall think fit.

Since the current incumbent was an unpopular Laudian cleric it is hardly surprising to find that the first appointment to Fishborne's lectureship in December 1628 was an outsider.[31] Similarly, between 1629 and 1640 the parishioners of St Peter upon Cornhill appointed a series of non-beneficed clergymen rather than their parson to give Sunday-afternoon lectures.[32]

There are a number of points at which the problem of non-beneficed lecturers touches the relations between the City fathers and the government of church and state. As early as 1617 the refusal of the bishop of London to accept the traditional aldermanic nomination of three lecturers (two of them Doctors of Divinity) to preach at St Mary's Hospital during Easter week had aroused sufficient resentment to precipitate an appeal from the aldermen to the privy council.[33] But the reign of Charles I and the Laudian ascendancy was the time of the sharpest contention. One of the *causes célèbres* of that reign was the case brought by the crown in 1633 against the so-called Feoffees for Impropriations, an active group of City Puritans, headed by the lord mayor, Sir Nicholas Rainton, and devoting itself to the purchase of impropriated ecclesiastical revenues

[31] London Guildhall MSS., 4384/1 (V.M., St Bartholomew-by-the-Exchange 1547–1643), fos. 364–5, 391, 406; Jordan, *Charities of London*, pp. 115, 287; Seaver, *Puritan Lectureships*, p. 143.

[32] London Guildhall MSS., 4165/1 (V.M., St Peter upon Cornhill 1574–1714), fos. 196, 200, 236, 259, 264. There are however a number of examples of *modi vivendi* being established even between Laudian incumbents and Puritan lecturers whereby the former, in return for a consideration, undertook not to make trouble (London Guildhall MSS., 4165/1, fos. 196, 200; ibid. 4425/1 (V.M., St Christopher-le-Stocks 1593–1731), fos. 19(b), 20, 20(b), 21(b), 24, 31, 32; C. Hill, *Society and Puritanism in Pre-Revolutionary England* (1964), pp. 110–11; D. A. Williams, 'London Puritanism: The Parish of St. Botolph without Aldgate', *Guildhall Miscellany*, II (1960), 32).

[33] *Remembrancia Index*, pp. 367–8.

and the application of them to godly causes. Amongst other things it was claimed that the Feoffees appointed lecturers over the heads of incumbents with the deliberate aim of countering their influence and breeding 'difference and Jarring'. It was the essence of Attorney-General Noy's case against the Feoffees that they showed a distinct preference for applying these revenues to the establishment of 'dative lecturers' removable at their pleasure rather than to the augmentation of the stipends of beneficed clergymen, except in the case of parsons of whose opinions they approved. In this the Feoffees, who were dissolved in 1633, were not the only, even if they were the most spectacular, offenders.[34]

The change in the attitude of the municipal government to the famous lectures at St Antholin Budge Row has been seen as one of a number of indications of the cooling of Puritan ardour among the City fathers in the face of the Laudian policies of the 1630s. In 1630 the City governors refused to renew their annual contribution of £40 which they had made since 1622 towards the cost of these lectures, a decision which has been interpreted as the conservative response of the aldermanic governors to the taking over of the management of the lectures by the Feoffees for Impropriations, who were themselves by this time the objects of suspicion to Laud and the government.[35] Now while it is more than likely that such considerations may have weighed quite heavily with cautious, if by no means altogether unsympathetic, aldermen for whom discretion in such matters was normally very much the better part of valour, it is worth emphasizing that the origin of the withdrawal of official City support for the lectures is historically to be found in a decision dating from before Laud's accession to the see of London. It therefore antedates by several years the beginnings of the questioning of the practices of the Feoffees. In 1627 the alder-

---

[34] I. M. Calder (ed.), *Activities of the Puritan Faction of the Church of England 1625–1633* (1957), pp. 59, 82–3; C. Hill, *Economic Problems of the Church*, pp. 258–63; Seaver, *Puritan Lectureships*, pp. 88–9; E. W. Kirby, 'The Lay Feoffees: A Study in Militant Puritanism', *J. Mod. Hist.*, XIV (1942), 1–25; Calder, 'A Seventeenth Century Attempt to Purify the Anglican Church', *Amer. Hist. Rev.*, LIII (1948), 760–75.

[35] Pearl, pp. 79, 164–5; D. A. Williams, 'Puritanism in the City Government 1610–1640', *Guildhall Miscellany*, I (1955), 3–8.

men had demanded as the price of their continued support that they should have the right to nominate to the lectureship next falling vacant, phrasing their demand in such a way that any thing but a negative reply from the parishioners would be taken to imply their consent. Accordingly the grant continued, no lectureship having fallen vacant. In the meantime, however, the management of the lectures had come into the hands of the Feoffees, so that when, in November 1630, following an aldermanic decision of the previous month to renew the grant, the court declared itself willing to renew it on condition of its having 'the nominacion and Choise of one of the Lecturers when any one of the said places shall . . . become voyd', this was in essence no more than a reiteration of the 1627 decision, which was now made necessary by the Feoffees' claim to control all the lectures. Faced by the unpleasant choice of losing either the City's or the Feoffees' contribution, it is hardly surprising that the parishioners chose the former, since the Feoffees had made it clear not only that they would withdraw their far more substantial financial support in the event of their being denied total control, but that they were willing to replace from their own resources any contribution from elsewhere which might either fall short or be withdrawn.[36]

Sabbatarianism is another of the issues frequently cited in support of the thesis of diminished City ardour for Puritan causes in the 1630s. More than once during the early 1620s the City authorities had sought to obtain the co-operation of their bishop in the suppression of 'divers abuses and disorders Comitted within this Cittye to the profanacion of the Sabboath daye'. Whatever the nature of the episcopal response to such appeals, there can be no doubt that the elevation of Laud, with his notorious enthusiasm for saints' days and dislike of Sabbatarianism, to the see of London in 1628 gave just grounds for misgivings. Indeed the lord mayor and his colleagues soon fell foul of the new bishop over their arrest of an apple woman for going about her business in Paul's churchyard on the Sabbath,

[36] C.L.R.O., Rep. xl, fo. 243; Rep. xli, fos. 366(b)–367; Rep. xliv, fo. 369; Rep. xlv, fos. 25(b)–26; Calder (ed.), *Puritan Faction*, pp. xvi, xx, 40, 70–2, 79, 83, 90–1, 96, 100, 136, and *Amer. Hist. Rev.*, liii (1948), 766–7; E. W. Kirby, *J. Mod. Hist.*, xiv (1942), 10–11.

and hereafter aldermanic zeal for the punishment of Sabbath-
breakers seems to have diminished, or at least to have been
repressed, re-emerging during the period of Puritan triumph
which followed Laud's downfall at the beginning of the next
decade. During the 1630s, therefore, the City fathers seem to
have toned down their Sabbatarian inclinations, and not to have
offered any resistance even to the insistence on the observance
of the saints' days which were so repellent to the Puritan conscience. The complaint of a London stationer in 1639 that,
while he dared not sell parchment on Ascension Day, he might
do so with impunity on the Sabbath probably echoed the feelings
of many godly tradesmen in those dark days.[37]

If there is one factor which is common to all the Laudian
policies which brought the hierarchy into conflict with the City
over some of the questions described above, it is the determination not only to improve the income but also to elevate the
status and dignity of the clergy. This central feature of Laudian-
ism also finds expression in a number of other matters at issue
between the City and the church. Some of these may seem
trivial and petty to the modern reader, but were crucially
significant in an age which attached enormous importance to
symbols of hierarchy and degree. Such were, for example, the
quarrels between the lord mayor and the dean and chapter of
St Paul's over the former's attempt to exercise civic jurisdiction within Paul's churchyard, and the disputes which came
to a head in 1633 about the bearing of the lord mayor's sword
at the head of the civic procession entering St Paul's for divine
service. Similar practices survive to this day on the occasion of
civic services in English cathedrals and churches, and this one
in particular was amply backed by tradition, despite the dean
and chapter's claim that it was 'contrary to the rightes and
customes of the said Church'. Although the matter was technically a dispute between the lord mayor and the dean and
chapter (rather than the bishop) it is difficult not to see the un-
compromising spirit of Laud behind the fortitude of the capitu-
lar body, and it may have been his elevation to Canterbury in

---

[37] C.L.R.O., Rep. xxxiv, fo. 324; Rep. xxxvi, fo. 4; Rep. xxxviii, fos. 9(b), 33;
Rep. lvi, fo. 1(b); Pearl, p. 79; C. Hill, *Society and Puritanism*, p. 158; D. A.
Williams, *Guildhall Miscellany*, i (1955), 8–9.

1633 which enabled the matter to slip quietly out of sight thereafter.[38]

However, there was another matter relating to the great cathedral church of London that was to be pressed even more insistently after Laud had left London to become primate of all England. This was his zeal for the reparation and re-edification of St Paul's cathedral. Although Elizabeth I had made a substantial contribution to the rebuilding of Paul's steeple after it had been struck by lightning in 1561, the shocking state of disrepair revealed by reports in the 1580s, with breaches in the walls and the gutter leads removed, is symptomatic of the neglect and indifference which characterized the attitude of so many Elizabethans to the care of the fabric of churches. James I began his reign by offering £500 as a gift to the City if it would undertake the repair of Paul's steeple and other works, but it was not until 1620, after an official visit of the king to hear a sermon in St Paul's, which had been heralded by the demolition of unsightly buildings in the immediate vicinity, that a royal commission was set up to manage the matter. But initial enthusiasm seems rapidly to have waned, and the really constructive and vital period of reform can be dated from Laud's translation to the bishopric of London in 1628. The verdict that the subsequent enthusiasm for the re-edification of London churches was due to the continuous prodding of a sullen and reluctant public by Laud and the privy council is certainly truer of St Paul's than it is of the many parish churches of the City and suburbs which underwent considerable improvement often at great expense. Nor was the expense of the operation the only objection to it. Inigo Jones's inspired creation of a new west front for the cathedral church, as well as other alterations, involved the demolition of some adjacent buildings, among them the parish church of St Gregory, whose parishioners were to clamour to the Long Parliament in July 1641 for repair of the damage, estimated at being likely to cost £3,000, and for proceedings to be taken against those responsible for it. Although the appeal for St Paul's had been made on a national basis, Laud and the government had hoped for a particularly generous response from the City not only on account of its great wealth but also because St Paul's after all lay in the very heart of the City itself. But, despite the very heavy and unwelcome pressure to which the City fathers were subjected, these expectations were very sadly disappointed. Particularly unwelcome no doubt to the lord mayor and his colleagues was the contrast which both Laud and the privy council were at pains to stress, between royal generosity and municipal parsimony, and the emphasis upon the 'scandall to our Religion & ... imputacion & disgrace vpon that Cittie in perticular' resulting from 'soe backward and could [*sic*] effects of deuocion in ye Cittie to repaire that famous & auncient Churche'. Pearl's observation that during the 1630s the City reversed the process of supporting Puritan causes in favour of contributing towards St Paul's and other churches ought not to be taken to imply that these contributions were simply the product of its openhanded enthusiasm.[39]

V

The end of Charles I's personal government was heralded by the outbreak of war with the Scots in 1639. In March, in response to a royal demand for financial assistance and for the secondment of 3,000 men from the City trained bands, the City grubbed together the totally inadequate sum of £5,000. If this had actually been offered to the king, it would almost certainly have been refused, since it had been common council's intention to present it along with a petition complaining of abuses such as monopolies, high prices and the requirement that citizens should serve in campaigns other than for the defence of London. Charles's attempt to raise a loan of £100,000 in June was a distinctly damp squib, and he was fobbed off

[39] C.L.R.O., Rep. xlv, fos. 499–500(b), 514; Rep. xlvi, fo. 203; Rep. xlviii, fos. 320–321(b); Remembrancia, vii, 88, 105, 122; Remembrancia, viii, 85, 122; *A.P.C. 1619–21*, p. 165; H.M.C., *Fourth Report*, pt i, 89; *H. of C. J.*, ii, 35–6, 216; *H. of L.J.*, iv, 321; *Remembrancia Index*, pp. 322–9; W. S. Simpson (ed.), *Documents Illustrating the History of St. Paul's Cathedral*, Camden Soc., n.s., xxvi (1880), 134–5; H. R. Trevor-Roper, *Archbishop Laud* (2nd edn, 1963), pp. 121–6, 346–7, 350–1, 428–9; Jordan, *Charities of London*, pp. 270, 294–7, 301–7; Pearl, p. 79.

with a free gift of £10,000 instead.[40] Certainly the attitude of many of the chief citizens was anything but co-operative. The refusal of the lord mayor, Sir Morris Abbot, merchant prince and royal concessionaire though he was, and of all but two of the aldermen to appear before the privy council when summoned there in the service of the loan; the fact by no means all of them appeared in response to a sharper summons three days later; the refusal of the lord mayor and fifteen of those who did appear on this occasion to do anything for the king; the comment of one of the lords of the council that the negative response of the aldermen would have been more convincing if they had sold their gowns and chains first – all these things suggest that a prolongation of the accumulated bitterness resulting from the disputes of the 1630s and an accentuation of that bitterness as a result of courtly tactlessness and arrogance[41] may have contributed very powerfully to the City's attitude. Doubtless Strafford's observation that the king's affairs might be expedited by hanging some of the more recalcitrant aldermen was made in exasperation and not intended to be taken literally, but he had a great deal to be exasperated about. The initial demand for a loan in April had coincided with the meeting of the Short Parliament, and the then lord mayor, Sir Henry Garway, whose sympathies with the government were never in doubt, had been ordered to compile a list of rich citizens who would contribute. Pressure was also applied to individual aldermen by the privy council, but with very indifferent success, and the situation was worsened by the royal dissolution of parliament. The incident which had provoked Strafford's outburst was the refusal of seven of the aldermen to draw up lists of the richest residents in their wards and the fact that many who complied did so with obvious reluctance. The final outcome was that the

[40] Pearl (pp. 96–8) explains this incident chiefly in terms of the prevailing tightness of credit in the City and the unsatisfactory securities offered for the loan. Since, however, she is normally ready to ascribe City *willingness* to lend to political sympathy with the government rather than to prevailing conditions in the money market and the worth of royal securities, parity of reasoning would suggest that other than financial considerations may well have been more important in City *reluctance* to lend than she is willing to concede.

[41] For examples see Bodleian Library, Clarendon MSS., 17, fos. 23, 24–24(b); also Ashton, *The Crown and the Money Market*, pp. 77, 180–1.

City agreed to lend £200,000, but only after it had been made clear that another parliament was to be called, and even then the £200,000 was to be doled out in carefully spaced instalments to ensure that this was not to be another Short or Addled Parliament.[42]

Although Pearl is obviously right to emphasize the rôle of the City parliamentary Puritans in ensuring the success of these delaying tactics, it would be a mistake to see the situation in terms of the polarization of extremes. There can, of course, be no doubt that among the aldermen were men like Alderman Abell, the notorious wine monopolist, and the lord mayor, Sir Henry Garway, who would have been happy to further the service of the loan without insisting on the political safeguards which were eventually secured. But by no means all of those who had opposed a loan in 1639 and who had insisted on such safeguards in 1640 were extremists at the opposite pole to Garway and Abell. And in this the temper of the City reflected that of the political nation. Just as in England in general many men who were ultimately to fight on the royalist side in the Civil War welcomed the summoning of the Long Parliament and supported its earlier measures limiting royal powers and restoring the imagined ancient constitutional equipoise, so were there among the City fathers men who, unlike the customs farmers and the monopolists, had everything to hope and nothing to fear from a reforming parliament, and looked back on the royal policies of the 1630s with distaste. If any general conclusion can be drawn from the developments which have been described in the last three chapters, it is that these developments must have contributed spectacularly to the growth of the influence and numbers of those holding such opinions.

[42] Ashton, *The Crown and the Money Market*, pp. 180–4; Sharpe, *London and the Kingdom*, II, 119–31; Pearl, pp. 94–104.

7

Conclusion

It is an established historical commonplace which finds regular expression in first-year-undergraduate and sixth-form essays that when the Long Parliament assembled in November 1640, the vast bulk of its members, including many who were ultimately to fight for the king in the Civil War, had been alienated from the existing régime of royal personal government, the dismantling of which over the succeeding months met with their complete approbation. Accordingly the central interest of the period of almost two years down to the outbreak of the war is correctly seen to reside in the need to explain the defection from the parliamentary cause of many of those who had opposed ship money and the centralizing tendencies of government in the 1630s, and who were delighted to get rid of Strafford and to vote for legislation which, while curtailing the royal prerogative and clipping the wings of the main instruments of the so-called eleven years' tyranny, ensured that parliament would be a regular feature of English constitutional life. Down to the recess in the autumn of 1641 the parliamentary reforms commanded very general approval. At the same time the king's concessions, albeit made under duress, fostered hopes of a new rapprochement between king and parliament. These hopes were shattered by the renewed offensive of Pym and his allies after the recess and a further and far less generally applauded assault on the prerogative. Thus it was that royal acquiescence in the early reforms of the Long Parliament combined with renewed parliamentary usurpation of the royal prerogative after the recess of 1641 to generate a flow of sympathy back to the king, and to ensure, for example, that the Grand Remonstrance passed the House of Commons on 22 November only by a handful of votes.

Clearly the conclusions of the last three chapters fit very comfortably into this general picture. Like the vast majority of the rest of the political nation, the City, with the exception of a small minority of concessionaires, was alienated. The relations of the majority of business concessionaires with the crown and court had been put to an intolerable strain. Already by the beginning of Charles I's experiment in personal rule in 1629, some measure of rapprochement had been achieved between the chief opponents of royal policies in the House of Commons and the privileged chartered companies. In this process company disillusionment about the unreliability of royal support and the constitutional disputes in the early parliaments of Charles I's reign on the subject of tonnage and poundage appear to have played crucial parts. Although some of the companies managed to regain part of the lost ground during the 1630s, developments such as the royal support for Courteen's rival East India association with its strong backing at court must have aroused uneasy recollections of that first great shock to company confidence, the Cockayne project of 1614. Accordingly the tentative alliance forged in the heat of the parliamentary crisis of 1628–9 seems to have survived into the Long Parliament, which certainly saw no sustained attack on the chartered companies to match those of its predecessors in 1604 and 1621 and its own onslaught on the patentees and the customs farmers. The period of a determined parliamentary assault on a crown-backed commercial exclusivism is the reign of James I, not that of his son. If the arguments of an earlier chapter about the loosening of the ties of economic interest between the court and important sectors of the concessionary interest are accepted, it must follow that only among domestic concessionaires such as patentees and customs farmers did such ties continue to carry much weight. And here it will be useful to recall our earlier findings about the concessionary interests of the aldermen.[1] Of the thirty aldermen in 1640–1, only nine held such domestic concessionary interests, a significant proportion of the whole, but nothing approaching a majority, let alone a preponderance. It is only if we include directoral

---

[1] See above, pp. 34–42.

interests in chartered companies that the proportion of aldermen with one sort of concessionary interest or another becomes
really striking, and the argument that such commercial interests did not necessarily dispose the directors in question
towards the court has already been sufficiently emphasized
and hardly requires stressing yet again. Similarly the municipal
government was involved during the 1630s in a wide variety of
disputes with the crown which would reinforce any general
sense of alienation which its members might share with the
overwhelming majority of their compatriots, who were falling
out of sympathy with the personal government of Charles I at
an alarming rate. It is no less difficult to reconcile these disputes
with the notion of a continued orientation of the City fathers
towards the court rather than the country without reducing
the issues to the status of minor irritants. If the account which
has been given of these disputes in the two preceding chapters
is to be credited, they were a great deal more than that.

While, therefore, there is nothing in these findings to contra-
dict the standard account of the rôle of the City in the genesis
of the Civil War, which argues that a pro-royalist municipal
government had to be captured by Pym's supporters in the
City before its support for parliament could be assured in the
forthcoming struggle, they do cast very serious doubts on its
generally accepted corollary that the City government was in
close alignment with the court during the 1630s and at the time
of the calling of the Long Parliament.[2] In actual fact the choice
before the aldermen in 1640 was far less stark and more complex than a simple decision to support either the earl of Strafford
or John Pym. To suggest that the events which form the subject
of a large part of this book might predispose most of the members of the aldermanic bench to support the destruction of

---

[2] Pearl, pp. 276–7. For a more extreme statement of this view, see Brenner,
P. & P., no. 58 (1973), 53–65, 72–6. Brenner, does, however, admit that
'significant numbers of citizens who were conservative in the municipal political
context seem to have been initially favourable to parliamentary reform at the
national level'. It is perhaps worth emphasizing that support for moderate
parliamentary reforms was a perfectly natural conservative stance. It was the
crown, or its advisers, it was argued, who had been guilty of innovation; in
which circumstances the early reforms of the Long Parliament might be seen as
the restoration of a constitutional equilibrium which had been shattered by the
eleven years' tyranny.

Strafford[3] and the dismantling of the machinery of royal personal government is not to equate them with radicals such as Henry Marten, John Pym or even Denzil Holles. For the reformist programme at this point also attracted the support of men such as Falkland and Hyde who were ultimately to fight against parliament in the Civil War. In other words, not the least attractive feature of this thesis is that it fits conveniently into the national picture. It offers an explanation of the royalism of many of the City fathers which harmonizes well with the central phenomenon of the political history of these months: the defection of a strong nucleus of constitutional royalists, led by Hyde and Falkland, from the cause of further parliamentary reform. In a word the municipal revolution of 1641–2 took place not because the aldermanry had been consistent supportors of royal absolutism from the beginning, but because the events of these months'had precipitated a significant move to the right in aldermanic circles.[4]

II

This rightward movement was a response to developments both in the City and at Westminster. As to the former, thanks to the researches of Pearl, the details of the radical offensive in the City are familiar enough and need only be summarized briefly here.[5] First came 'the most extreme stir about choosing a Lord Mayor that ever was known' in September 1640, when Common Hall refused to follow the long-accepted practice of electing the senior alderman to the mayoral chair, since in this case

[3] After all it was Strafford who had threatened to hang recalcitrant aldermen (see above, p. 199, and Pearl, p. 100). Although the London petition of April 1641 against Strafford, of which the number of signatories was variously computed at 8,000, 20,000 and 30,000, emanated from radical elements rather than from the aldermen, it is unnecessary to postulate aldermanic hostility to the parliamentary reformers from the beginning of the Long Parliament. Even Sir Henry Garway, the royalist lord mayor, one recalls, gave evidence against Strafford at his trial (H.M.C., *Twelfth Report*, pt II, pp. 278, 280; Pearl, pp. 100, 205, 216, 300).

[4] At least one contemporary regarded the election of the strongly royalist Richard Gurney as lord mayor in 1641 as a clear sign of the turn of the tide and an example which might well be followed elsewhere (*Cal. S.P.D. 1641–3*, p. 132).

[5] Pearl, pp. 107–59, 237–84.

the senior alderman happened to be Sir William Acton who 'would not be endured; the good service he did in the business of poundage and tonnage sticks yet in the city's stomachs'. The significance of this incident was certainly not lost on the king and the privy council.[6] Then there was the securing via elections in Common Hall of a radical representation for the City in what was to become the Long Parliament, and several months after this, in June 1641, the claim of Common Hall – again running contrary to constitutional practice – to elect both of the sheriffs as well as the city chamberlain, bridgemaster and the auditors of accounts, a claim which, in the case of the sheriffs, was upheld by the House of Lords to the consternation of the lord mayor and the more conservative aldermen.[7]

The crucial breakthrough came with the elections to common council in December 1641, when that body was effectively captured for the radical party. According to one observer who approved of the change, the old displaced common councilmen were 'so superbious in their Offices, *that they did tyrannicallie* insult over others . . . so inexcusable, delinquent and peccant, [that] they were incontinently excluded from their corrupt Offices and New Common-Councell-men elected in their Places'.[8] Needless to say, not everyone took the same view.

Now [wrote one later royalist sympathizer] outgoe all the grave, discreet, well-affected Citizens . . . and in their Stead are chosen *Fowke* the Traytor, *Ryley* the Squeeking Bodyes-maker, *Perkins* the Taylor, *Norminton* the Cutler, young beardlesse *Coulson* the Dyer,

---

[6] *Cal. S.P.D. 1640–1*, p. 115; H.M.C., *Montagu of Beaulieu MSS.*, p. 128; *Clarendon S.P.*, II, 124, 125, 128; *Cal. Clarendon S.P.*, I, 207–8. After some confusion Alderman Edmund Wright was chosen. For Acton's part in the tonnage and poundage dispute of 1628–9, see above, pp. 184–5.

[7] *H. of L. J.*, IV, 292, 293, 303–4, 316, 329, 334, 336, 364, 373, 376–7; H.M.C., *Fourth Report*, pt I, pp. 79, 84, 88, 91, 92, 95, 97, 98, 99.

[8] J. Bond, *The Downfall of the Old Common-Counsel Men* (1642) (London Guildhall pamphlet, no. 2588). For decisions about the disputed common-council elections, see C.L.R.O., Jor. XL, fos. 16, 21–3, 24(b), 26–26(b). For two quite different views of the significance of these elections, see Wren, *Eng. Hist. Rev.*, LXIV (1949), 34–52, and Pearl, pp. 132–9. While the arguments of the preceding chapters of this book must make it clear that I have much sympathy with Wren's view that municipal disquiet at royal policies had been increasing since the beginning of the reign, I am not convinced by his argument that the changes wrought in December 1641 were of relatively minor significance.

Gill the Wine-Cooper, and *Jupe* the Laten-man in *Crooked-Lane*, *Beadle* of the Ward, in the Place of *Deputy Withers*.[9]

After this great radical victory constitutional changes followed thick and fast, and the reader is referred to Pearl's account for the full details. Among the most important changes were the establishment by the new common council in January 1642 of a committee of safety, again containing a preponderance of radicals. This in turn paved the way for a parliamentary order which usurped the mayoral prerogative of summoning common council by ordering that the lord mayor must do this whenever the committee of safety required it. The parallel between events at Westminster and in the City was becoming all too plain. Just as the Triennial Act and the Act that parliament could not be dissolved without its own consent, though applauded by most moderates, destroyed the royal prerogative of summoning and dissolving parliament, so was the lord mayor, in Mercurius Civicus' words, 'not left to his own Judgement, when to call or not to call a Common-Councell, but must doe it as oft as the Men of this Faction shall command him.[10]

In March the House of Commons replied to the lord mayor's plea that illness had prevented him from calling a meeting of common council when required to do so by the committee of safety by commanding him to appoint a *locum tenens*, and, faced by his unwillingness to do so, the appointment was taken out of his hands.[11] Regular meetings of the now radical common council having been secured, it only remained to Pym's supporters in the City to emasculate the constitutional powers of the court of aldermen, though the need to do this became less urgent in proportion as the aldermanic bench was gradually reconstituted between January 1642 and May 1643, as its more conservative members died, resigned or were discharged for delinquency or neglect. In the meantime in the summer of 1642 the pro-royalist lord mayor, Sir Richard Gurney, had been deposed and replaced by the radical City M.P., Alderman

[9] 'A Letter from Mercurius Civicus', p. 407.
[10] *H. of L. J.*, IV, 510; *H. of C. J.*, II, 662–3; 'A Letter from Mercurius Civicus', p. 411.
[11] *H. of L. J.*, V, 210, 229; *H. of C. J.*, II, 688; H.M.C., *Fifth Report*, pt I, pp. 37, 39.

Isaac Penington, and the recorder, Sir Thomas Gardiner, suffered the same fate.[12]

The capture of the machinery of City government by Pym's supporters was, in some measure at least, due to their fear that the all too evident disenchantment of many of the City fathers with the cause of reform might impel them to defect to the court. For those whose sympathies were moving in this direction and who shied away from a further dose of reform and a further assault on the royal prerogative, two distinct sets of considerations probably loomed largest. The first of these related to what they increasingly came to regard as the extremism of Pym and his associates and the social dangers of their political radicalism. The second was Charles's own new-found reasonableness, 'his gracious concurrance with the *Parliament*, in extirpating the Recusant party and devoting his Popish Lords and Bishops from the House of Peers, and desiring his longer continuance with them in the establishing of the weighty and impendent affairs of the Kingdome'.[13] While it is certainly true that some of the king's actions during these crucial months belied the image of a moderate and constitutional monarch which Hyde and his other parliamentary associates were endeavouring so painfully to create, royalist propaganda at its most skilful and accomplished offered a convincing explanation of royal policies which made much both of the royal willingness to accept parliamentary reforms and of the impossibility of conciliating Pym and his allies.[14] Such considerations were no less influential in winning support in the City than they were in parliament and in the country as a whole, but they were supplemented by autonomous factors relating to the royal

[12] C.L.R.O., Rep. LV, fo. 456(b); *H. of L. J.*, V, 72, 192, 280, 284; *H. of C. J.*, II, 484, 492, 499, 657, 662–3; H.M.C. *House of Lords MSS.*, XI, *Addenda 1514–1714*, 320; H.M.C., *Fifth Report*, pt I, pp. 24, 36, 37, 42; H.M.C., *Twelfth Report*, pt II, p. 321; 'A Letter from Mercurius Civicus', p. 412; *A Continuation of the True Diurnall of All the Passages in Parliament, number 10* (1642), p. 67; *A Perfect Diurnall of the Passages in Parliament... number 11* (1642), p. 4; *The King's Majestie's Resolution Concerning the Lord Maior of London* (1642).

[13] Bond, *The Parliament's and London's Preparations for His Majesties Return...* (1641) (London Guildhall pamphlet, no. 2578).

[14] See, for instance, *A Collection of Severall Speeches, Messages and Answers* (1642), pp. 55–6. A superb example, though somewhat late for our purposes, is *His Majesties Declaration to All His Loving Subjects of August 12, 1642* (Cambridge, 1642), *passim*.

relations with the City and the king's determination to undo some of the damage which these relations had suffered during the two previous decades. There were, for instance, some indications of a change in royal policy towards commercial concessionaires. The repudiation of the Courteen adventurers at the end of 1639 was followed in 1641 by a further attempt at rapprochement with the East India Company, when the king made a determined attempt to bring to a conclusion the apparently interminable wranglings about compensation for the Amboyna massacre and other Dutch acts of aggression. And in complete contrast to the still-remembered royal intransigence over tonnage and poundage in 1629 was the king's letter from Scotland to the lord keeper on 7 September 1641, urging him to take pains to emphasize to the citizens that 'though their own burgesses forget them in Parliament', he would make sure that certain clauses which had been left out of the current tonnage and poundage bill to the detriment of mercantile interests would be put back into it.[15]

But the most striking example of the king's conciliatoriness towards the City is to be found in Charles's relations with the municipal government. It has already been argued that, far from being the enthusiastic and faithful partner in royal absolutism, the City government had been battered and disillusioned as a result of the events of the 1630s. It is indeed difficult to imagine a more striking contrast than that between the brutal and tactless behaviour of the crown in this decade and the new look of royal policies in the ten months before the outbreak of the Civil War, when the City was assiduously courted. Charles had learned at last and it was still not too late. The City fathers were assured that their king was not so ignorant of the state of affairs prevailing in his capital city as to be unaware of the distinction between their loyalty and affection and the radical predispositions of 'the meaner sort of the people', a distinction which Charles was to continue to stress down to the summer of 1642. Nor was it simply a matter of empty compliments and the replacing of the hard words of the 1630s by soft. The lord mayor and his colleagues were given

---

[15] P.R.O., P.C.R., P.C. 2, LI, fos. 165-8; *C.M.E.I.C. 1635-9*, pp. 340-2, 351-2; *C.M.E.I.C. 1640-3*, pp. 23-7, 134-5; Gardiner, History, x, 28; Pearl, p. 122.

solid grounds for hope that much of the damage wrought to the City by royal actions in the previous decade would be put right. Hopes were held out that the City's confiscated estates in Ulster would be restored; that the detested Corporation of the Suburbs would disappear into limbo; and that there would be welcome alterations to the City's charter, including 'the bringing of the election to a less company and adding all the suburbs to their government'. The policy of conciliation and rapprochement reached its high point in the magnificent banquet given to the king by the City on 25 November 1641. After having displayed in better times a contemptuous disregard for the City's desire to fête him in the traditional manner,[16] the king at last made amends, and the lord mayor was officially informed by the queen earlier in the month of Charles's intention to pass through the city on his return from Scotland. The royal timing could hardly have been better, and the aldermen resolved that the king was to be received 'in as great shew & glory as at any time heretofore hath been performed to any Prince'. The king was met by the citizens near Balmes, the country house of Alderman Sir George Whitmore, a former lord mayor, and from there conducted to and through the City. The day's pageantry culminated in the banquet at Guildhall;

the whole day seemed to be spent in a kind of emulation . . . between their Majesties and the city: the citizens blessing and praying for their Majesties and their princely issue, and their Majesties returning the same blessings upon the heads of the citizens . . . Insomuch that it is hard to resolve whether the citizens were more joyed with the gracious acceptance of their weak, though hearty and loyal endeavours, or their Majesties with the performance of the day's seasonable service.

The net result of all this would be, calculated Secretary Nicholas, the capture of the citizens' hearts by King Charles and their loss to King Pym, whose own affairs had just reached a very critical juncture as he prepared to launch the Grand Remonstrance in parliament.[17]

---

[16] See above, pp. 172–3.
[17] C.L.R.O., Jor. XL, fos. 10–10(b); Rep. LV, fos. 227–227(b); *Cal. S.P.D. 1641–3*, pp. 177–8, 184; H.M.C., *Buccleuch and Queensbury MSS.*, I, 286; Rushworth (ed.), *Historical Collections*, IV (1691), 429–34; Bond, *Parliament's and London's Prepar-*

Yet, as in the case of the growth of support for the king in the Long Parliament, the most potent reasons for the growth of aldermanic support for Charles I and revulsion from Pym probably stemmed from their fear of extremism and the chaos and anarchy unloosed by the events of 1641–2. And there can be no doubt that the growth of religious radicalism played an important part in this process. Many moderate and conservative men increasingly found the pace of religious change alarmingly fast. In January 1642 the gentlemen of the Inns of Court petitioned the House of Commons against 'the exorbitances of the Separatists and disorderly persons, that thereby the City of London and the Suburbs may be disburthened from their continuall care and feares'. It was not only royalist pamphleteers like Mercurius Civicus who emphasized the connection between religious radicalism and social radicalism, as Puritan preachers 'to further the Rebellion intended . . . cause the very Dregs and Scum of every Parish to petition against the Orthodox Clergy'; or Sir Edward Dering who complained that 'Taylers, Shoomakers, Braziers [and] Feltmakers do climbe our publick Pulpits'. There can be no doubt that the fears of cultivated and civilized moderates like Dering were enormously accentuated by what they correctly perceived to be a threat to civilization and culture if the many-headed multitude took over. It was not for nothing that among the requests of the gentlemen of the Inns of Court in their petition of 11 January was that the House of Commons 'will not suffer learning to be defaced, nor discountenanced by the ignorant, but rather that you will be pleased to advance it to its dignity, it being the maine supporter of lawfull obedience, of Order, civility, and regularity in all sorts'. Dering offers the following version of part of one of his speeches made in the House of Commons on 20 November 1641.

I started with wonder and with anger to heare a bold Mechanike tell me that my *Creed* is not my *Creed*. He wondred at my wonder and said, *I hope your worship is too wise to beleaue that which you call your*

Creed . . . One absurdity leads in a thousand and when you are down the Hill of errour, there is no bottom, but in Hell and that is bottom-lesse too.

If such things shocked the man who had been chosen to introduce the Root and Branch Bill in the House of Commons, they were likely to have an even more violent impact on conservative citizens who had opposed prelacy and supported moderate reform, but were horrified by tales of sects using extempore prayers or worshipping stark naked. Some of these accounts were no doubt fabricated, but none of them lost anything in the telling.[18]

Of course while the susceptibilities of the lord mayor and most of the aldermen of 1641 and the early part of 1642 might well be outraged by such occurrences, once Gurney had been removed and replaced by the radical Penington in the summer of 1642 the lord mayor himself was not above suspicion of countenancing such things. Penington might deny, with Pym's support, that he and his colleagues were 'countenancers of Brownists and Anabaptists and all manner of sectaries'. But such accusations were at least sufficiently plausible to convince some, and, while not going to these extremes, Sir Henry Garway was reported to have challenged Pym's views about Penington's religious orthodoxy in a – possibly apocryphal – speech made at Common Hall on 17 January 1643.

Did not my lord mayor first enter upon his office, with a speech against the book of common-prayer? Hath the common-prayer ever been read before him? Hath not Captain Venn said that his wife could make prayers worth three of any in that book?

This, of course, is to anticipate, but there can be little doubt that the excesses of the sectaries were an important factor influencing the attitude of the City fathers, most of whom probably regarded even presbyterianism as a dangerous form of religious radicalism, during the latter part of 1641 and the first half of 1642.[19]

[18] *Cal. S.P.D. 1641–3*, pp. 424–5; 'A Letter from Mercurius Civicus', p. 415; 'Mr. Edward Hydes Speech', pp. 36–7; *His Majesties Declaration*, pp. 21–2, 48, 68–9; Sir Edward Dering, *A Collection of Speeches* (1642), pp. 101, 105. For details of religious radicalism in London, see Gardiner, *History*, ix, 266, 394–5, x, 29–31; Pearl, p. 124.

[19] 'Two Speeches . . . by the Earl of Manchester and John Pym Esq. . . . . the

H

In the view of the more conservative and even of many moderate citizens Pym and his colleagues and their allies in the City appeared to be irresponsibly unleashing forces which might easily get out of hand and threaten the whole social order. This is instanced by the numerous petitions to parliament which were organized by the radical leaders. As Pearl has shown in her admirable account of these petitions,[20] they had no official *locus standi* and had not been approved, as constitutional practice required, by the City government, which is hardly surprising, since they pressed upon parliament the need to pursue radical courses of action with which the City fathers were increasingly totally out of sympathy. Indeed the organizers of one of these petitions, a petition against the temporal authority of the bishops which was presented to the House of Commons by John Fowke on 11 December 1641, claimed that it had 'some 15,000 names sett to it, soe it was three quarters of a yard in breadth and 24 yards in length', and would have contained many more signatures but for the 'many obstructions and much opposition from the Lord Mayor and others'.[21] No wonder that Lord Digby in the debate on 9 February on the Root and Branch Petition protested that 'I look not upon this Petition as a Petition from the City of *London,* but from I know not what 15,000 *Londoners,* all that could be got to subscribe'.[22] Clarendon's well-known denunciation of 'a strange uningenuity and mountebankry that was practised in the procuring of those petitions', whereby men's signatures were affixed to petitions quite different from and far more radical in tone and content than those which they had assumed they were signing, may have been overdone and is certainly not free from *parti pris,* but his was only one of many objections against them.[23] And prominent among the ways in which signatures were obtained

Thirteenth of January 1642 [viz. 1643]', *Harleian Miscellany,* v (1810), 221; 'A Speech Made by Alderman Garroway at a Common Hall on Tuesday the Seventeenth of January' (1642, viz. 1643), ibid. p. 228; *An Humble Remonstrance . . . to the Kings Most Excellent Majesty in Vindication of the Honorable Isaak Pennington, Lord Maior . . .* (1643) (London Guildhall, A4, no. 37), p. 9.

20 Pearl, pp. 210–36.
21 Coates (ed.), *D'Ewes's Journal,* pp. 271, 319–20; Gardiner, *History,* x, 98–9.
22 Rushworth, *Historical Collections,* IV, 171.
23 Clarendon, *History of the Rebellion* (Oxford, 1958 edn), I, 271–2.

were various forms of coercion, intimidation and violence. One night during the late autumn of 1641 one William Hobson summoned a number of his fellow parishioners to his house in Ave Mary Lane and told them that if they refused to sign the radical petition which was currently circulating in London they were neither Christians nor honest men well affected to the commonwealth. Edward Curle, a druggist dwelling in Bucklersbury, alleged on 11 December that he had been informed by John Greensmith, a tobacconist, that he was likely to have his throat cut as a result of his refusal to subscribe to a petition against bishops.[24] Nor was it simply in the obtaining of names to petitions that the threat of violence was a factor to be reckoned with. The practice of tumultuous assembly and public demonstration is not a twentieth-century innovation, and, as in the use of the Paris mob by the radicals in another revolution, it was to prove a valuable weapon used from time to time by Pym and his colleagues as a means of coercing parliamentary opinion. It could, however, be counter-productive, and a contemporary observer may have been correct in his assertion that the presentation of the petition of 11 December by respectable bourgeois 'to the number of 400 . . . all riding out of the *Citie* of London in 50 Coaches or thereabouts to the *Parliament House*' was designed to create an impression of respectability and 'to prevent the aspersion that they were of the basest sort of people only which were that way affected'. But the dangers of disturbances from a more turbulent multitude were never far from people's minds, and the radical party was not averse from making use of them. When a guard of some two hundred men armed with halberds made its appearance at Westminster in December 1641 there were strong protests from this quarter in the House of Commons that this was designed to prevent the apprentices from delivering their petition against episcopacy.[25]

On 26 December 1641 in response to similar mass agitation the king substituted the name of Sir John Byron for that of

[24] *Cal. S.P.D. 1641–3*, pp. 193, 197.
[25] Bodleian Library, Clarendon MSS., 20, fo. 129; *Cal. S.P.D. 1641–3*, p. 202; H.M.C., *Montagu of Beaulieu MSS.*, pp. 134, 135; *The Humble Petition of the Aldermen, Aldermen's Deputies, Marchants . . . and Citizens of Good Ranke and Quality* (1642) (London Guildhall pamphlet, no. 7615); Gardiner, *History*, x, 98–9. Despite its title the petition did not have the approval of the court of aldermen.

Colonel Lunsford whom he had recently appointed as lieutenant of the Tower, but the agitators were not placated. On 27 December 'many thousands of the meaner sort of citizens' appeared at Westminster demanding the re-appointment of Lunsford's predecessor, Sir John Balfour, and the abolition of episcopacy. On the following day they were to strike a shrewd blow in the latter cause when 'There were certain Bishops coming to the House [of Lords] and the apprentices cried "a bishop, a bishop", and so with cries kept them from landing, they rowing up and down about an hour, and at last went back.' This was, needless to say, an outrageous interference with the privileges of parliament. Both of these days had seen unseemly and bloody skirmishes between apprentices and groups of cavaliers, and violence appeared to be escalating dramatically. It was not only the king who was alarmed at the news in the early days of January 1642 that persons of mean quality were hoarding arms and ammunition in their dwellings, in which circumstances his claim that he had taken armed men with him to protect him against the multitude when he had tried to set in motion the impeachment of the five members on 4 January was perhaps less implausible than may appear at first sight. Even commentators who were by no means entirely unsympathetic to the aims of Pym expressed alarm at the disorders which seemed to be getting out of hand. 'The apprentices behave themselves rudely' was the comment of one news-letter writer describing the events of the Christmas period 1641. 'I wish the House of Commons and the Kingdom repent not this connivance. I do not think London a place of that safety that I formerly did.'[26]

While the use of the mob and the practice of tumultuary petitioning were undoubtedly used ruthlessly by Pym and his radical City allies, it is more than likely that the atmosphere created by such happenings did more to win support for the king than for his opponents. Royalist propaganda was certainly to make the most of the opportunities presented by these incidents. How, it was to be argued, could Pym and his friends argue with conviction about royal violation of parliamentary privilege

---

[26] *Cal. S.P.D. 1641–3*, p. 237; H.M.C., *Montagu of Beaulieu MSS.*, pp. 137–8, 141.

when Alderman *Pennington* and Captain *Venne* brought down their Myrmidons to assault and terrifie the Members of both Houses, whose faces or whose opinions they liked not . . . when those rude multitudes published the names of the Members of both Houses, as enemies to the Commonwealth, who would not agree to their frantick propositions; when the names of those were given by Members of the House, that they might be proscribed, and torn in pieces by those Multitudes, when many were driven away for fear of their lives from being present at those consultations?

Lord Digby was a politician who was to be as much distrusted by moderate royalists as he was to be execrated by parliamentarians. Nevertheless there were many men of the still uncommitted centre in 1641–2 who would surely agree with his statement about tumultuary petitioning in his speech in the House of Commons on 9 February 1641, when he emphasized that 'there is no man of Judgment, that will think it fit for a Parliament under a *Monarchy* to give Countenance to irregular and tumultuous Assemblies of people, be it for never so good an end'. The king was only slightly exaggerating when he declared that 'any disorderly persons (let their intentions and demeanours be never so seditious) are above the reach of Law and Justice if they please to say they meet to prepare any Petition to the House of Commons'. This serves to emphasize that the historian needs to distinguish carefully between those tumults which were unconnected with the implementation of the policies of Pym and his parliamentary allies, or at least were not encouraged or countenanced by them, and those which were deliberately used as instruments of policy. But the distinction, though a real one, would offer little comfort to those who were becoming more and more convinced that things were going too far, and that the latter sort of disturbance simply encouraged the former. Charles I's oft-reiterated plea that it was such tumults which had driven him from London, and fear of them which prevented his return, probably fell upon increasingly receptive ears.[27]

Of course, once the revolution in control of City government

---

[27] C.L.R.O., Jor. xl, fos. 10–10(b); Rushworth, *Historical Collections*, iv, 171, v, 395–6; 'Mr. Edward Hydes Speech', pp. 16–17, 53; *A Collection of Severall Speeches*, pp. 54, 55, 63, 64–5, 80–1; *His Majesties Declaration*, pp. 16–17, 29–33, 39–40, 70–1.

which was set in motion by the common council elections of December 1641 had been completed, radical petitions for the most part no longer needed to bypass the City authorities, and the seal of official civic approval could be set on their work. But there was a long period of uncertainty and confusion during which the unregenerate court of aldermen and the common council, which had been captured by the radicals, were at daggers drawn. The aldermen made a determined attempt to stave off the inevitable when they ordered on 10 March 1642 that all petitions presented in common council must first be approved by them.[28] This was nothing more than the traditional procedure, but it was now doomed. And even when the process of transfer of power had been accomplished, uncertainty was by no means completely removed. To some extent, of course, the situation which had obtained previously was reversed, and it was now the official City petitions which were designed to further radical courses of action, and many at least of the unofficial ones which argued for the opposite. But those more conservative citizens who attempted to emulate the radical actions of a few months earlier quickly learned that the once boasted freedom to petition applied to some petitions but not to others. The earliest indication of this was the fate of Sir George Benion, one of the common councilmen who had been displaced in the elections of December 1641, and his fellow petitioners who received very short shrift from the House of Commons in connection with their petition of 24 February 1642 complaining of the removal of the command of the City militia from the lord mayor and the placing of it in the hands of men of mean estate. In addition to the rejection of this petition, Benion was later fined and imprisoned, and the municipal authorities seem to have made no effort to punish the ringleaders of the mob who defaced and looted his splendid city house.[29] Nevertheless, that the triumphant City supporters

---

[28] C.L.R.O., Rep. LV, fo. 393(b); H.M.C., *Twelfth Report*, pt II, p. 311.

[29] C.L.R.O., Jor. XL, fos. 25–6, 27–28(b); *H. of C. J.*, II, 489, 499, 501, 502; *H. of L. J.*, IV, 651–2; *A Perfect Diurnall*, pp. 1–2; 'A Letter from Mercurius Civicus', pp. 413–14. On 9 August it was reported that money belonging to Benion to the value of £4,000 or £5,000 had been intercepted when about to be dispatched to the king at York (*Cal. S.P.D. 1641–3*, p. 368).

of Pym[30] did not succeed in completely extirpating unofficial petitions is brought out by a reference in a petition to common council of 12 December 1642 to 'the vnhappy Jarrs that are lately risen within this Cittye through diuersitye and seeming contrarietye of Peticions about the matter of peace'.[31] Moreover, there were still some radical petitions which were submitted to parliament without municipal approval, though parliament sometimes took a stiffer line with such petitioners than it had done with their predecessors in 1641 and the opening weeks of 1642. Such a case was the petition presented in December 1642 by Sir David Watkins and others, protesting against the terms of the current parliamentary proposals for accommodation with the king and asking for a more vigorous prosecution of the war. When the House of Commons discovered that the petition had not been sanctioned by the civic authorities, it was referred by them to common council, but that body refused to countenance it, an indication perhaps of changing currents of opinion among the City governors.[32] But if Watkins and the other radical petitioners had got no change out of either the House of Commons or the common council, their treatment was mild compared with that meted out to a deputation attending at Guildhall in the same month to further a petition of a quite different nature. It may well be that this meeting was less than orderly and that the petitioners were not quite the lambs of their own picture brutally committed to the slaughter by their opponents. At least they seem to have succeeded in disarming some twenty soldiers who attacked them with shouts of '*on, on, strike now or never, Let us destroy those malignant Doggs that would have PEACE, let us cut the throates of these Papist Rogues*'. But the petitioners claimed that this was only the prelude to a more violent onslaught. However, despite the pandemonium 'a strange deafenesse' seemed to possess the members of the common council who were debating upstairs, and the molested petitioners alleged that they were

---

[30] This is perhaps a little misleading. As Pearl has shown, Penington and Venn, for example, were if anything to the left of Pym. In terms of Hexter's parliamentary groupings, they were of the war rather than the middle party.

[31] C.L.R.O., Jor. XL, fo. 43.

[32] *The True and Originall Copy of the First Petition Which Was Delivered by Sir David Watkins, etc. . . . Together with the House of Commons Answer to the Said Petition* (1643).

forced to break into the council chamber and beg for protection. They were assured that they could depart unmolested, but no sooner did they get outside than they were brutally set upon by the soldiers and the mob which had been lying in wait for them. Not all of them were so lucky as one of their number who succeeded in escaping from his pursuers only by leaping from one rooftop to another.[33]

On the last day of 1641, when the old common council had been on the eve of transformation, it had condemned in forthright terms 'such disorders & tumultuary Assemblies that bee permitted in such a Citty as this, formerly famous for the good & quiett gouerment thereof'. There can be little doubt that at that time a substantial body of influential citizens would have endorsed this condemnation, and perhaps especially common council's statement that one of the most alarming consequences of this disorderly behaviour was 'the great disrespect of Magistracy & Contempt of gouernment' in the City.[34] For authority and order were indivisible. The decline in the respect accorded to monarchs and lord mayors – and the two processes at that time appeared to be proceeding *pari passu* – would set in motion a parallel process bringing authority in general into disrepute; the authority, for instance, of masters over their servants and fathers over their families. Of course, such incidents as the committal of the innholder Richard Jenkins to Newgate on 29 September 1641, for 'vttering Certaine malapart & saucy speeches in Contempt of the Lord Maior and his authority',[35] were by no means unknown before this time, but the heady atmosphere of 1641–2 was especially conducive to their proliferation, which was an important factor helping to shock into reaction many of those who had been moderate reformers a few months earlier. It also may have prompted reflections of the sort to which the royalist pamphleteer Mercurius Civicus

---

[33] *The Humble Petition and Remonstrance of Divers Citizens and Other Inhabitants of the City of London and Borough of Southwark* . . . (1642, viz. 1643) (London Guildhall pamphlet, no. 1667). In fairness it ought to be pointed out that the official record of the common council describes the matter very differently, and gives the impression that it was the disorderly multitude of petitioners rather than the violence of the soldiers and the anti-peace mob which was the real occasion of the tumult (C.L.R.O., Jor. XL, fos. 43–4).

[34] C.L.R.O., Jor. XL, fo. 10(b).

[35] C.L.R.O., Rep. LV, fos. 197(b)–198.

was later to give such effective expression about the consequence of promoting men of meaner estate to the higher civic positions.[36] Whatever the authenticity of Sir Henry Garway's alleged outburst at Common Hall on 17 January 1643, the views expressed in it would have awoken some very sympathetic echoes among many senior citizens long before the beginning of 1643.

I am not willing to speak slightly of any persons gotten into authority; only we may say, there be some amongst us, we did not think two years ago to have met here, and yet we were wont to see an alderman coming a dozen years off . . . I have been lord mayor myself, in a pleasanter time than this, and should have some share still in the government; before God, I have no more authority in the city, than a porter, not so much as an Aldermanbury porter. If to be governed by people whose authority we know not, and by rules which no body ever heard of, or can know, be a sign of arbitrary power, we have as much of it as heart can wish.[37]

As the fears of social disruption and chaos loomed larger in the consciousness of most of the aldermen, so did the significance of the royal aggression, from which the City fathers had been among the principal sufferers in the 1630s, shrink to relative insignificance. The moderate reformers of 1640 became the fearful and threatened men of 1642, and as their natural conservatism reasserted itself, they clung the more tenaciously to the king as the supreme symbol of that order and authority which appeared to be threatened on all sides. More particularly, their own position was under threat, not simply from the constitutional assault on their prerogatives which was set in motion by the election of a more radical common council, but also by parallel developments in parliament, as Pym and his associates increasingly voiced criticisms of their alleged rôle as instruments of royal policy before and during the eleven years' tyranny; in the imprisoning of Nicholas Clegate in 1628;[38] in imprisoning those who refused to contribute to the unparliamentary levies of ship money and tonnage and poundage; and in rendering assistance to the court of high commission. Certainly there is a suggestive parallel between the diminution of the royal preroga-

---

[36] 'A Letter from Mercurius Civicus', pp. 399–400, 407, 412.
[37] 'Two Speeches', p. 226.
[38] See above, pp. 180–1.

I

tive as a result of the legislation of the Long Parliament and the subsequent assault on the civic prerogative of the lord mayor and aldermen in the City with the full co-operation of the radical party in parliament. In the for once strictly accurate judgment of Mercurius Civicus, 'a Faction in the *City* conspired with a Faction in the *Parliament,* and this Faction in the *Parliament* with that in the *City*'. Thus

as two Strings set to the same Tune, though on two severall *Violls* . . . if you touch one, the other by Consent renders the same Sound, so, the *House* of *Commons,* and the *Common-Councell* of this City, were now grown to such a Sympathy, that the Motions and Endeavours of one, were the work of both.[39]

Nowhere is this better illustrated than in the matter of the controversy over the control of the militia, in which the parliamentary usurpation of the royal prerogative was reproduced in microcosm in the constitutional usurpation of the common council and committee of safety in taking control of the City trained bands from the lord mayor and aldermen. What more natural than that the latter should connect their own lost authority with that of the crown and the usurped authority of their inferiors with that of the parliament?

To conclude then, the onslaught on the civic oligarchy which began with the common-council elections of December 1641 was not directed against an aldermanic bench of which a majority had been consistent supporters of royal policies and opponents of reform. On the contrary it was designed to forestall the possibility of an aldermanic counter-revolution which, like the constitutional royalist counter-revolution at Westminster, had been brought about by a complex concatenation of circumstances, the chief of which were the combined factors of royal conciliation and fears that events were getting out of hand. Both of these things highlighted the significance of the crown as the symbol and safeguard of that order which radical policies in both parliament and the City were placing at hazard. It was considerations such as these which brought back so many of the City fathers to that natural alliance with the crown from which they had been detached for more than a

---

[39] 'A Letter from Mercurius Civicus', pp. 407, 412.

decade as a result of royal policies which had alienated them in their twin capacities as members of both a municipal and a business élite. And it was this tide of returning civic support which necessitated a revolution in London if the parliamentary cause in the nation as a whole was to have any real prospect of success.

Sources and bibliography

(Place of publication is London unless otherwise stated)

A. MANUSCRIPT SOURCES

(1) In the British Library

(a) Parliamentary diaries

Additional MSS., vol. 18,597 (Earle's diary).

Additional MSS., vol. 26,639 (Pym's diary).

Additional MSS., vol. 48,091 (proceedings in the House of Commons 1625).

Harleian MSS., vol. 159 (D'Ewes's diary).

Harleian MSS., vol. 6383 (Holles's diary).

Harleian MSS., vol. 6799 (Pym's diary).

(b) Other materials

Additional MSS., vol. 36,825.

Cottonian MSS., Titus Bv.

Egerton MSS., vol. 2544.

Harleian MSS., vols. 1769, 1878, 2243, 4771.

Lansdowne MSS., vols. 92, 106, 151, 152, 160, 165, 169, 172, 487.

Sloane MSS., vol. 3515.

Stowe MSS., vol. 326.

(2) In the Public Record Office

Audit Office A.O. 1/1948/1 (purchase and sale of pepper).

Audit Office A.O. 1/594/2–5; A.O. 1/595/6–10; A.O. 1/596/11–14; A.O. 1/597/15–18(a); A.O. 1/598/19–22; A.O. 1/599/23–7; A.O. 1/600/28–32; A.O. 1/601/33–7; A.O. 1/602/38–42; A.O. 3/297 (customs farmers' declared accounts).

Declared Accounts, Pipe Office, E. 351/609–42, 673–7 (customs farmers' declared accounts).

Close Rolls, James I and Charles I (C.54).

Patent Rolls, James I and Charles I, (C.66).

Privy Council Register (P.C. 2), vols. 41–52.

State Papers Domestic James I (S.P. 14, vols. 1–213).

State Papers Domestic Charles I (S.P. 16, vols. 1–539).
State Papers Domestic (S.P. 15).
State Papers Docquets (S.P. 38, bdls. 7–18).
Collected Sign Manual Grants and Warrants (S.P. 39, vols. 1–32).
State Papers 105/143 (Register Book of Levant Company).
State Papers 105/147 (General Court Book of Levant Company).
MS. Calendar of Sackville MSS. compiled by A. P. Newton.

(3) In the Bodleian Library

(a) Parliamentary diary
Tanner MSS., vol. 392 (Holland's diary).

(b) Other materials
Bankes MSS., bdls. 5, 6, 11, 12.
Clarendon MSS., vols. 17, 20.
Rawlinson MSS., A1.
Tanner MSS., vol. 65.

(4) In the Record Office of the Corporation of London

Journals of the Court of Common Council, vols. 24–40.
Repertories of the Court of Aldermen, vols. 25–57.
Remembrancia, vols. 1–7.
Minutes of the Committee for Sale of the Royal Contract Estates
    1632–64.
Royal Contract Estates Papers.

(5) In the Library of the Guildhall of the City of London

Guildhall MSS., 4165/1 (V.M., St Peter upon Cornhill 1574–1714).
Guildhall MSS., 4384/1 (V.M., St Bartholomew-by-the-Exchange
    1547–1643).
Guildhall MSS., 4425/1 (V.M., St Christopher-le-Stocks 1593–1731).
Guildhall MSS., 5186 (informations laid against unauthorized
    bakers of white bread).
Guildhall MSS., 5614/1 (Coopers' Quarterage Books).
Court Minute Books of the Barber–Surgeons' Company 1605–51
    (2 vols.).
Court Minute Books of the Blacksmiths' Company 1605–31 (2 vols.).
Court Minute Books of the Brewers' Company 1604–42 (4 vols.).
Court Books of the Carpenters' Company 1600–35 (2 vols.).
Court Minute Book of the Coopers' Company 1597–1627 (1 vol.).
Court Ledgers of the Fishmongers' Company 1592–1631 (2 vols.).
Court Books of the Turners' Company 1605–38 (2 vols.).
Court Minute Book of the Weavers' Company 1610–41 (1 vol.).

Court Minute Books of the Whitebakers' Company 1592–1648 (2 vols.).

(6) In the custody of the London livery companies

Goldsmiths' Company, Wardens' Accounts and Court Minutes 1599–1629 (4 vols.).
Court Book 1639–42.
Grocers' Company, Orders of the Court of Assistants 1591–1668 (3 vols.).
Haberdashers' Company, Court of Assistants' Minutes 1583–1652.
Mercers' Company, Acts of Court 1513–1629 (2 vols.).
Repertories or Acts of Court 1625–41 (3 vols.).
Merchant–Tailors' Company, Court Minutes, vols. 5–9.
Skinners' Company, Court Books 1551–1651 (3 vols.).
Vintners' Company, MS. transcripts of Court Minute Books for 1608–42.

B. PRINTED SOURCES, CALENDARS AND COLLECTIONS OF CONTEMPORARY MATERIALS

(1) Parliamentary diaries and records

A Continuation of the True Diurnall of All the Passages in Parliament, number *10* (1642).
A Perfect Diurnall of the Passages in Parliament . . . number 11 (1642).
Bruce, J. (ed.), *The Verney Papers: Notes of Proceedings in the Long Parliament . . . by Sir Ralph Verney, Knight, Member for the Borough of Aylesbury,* Camden Soc., o.s., XXXI (1845).
Coates, W. H. (ed.), *The Journal of Sir Simonds D'Ewes from the First Recess of the Long Parliament to the Withdrawal of King Charles from London* (New Haven, Conn., 1942).
Gardiner, S. R. (ed.), *Debates in the House of Commons in 1625,* Camden Soc., n.s., VI (1873).
Grosart, A. B. (ed.), *An Apology for Socrates and Negotium Posterorum by Sir John Eliot,* 2 vols. (1881).
Johnson, R. C., M. F. Keeler, M. J. Cole, and W. B. Bidwell (eds.), *Commons Debates 1628,* 3 vols. (New Haven, Conn., 1977).
Journals of the House of Commons, vols. I–II.
Journals of the House of Lords, vols. IV–V.
Notestein, W. (ed.), *Journal of Sir Simonds D'Ewes from the Beginnings of the Long Parliament to the Opening of the Trial of the Earl of Strafford* (New Haven, Conn., 1923).
Notestein, W. and F. H. Relf (eds.), *The Commons Debates for 1629* (Minneapolis, Minn., 1921).

Notestein, W., F. H. Relf, and H. Simpson (eds.), *Commons Debates 1621*, 7 vols. (New Haven, Conn., 1935).
Willson, D. H. (ed.), *The Parliamentary Diary of Robert Bowyer 1606–1607* (Minneapolis, Minn., 1931).

(2)   Calendars etc.

Acts of the Privy Council of England 1601–4 (vol. XXXII).
Acts of the Privy Council of England 1613–31 (vols. XXXIII–XLVI).
Analytical Index to the Series of Records Known as the Remembrancia. Preserved among the Archives of the City of London (1878).
Birdwood, G. and W. Foster (eds.), *The Register of Letters . . . of the Governor and Company of Merchants . . . Trading into the East Indies, 1600–1619* (1893).
Calendar of State Papers, Colonial Series, vol. I, *America and West Indies 1574–1660*; vols. II–IV, *East Indies, China and Japan* 1513–1624; vol. VI, *East Indies, China and Persia 1625–9*; vol. VIII, *East Indies and Persia 1630–4*.
Calendar of State Papers Domestic 1595–7.
Calendar of State Papers Domestic 1598–1601.
Calendar of State Papers Domestic 1603–1625 (4 vols.).
Calendar of State Papers Domestic Addenda 1580–1625.
Calendar of State Papers Domestic 1625–43 (18 vols.).
Calendar of State Papers Domestic Addenda 1625–49.
Calendar of State Papers . . . Existing in the Archives and Collections of Venice and in Other Libraries in Northern Italy, 1603–47 (18 vols.).
Historical Manuscripts Commission, *Fourth Report*, pt I (1874).
Historical Manuscripts Commission, *Fifth Report*, I vol. in 2 pts (1876).
Historical Manuscripts Commission, *Eighth Report*, app. II (1881).
Historical Manuscripts Commission, *Eleventh Report*, pt I (1887).
Historical Manuscripts Commission, *Twelfth Report*, pts II & IV (1890).
Historical Manuscripts Commission, *Calendar of Manuscripts of the House of Lords*, vol. XI, *Addenda 1514–1714* (1962).
Historical Manuscripts Commission, *Calendar of the Manuscripts of Major-General Lord Sackville . . .*, 2 vols. (1940–60).
Historical Manuscripts Commission, *Calendar of the Manuscripts of the Most Hon. the Marquess of Salisbury . . .* vols. V, IX–XIX (1894, 1902–65).
Historical Manuscripts Commission, *Report on the Manuscripts of Lord Montagu of Beaulieu* (1900).
Historical Manuscripts Commission, *Report on the Manuscripts of the Marquis of Downshire*, vol. II (1936).

Historical Manuscripts Commission, *The Manuscripts of His Grace the Duke of Buccleuch and Queensberry*, vol. 1 (1897).

Kingsbury, S. M. (ed.), *The Records of the Virginia Company of London*, 4 vols. (Washington, D.C., 1906–35).

Lambert, J. J. (ed.), *Records of the Skinners of London: Edward I to James I* (1933).

Larkin, J. F. and P. C. Hughes (eds.), *Stuart Royal Proclamations*, vol. 1 (Oxford, 1973).

Laughton, J. K. (ed.), *State Papers Relating to the Defeat of the Spanish Armada anno 1588*, Navy Record Soc., vols. 1–11 (1894).

Lefroy, W. (ed.), *Memorials of the Discovery and Early Settlement of the Bermudas or Somers Islands 1615–1685*, 2 vols. (1877–9).

Londonderry and the London Companies 1609–1629, Being a Survey and Other Documents Submitted to King Charles I by Sir Thomas Phillips (Belfast, 1928).

Ogle, O. and W. H. Bliss (eds.), *Calendar of the Clarendon State Papers Preserved in the Bodleian Library*, 3 vols. (Oxford, 1872).

Rushworth, J. (ed.), *Historical Collections*, vols. 1 (1682), 11–111 (1680), 1v–v (1691).

Sainsbury, E. B. (ed.), *Calendar of Court Minutes of the East India Company 1635–43*, 2 vols. (Oxford, 1907–38).

Scrope, R. and T. Monkhouse (eds.), *State Papers Collected by Edward, Earl of Clarendon, Commencing 1621*, 3 vols. (Oxford, 1767–86).

Steele, R. R. (ed.), *Bibliotheca Lindesiana: A Bibliography of Royal Proclamations of the Tudor and Stuart Sovereigns . . . 1485–1714*, 2 vols. (Oxford, 1910).

Stevens, H. (ed.), *The Dawn of English Trade to the East Indies* (1886).

(3)   Other printed sources

A Brief Narrative of the Cases of Sir William Courteen and Sir Paul Pindar (n.d.).

A Collection of Severall Speeches, Messages and Answers (1642).

'A Letter from Mercurius Civicus to Mercurius Rusticus . . .' (1643), *Lord Somers' Tracts*, 2nd. coll., 1 (1750), 397–420.

An Humble Remonstrance to the Kings Most Excellent Majesty in Vindication of the Honorable Isaak Pennington, Lord Maior . . . (1643) (London Guildhall A4, no. 37).

Ashton, R. (ed.), *James I by His Contemporaries* (1969).

'A Speech Made by Alderman Garroway at a Common Hall on Tuesday the Seventeenth of January' (1642, viz. 1643), *Harleian Miscellany*, v (1810), 224–31.

A True Discovery of the Proiectors of the Wine Proiect (1641).

Batho, G. R. (ed.), *The Household Papers of Henry Percy, Ninth Earl of*

Northumberland (1564–1632), Camden Soc., 3rd ser. xcIII (1962).

Bond, J., *The Downfall of the Old Common-Counsel Men* (1642) (London Guildhall pamphlet, no. 2588).

The Parliament's and London's Preparations for His Majesties Return ... (1641) (London Guildhall pamphlet, no. 2578).

Calder, I. M. (ed.), *Activities of the Puritan Faction of the Church of England 1625–1633* (1957).

Carew, G., *A Vindication of the Several Actions at Law Brought against the Heirs of Sir Peter Courten and Peter Boudaen* (Middelburgh, 1675).

Carew, T. *Hinc Illae Lacrimae: or An Epitome of the Life and Death of Sir William Courteen and Sir Paul Pindar* (1681).

Carr, C. T. (ed.), *Select Charters of Trading Companies*, Selden Soc., vol. xxvIII (1913).

Clarendon, Edward, Earl of, *The History of the Rebellion and Civil Wars in England*, 6 vols., ed. W. D. Macray (Oxford, 1888).

Dale, T. C. (ed.), *The Inhabitants of London in 1638* (1931).

Dering, Sir Edward, *A Collection of Speeches* (1642).

Gardiner, S. R. (ed.), *The Constitutional Documents of the Puritan Revolution 1625–1660* (3rd edn, Oxford, 1962).

Goodman, G., *The Court of King James I*, 2 vols., ed. J. Brewer (1839).

Halliwell, J. O. (ed.), *The Autobiography and Correspondence of Sir Simonds D'Ewes Bart. during the Reigns of James I and Charles I*, 2 vols. (1845).

Hill, L. M. (ed.), 'Sir Julius Caesar's Journal of Salisbury's First Two Months and Twenty Days as Lord Treasurer, 1608', *Bull. Inst. Hist. Res.*, xLV (1972), 311–27.

His Majesties Declaration to All His Loving Subjects of August 12, 1642 (Cambridge, 1642).

McClure, N. E. (ed.), *The Letters of John Chamberlain*, 2 vols., (Philadelphia, 1939).

'Mr. Edward Hydes Speech at a Conference betweene Both Houses, on Tuesday the 6th of July, 1641, at the Transmission of the Severall Impeachments against the Lord Chiefe Baron Davenport, Mr. Baron Trevor and Mr. Baron Weston', *Lord Somers' Tracts*, 2nd coll., II (1750), 275–9.

'Ovatio Carolina. The Triumph of King Charles, or the Triumphant Manner and Order of Receiving His Majesty into the City of London on Thursday the Twenty-Fifth Day of November, Anno Dom. 1641, upon His Safe and Happy Return from Scotland', *Harleian Miscellany*, V (1810), 86–103.

Ramsay, G. D. (ed.), 'The Report of the Royal Commission on the Clothing Industry, 1640', *Eng. Hist. Rev.*, LVII (1942), 482–93.

Simpson, W. S. (ed.), *Documents Illustrating the History of St. Paul's Cathedral*, Camden Soc., n.s., xxvi (1880).

Spedding, J., *The Life and Letters of Francis Bacon*, 7 vols. (1861–74).

Stow, J., *A Survey of London by John Stow Reprinted from the Text of 1603*, 2 vols., ed. C. L. Kingsford (Oxford, 1908).

A Survey of London (1618 edn.).

Tawney, R. H. and E. Power (eds.), *Tudor Economic Documents*, 3 vols. (1924).

The Humble Petition and Remonstrance of Divers Citizens and Other Inhabitants of the City of London and Borough of Southwark ... (1642, viz. 1643) (London Guildhall pamphlet, no. 1667).

The Humble Petition of the Aldermen, Aldermen's Deputies, Merchants ... *and Citizens of Good Ranke and Quality* (1642) (London Guildhall pamphlet, no. 7615).

The King's Majestie's Resolution Concerning the Lord Maior of London (1642).

The Petition and Remonstrance of the Governor and Company ... *Trading to the East Indies Exhibited to the Honourable House of Commons* ... *Anno 1628* (1628).

The True and Originall Copy of the First Petition Which Was Delivered by Sir David Watkins etc. ... *Together with the House of Commons Answer to the Said Petition* (1643).

The Vintners' Answer to Some Scandalous Pamphlets (1642).

'Two Speeches ... by the Earl of Manchester and John Pym Esq. ... the Thirteenth of January 1642 [viz. 1643]', *Harleian Miscellany*, v (1810), 218–23.

Wilson, Arthur, 'The History of England, Being the Life and Reign of James the First' (1653), in White Kennet, *The Complete History of England* ... ii (1719), 661–792.

C. MODERN WORKS

Abrams, M. A., 'The English Gold and Silver Thread Monopolies', *J. Ec. B. H.*, iii (1931), 382–406.

Andrews, K. R., *Elizabethan Privateering: English Privateering during the Spanish War 1585–1603* (Cambridge, 1964).

Ashdown, C. H., *A History of the Worshipful Company of Glaziers of the City of London* (1919).

Ashton, R., 'Charles I and the City', in F. J. Fisher (ed.), *Essays in the Economic and Social History of Tudor and Stuart England* (Cambridge, 1961), pp. 138–63.

'Conflicts of Concessionary Interest in Early Stuart England', in D. C. Coleman and A. H. John (eds.), *Trade Government and Economy in Pre-Industrial England* (1976), pp. 113–31.

'Jacobean Free Trade Again', *P. & P.*, no. 43 (1969), 151–7.

'Revenue Farming under the Early Stuarts', *Econ. Hist. Rev.*, 2nd ser., VIII (1956), 310–22.

The Crown and the Money Market 1603–1640 (Oxford, 1960).

'The Disbursing Official under the Early Stuarts: The Cases of Sir William Russell and Philip Burlamachi', *Bull. Inst. Hist. Res.*, XXX (1957), 162–74.

The English Civil War: Conservatism and Revolution 1603–1649 (1978).

'The Parliamentary Agitation for Free Trade in the Opening Years of the Reign of James I', *P. & P.*, no. 38 (1967), 40–55.

'Usury and High Finance in the Age of Shakespeare and Jonson', *Ren. & Mod. Stud.*, IV (1960), 14–43.

Aylmer, G. E., *The King's Servants: The Civil Service of Charles I 1625–1642* (1961).

Bagwell, R., *Ireland under the Stuarts*, 3 vols. (1962 repr.).

Barnes, T. G., *Somerset 1625–1640: A County's Government under the Personal Rule* (1961).

Barrett, C. R. B., *History of the Society of Apothecaries of London* (1905).

Beaven, A. B. (ed.), *The Aldermen of the City of London*, 2 vols. (1908–13).

Bergeron, D. M., 'Charles I's Royal Entries into London', *Guildhall Miscellany*, III (1970), 91–7.

English Civic Pageantry (1971).

Boynton, L., *The Elizabethan Militia 1558–1638* (1967).

Brenner, R., 'The Civil War Politics of London's Merchant Community', *P. & P.*, no. 58 (1973), 53–107.

Brett-James, N. G., *The Growth of Stuart London* (1935).

Calder, I. M., 'A Seventeenth Century Attempt to Purify the Anglican Church', *Amer. Hist. Rev.*, LIII (1948), 760–75.

Cameron, H. C., see Wall, C.

Chaudhuri, K. N., *The English East India Company* (1965).

Cliffe, J. T., *The Yorkshire Gentry from the Reformation to the Civil War* (1969).

Cokayne, G. E., *Some Account of the Lord Mayors and Sheriffs of London (1601–1625)* (1897).

Consitt, F., *The London Weavers' Company* (Oxford, 1933).

Cooper, J. P., 'Economic Regulation and the Cloth Industry in Seventeenth-Century England', *Roy. Hist. Soc. Trans.*, 5th ser., XX (1970), 73–99.

Craven, W. F., *Dissolution of the Virginia Company* (Gloucester, Mass., 1964 edn).

Croft, P., 'Free Trade and the House of Commons 1605–6', *Econ. Hist. Rev.*, 2nd ser., XXVIII (1975), 17–27.

Dale, H. B., *The Fellowship of Woodmongers* (1924).

Dictionary of National Biography.

Dietz, F. C., *English Public Finance 1558–1641* (2nd edn, 1964).

Englefield, W. A. D., *The History of the Painter–Stainers' Company of London* (1923).

Everitt, A. M., *The Community of Kent and the Great Rebellion 1640–60* (Leicester, 1966).

Fisher, F. J., 'Commercial Trends and Policy in Sixteenth-Century England', *Econ. Hist. Rev.*, X (1940), 95–117.

'London's Export Trade in the Early Seventeenth Century', *Econ. Hist. Rev.*, 2nd ser., III (1950), 151–61.

Fisher, F. J. (ed.), *Essays in the Economic and Social History of Tudor and Stuart England* (Cambridge, 1961).

Foster, F. F., *The Politics of Stability: A Portrait of the Rulers of Elizabethan London* (1977).

Foster, W., 'Charles I and the East India Company', *Eng. Hist. Rev.*, XIX (1904), 456–63.

Friis, A., *Alderman Cockayne's Project and the Cloth Trade: The Commercial Policy of England in Its Main Aspects* (1927).

Gardiner, S. R., *History of England from the Accession of James I to the Outbreak of the Civil War, 1603–1642*, 10 vols. (1883–4).

Gould, J. D., 'The Trade Depression of the Early 1620s', *Econ. Hist. Rev.*, 2nd ser., VII (1954), 81–90.

Gould Walker, G., *The Honourable Artillery Company* (1926).

Gras, N. S. B., *The Evolution of the English Corn Market from the Twelfth to the Eighteenth Century* (Cambridge, Mass., 1915).

Grassby, R., 'English Merchant Capitalism in the Late Seventeenth Century. The Composition of Business Fortunes', *P. & P.*, no. 46 (1970), 87–107.

'The Personal Wealth of the Business Community in Seventeenth-Century England', *Econ. Hist. Rev.*, 2nd ser., XXIII (1970), 220–34.

Herbert, W., *The History of the Twelve Great Livery Companies of London*, 2 vols. (1837).

Hexter, J. H., *The Reign of King Pym* (Cambridge, Mass., 1941).

Hill, C., *Economic Problems of the Church from Archbishop Whitgift to the Long Parliament* (Oxford, 1956).

Society and Puritanism in Pre-Revolutionary England (1964).

Hinton, R. W. K., *The Eastland Trade and the Common Weal in the Seventeenth Century* (Cambridge, 1959).

Johnson, A. H., *A History of the Worshipful Company of Drapers of the City of London*, 5 vols. (Oxford, 1914–22).

Johnson, D. J., *Southwark and the City* (1969).

Jones, J. R., 'The Clegate Case,' *Eng. Hist. Rev.*, XC (1975), 262–86.

Jones, P. E., *The Worshipful Company of Poulters of the City of London* (1939).
Jordan, W. K., *The Charities of London 1480–1660* (1960).
   The Charities of Rural England 1480–1660 (1961).
Ketton-Cremer, R. W., *Norfolk in the Civil War: A Portrait of a Society in Conflict* (1969).
Kirby, D. A., 'The Radicals of St. Stephen's Coleman Street, London, 1624–1642', *Guildhall Miscellany*, III (1970), 98–119.
Kirby, E. W., 'The Lay Feoffees: A Study in Militant Puritanism', *J. Mod. Hist.*, XIV (1942), 1–25.
Knowles, J. A., 'Additional Notes on the History of the Worshipful Company of Glaziers', *Antiquaries Journal*, VII (1927), 282–93.
Lang, R. G., 'London's Aldermen in Business 1600–1625', *Guildhall Miscellany*, III (1971), 242–64.
   'Social Origins and Social Aspirations of Jacobean London Merchants', *Econ. Hist. Rev.*, 2nd ser., XXVII (1974), 28–47.
   'The Greater Merchants of London in the Early Seventeenth Century', D.Phil. thesis, University of Oxford (1963).
Lipson, E., *The Economic History of England*, 3 vols. (9th edn of vol. I and 4th edn of vols. II & III, 1947).
Lloyd, H. A., *The Gentry of South-West Wales 1540–1640* (Cardiff, 1968).
Moir, T. L., *The Addled Parliament of 1614* (Oxford, 1958).
Moody, T. W., *The Londonderry Plantation 1609–1641* (Belfast, 1939).
Morrill, J. S., *Cheshire 1630–1660: County Government and Society during the 'English Revolution'* (1974).
Newton, A. P., 'The Establishment of the Great Farm of the English Customs', *Roy. Hist. Soc. Trans.*, 4th ser., I (1918), 129–56.
Nicholl, J., *Some Account of the Worshipful Company of Ironmongers* (1866).
Pearl, V., *London and the Outbreak of the Puritan Revolution: City Government and National Politics* (1961).
Prestwich, M., *Cranfield: Politics and Profits under the Early Stuarts* (Oxford, 1966).
Price, W. H., *The English Patents of Monopoly* (Boston, Mass., 1906).
Prideaux, W. S., *Memorials of the Goldsmiths' Company . . . between 1335 and 1815*, 2 vols. (1896).
Quinn, D. B., *Raleigh and the British Empire* (1947).
Rabb, T. K., *Enterprise and Empire: Merchant and Gentry Investment in the Expansion of England, 1575–1630* (Cambridge, Mass., 1967).
   'Free Trade and the Gentry in the Parliament of 1604', *P. & P.*, no. 40 (1968), 165–73.
   'Sir Edwin Sandys and the Parliament of 1604', *Amer. Hist. Rev.*, LXIX (1964), 646–70.

Raikes, G. A., *A History of the Honourable Artillery Company*, 2 vols. (1878–9).

Ramsay, G. D., *English Trade during the Centuries of Emergence* (1957).

Reddaway, T. F., 'Goldsmith's Row in Cheapside, 1558–1645', *Guildhall Miscellany*, II (1963), 181–206.

Scott, W. R., *The Constitution and Finance of English, Scottish and Irish Joint-Stock Companies to 1720*, 3 vols. (Cambridge, 1910–12).

Seaver, P. S., *The Puritan Lectureships: The Politics of Religious Dissent 1560–1662* (Stanford, Calif., 1970).

Sharpe, R. R., *London and the Kingdom*, 3 vols. (1894–5).

Stewart, H., *History of the Worshipful Company of Gold and Silver Wire-Drawers . . .* (1891).

Stone, L., 'State Control in Sixteenth-Century England', *Econ. Hist. Rev.*, XVII (1947), 103–20.

The Crisis of the Aristocracy, 1558–1641 (Oxford, 1965).

'The Fruits of Office: The Case of Robert Cecil, First Earl of Salisbury, 1596–1612', in F. J. Fisher (ed.), *Essays in the Economic and Social History of Tudor and Stuart England* (Cambridge, 1961), pp. 89–116.

'The Peer and the Alderman's Daughter', *History Today*, XI (1961), 48–55.

Stonehewer, M., 'Economic Policy and Opinion in the House of Commons, 1621', B.A. dissertation, University of Nottingham (1955).

Supple, B. E., *Commercial Crisis and Change in England 1600–1642* (Cambridge, 1959).

Tawney, R. H., *Business and Politics under James I: Lionel Cranfield as Merchant and Minister* (Cambridge, 1958).

See also Unwin, G.

Thrupp, S., *A Short History of the Worshipful Company of Bakers of London* (1933).

Trevor-Roper, H. R., *Archbishop Laud* (2nd edn, 1963).

Underwood, C. A., see Wall, C.

Unwin, G., *Industrial Organization in the Sixteenth and Seventeenth Centuries* (2nd impr., 1957).

Studies in Economic History, ed. R. H. Tawney (1927).

The Gilds and Companies of London (4th edn, 1963).

Upton, A. F., *Sir Arthur Ingram c. 1565–1642: A Study of the Origins of an English Landed Family* (1961).

Wadmore, J. F., *Some Account of the Worshipful Company of Skinners of London* (1902).

Wall, C., H. C. Cameron, and E. A. Underwood, *A History of the Worshipful Society of Apothecaries of London*, vol. I, *1617–1815* (1963).

Welch, C., *History of the Cutlers' Company of London and the Minor Cutlery Crafts*, 2 vols. (1916–23).

History of the Worshipful Company of Paviors of the City of London (1909).

History of the Worshipful Company of Pewterers of the City of London, 2 vols. (1902).

The Bibliography of the Livery Companies of the City of London, (1890).

Willan, T. S., *The Early History of the Russia Company 1553–1603* (Manchester, 1956).

Williams, D. A., 'London Puritanism: The Parish of St. Botolph without Aldgate', *Guildhall Miscellany*, II (1960), 24–38.

'London Puritanism: The Parish of St. Stephen, Coleman Street', *Church Q. R.*, CLX (1959), 464–82.

'Puritanism in the City Government 1610–1640', *Guildhall Miscellany*, I (1955), 2–14.

Williams, W. M., *Annals of the . . . Founders . . . of London* (1867).

Wood, A. C., *A History of the Levant Company* (2nd impr., 1964).

Wren, M. C., 'London and the Twenty Ships', *Amer. Hist. Rev.*, LV (1950), 321–35.

'The Disputed Elections in London in 1641', *Eng. Hist. Rev.*, LXIV (1949), 34–52.

Young, S., *The Annals of the Barber Surgeons of London* (1890).

Index